Public Policy and Politics

Series Editors: Colin Fudge and Robin Hambleton

Public policy-making in Western democracies is confronted by new pressures. Central values relating to the role of the state, the role of markets and the role of citizenship are now all contested and the consensus built up around the Keynesian welfare state is under challenge. New social movements are entering the political arena: electronic technologies are transforming the nature of employment; changes in demographic structure are creating heightened demands for public services; unforeseen social and health problems are emerging; and, most disturbing, social and economic inequalities are increasing in many countries.

How governments – at international, national and local levels – respond to this developing agenda is the central focus of the Public Policy and Politics series. Aimed at a student, professional, practitioner and academic readership, it aims to provide up-to-date, comprehensive and authoritative analyses of public policy-making in practice.

The series is international and interdisciplinary in scope, and bridges theory and practice by relating the substance of policy to the politics of the policy-making process.

Public Policy and Politics

Series Editors: Colin Fudge and Robin Hambleton

PUBLISHED

Danny Burns, Robin Hambleton and Paul Hoggett, *The Politics of Decentralisation: Revitalising Local Democracy*

Stephen Glaister, June Burnham, Handley Stevens and Tony Travers, *Transport Policy in Britain* (second edition)

Christopher Ham, *Health Policy in Britain: The Politics and Organisation of the National Health Service* (fifth edition)

Ian Henry, *The Politics of Leisure Policy* (second edition)

Christopher C. Hood and Helen Z. Margetts, *The Tools of Government in the Digital Age*

Peter Malpass and Alan Murie, *Housing Policy and Practice* (fifth edition)

Robin Means, Sally Richards and Randall Smith, *Community Care: Policy and Practice* (fourth edition)

David Mullins and Alan Murie, *Housing Policy in the UK*

Gerry Stoker, *The Politics of Local Government* (second edition)

Marilyn Taylor, *Public Policy in the Community*

Kieron Walsh, *Public Services and Market Mechanisms: Competition, Contracting and the New Public Management*

FORTHCOMING

Rob Atkinson and Simin Davoudi with Graham Moon, *Urban Politics in Britain: The City, the State and the Market* (second edition)

Robin Hambleton, *Reinventing Local Governance*

Public Policy and Politics
Series Standing Order
ISBN 13: 978–0–3370–1705–9 hardback
ISBN 13: 978–0–3336–9349–0 paperback
(*outside North America only*)

You can receive future titles in this series as they are published. To place a standing order please contact your bookseller or, in the case of difficulty, write to us at the address below with your name and address, the title of the series and an ISBN quoted above.

Customer Services Department, Macmillan Distribution Ltd
Houndmills, Basingstoke, Hampshire RG21 6XS, England

Community Care
Policy and Practice

Fourth Edition

Robin Means
Sally Richards
and
Randall Smith

palgrave
macmillan

First edition 1994
Second edition 1998
Third edition 2003
Fourth edition 2008

Published by
PALGRAVE MACMILLAN
Houndmills, Basingstoke, Hampshire RG21 6XS and
175 Fifth Avenue, New York, N.Y. 10010
Companies and representatives throughout the world

PALGRAVE MACMILLAN is the global academic imprint of the Palgrave Macmillan division of St. Martin's Press, LLC and of Palgrave Macmillan Ltd. Macmillan® is a registered trademark in the United States, United Kingdom and other countries. Palgrave is a registered trademark in the European Union and other countries.

ISBN-13: 978-0-230-00674-4
ISBN-10: 0-230-00674-4

This book is printed on paper suitable for recycling and made from fully managed and sustained forest sources. Logging, pulping and manufacturing processes are expected to conform to the environmental regulations of the country of origin.

A catalogue record for this book is available from the British Library.

A catalog record for this book is available from the Library of Congress.

10   9   8   7   6   5   4   3   2   1
17 16 15 14 13 12 11 10 09 08

Printed and bound in China

To **Deborah Means** and **Jim Malcomson** –
for all their support

To **Brenda Ward** *– in memory of a resilient
and spirited aunt*

Contents

List of Tables, Figures and Boxes

Tables

Figures

Boxes

Preface

Such is the continued pace of change in the world of health, housing and social policy and practice in Britain that the need for a fourth edition of this book became apparent within a couple of years of the appearance of the third edition in 2003. Whilst changes have taken place in all parts of Britain, the focus of the book (apart from Chapter 8) is primarily on the impact of change on adult social care services in England. The authors recognise that the world of community care policy and practice has still not settled into a stable state, so it is important for readers to recognise that the 'story' in this edition ends in Spring 2007.

ROBIN MEANS
SALLY RICHARDS
RANDALL SMITH

Acknowledgements

The production of this book has been greatly helped by advice from a wide range of people. Specifically we would like to thank the following for their very helpful guidance: John Baldock, Sophie Beaumont, Steen Bengtsson, Michael Fine, Jon Glasby, Caroline Glendinning, Ingrid Eyers, Hubert Heinelt, Frances Heywood, Andreas Hoff, Rachel Hurst, Anne Jamieson, Hans-Joachim von Kondratowitz, George Leeson, Mark Priestley, Thomas Scharf, Judy Triantafillou and Miguel Angel Verdugo.

Writing a book is a long and arduous business. So is producing a new edition of a book in a rapidly changing policy climate. We would like to thank family and friends for their encouragement and for putting up with bouts of evening and weekend work. We would also like to thank the forbearance of our publisher, Steven Kennedy. Finally, our ability to pull the book together has owed much to secretarial support from Linda Price, Angela Torrington and, above all, Lisa Sinfield.

R.M.
S.R.
R.S.

The authors and publishers wish to thank the following who have kindly given permission for the use of copyright material: C. Jagger at the Leicester Nuffield Research Unit for Table 1.3; the King's Fund for Figure 1.1; M. Knapp for Table 3.1, Blackwell Publishers for Boxes 3.1 and 3.3; the Editor of *Community Care* for Box 5.3; the Joseph Rowntree Foundation for Box 6.3; the University of the West of England for Box 6.4.

Crown Copyright material in Tables 1.1, 1.2, 4.1, 5.1, 6.1, 6.2 and Boxes 3.2, 5.1, 5.2, 6.2, 9.1 is reproduced with the permission of the controller of Her Majesty's Stationery Office under Click Use Licence CO1W0000276.

Every effort has been made to contact all the copyright-holders, but if any have been inadvertently omitted the publishers will be pleased to make the necessary arrangements at the earliest opportunity.

Chapter 1

Introducing Community Care

The first two editions of *Community Care: Policy and Practice* focused upon progress and problems in the implementation of the far-reaching changes introduced by the National Health Service and Community Care Act 1990. The 1990 Act had given the lead agency role to social services authorities for all the main 'core' groups of service users and required the stimulation of a mixed economy of care through encouraging independent providers. At a strategic level, this was to be achieved through the publication of community care plans on the basis of wide consultation with key agencies and groups, including service users and carers. Care management was to be used at the operational level to ensure service users were offered flexible packages of care which were to draw heavily upon the independent sector.

The third edition was published in 2003 and continued to focus on the 1990 Act but in the context of eight years of Labour Government. By 2003, three themes were beginning to dominate, namely:

- the growing emphasis by the government upon user empowerment;
- the speed of policy change leading to implementation problems which we called 'modernisation muddles';
- the growing emphasis upon the pivotal role of health/primary care leading us to question whether it would soon be 'the end for social services' as the lead agency in community care.

These three themes lie at the heart of this fourth edition. How far is the government willing to push its commitment to user empowerment? Has the pace of policy change slowed and are the numerous changes beginning to finally 'bed down'? Is it no longer appropriate to think in terms of lead agency roles in community care?

1

These crucial questions will be tackled by providing both a critique of key policy documents such as the Green Paper on Adult Social Care (Department of Health, 2005a) and also a review of the research evidence. However, as with previous editions, this one will be set within a context that is much wider than just contemporary community care policy and practice in the UK. This broader context will embrace historical perspectives (how much change is really occurring?), comparative perspectives (what is happening in other countries?) and theoretical perspectives (can we understand what is happening more clearly by drawing upon theories and organisational developments from outside community care?).

The third edition concluded with the following comments:

> New Labour's programme of modernisation seeks to achieve quality services that put the interests of the service user first. Whether this can be achieved by the top-down implementation of the current plethora of reforms and initiatives is likely to form the subject of any future edition of this book. (Means *et al.*, 2003, p. 222)

The overall task of the fourth edition is to assess whether such quality services have emerged or whether confusion remains the dominant feature of the community care policy and practice landscape in the UK.

What is community care? What is social care?

Since the late 1960s, community care has come to be almost universally espoused as a desirable objective for service users and a central pillar of policy for governments and politicians of all persuasions. An obvious starting point is for the authors to offer a clear statement about what they understand by the term 'community care'. Which groups will be covered? Will the book cover unpaid care as well as paid care? Does it include institutional care as well as domiciliary services? Which health care services are included? What does 'community' mean in the context of the term 'community care'? How does 'community care' relate to the growing use of the term 'social care' by government? These are simple questions but do they not necessarily have simple answers. 'Community care' has long been a contested term used by different people in different ways at different points in time.

The starting point in this definitional quest has to be the loaded power of the word 'community' within the term 'community care'. Titmuss (1968) described community care as 'the ever-lasting cottage-garden trailer' and went on to remark:

> Does it not conjure up a sense of warmth and human kindness, essentially personal and comforting, as loving as the wild flowers so enchantingly described by Lawrence in *Lady Chatterley's Lover*? (p. 104)

But where does the positive power of the term 'community care' come from? Baron and Haldane (1992) argued that it flows from the fact that 'community' is what Raymond Williams (1976) called a keyword in the development of culture and society. From the ninth century BC through to the twentieth century AD, Williams traced the use of the term 'community' to grieve for the recent passing of a series of mythical golden ages; each generation perceiving the past as organic and whole compared to the present. As Baron and Haldane point out, the term 'community' thus enables 'the continuous construction of an idyllic past of plenty and social harmony which acts as a critique of contemporary social relations' (p. 4). Thus the call by politicians and policy-makers to replace present systems of provision with community care feeds into this myth by implying that it is possible to recreate what many believe were the harmonious, caring and integrated communities of the past.

Taylor (2003) argues that it is possible to identify three different uses of the term community:

- descriptive: a group or network of people who share something in common or interact with each other;
- normative: community as a place where solidarity, participation and coherence are found;
- instrumental: (a) community as an agent acting to maintain or change its circumstances; (b) the location or orientation of services and policy interventions. (p. 34)

This perspective helps to explain the popularity of policy initiatives such as community care, community schools and community policing with politicians and policy-makers. Such policies use community in an instrumental way, justified by descriptions of community which stress their assumed normative strengths. Indeed, a strong feature of the Labour Governments since 1997 has been the stress upon neighbourhood and community renewal from a belief that 'healthy' communities are a prerequisite for a successful society (Department of Communities and Local Government, 2006). A key objective of this book is to delve behind the rhetoric of community care and caring communities. For example, several authors have pointed out that individuals and not communities carry out caring work, and that unpaid care is primarily carried out by female relatives (see Chapters 2 and 7). Equally, most people, including the users of community care services, have a highly complex notion of community. For some it is a small number of local streets, and for others their sense of community may come from work or leisure networks which are not geographically based (see Chapter 6). Indeed research suggests that as many as one in three people have no strong attachment to the 'community' in which they live (Taylor, 2003). Equally the provision of community care services based on local authority boundaries rarely reflects how service users perceive community. A day centre may not seem like a community service to a user if they have to travel three miles by specialist bus to reach it.

An important starting point for this analytical approach to community care is to trace the emergence of the term and its changing use over time. Yet it is very difficult to pin down the exact source. In a 1961 lecture delivered to the National Association of Mental Health, Titmuss (1968) claimed he had tried and failed to discover in any precise form its social origins, but went on to reflect that:

> institutional policies, both before and since the Mental Health Act of 1959, have, and without a doubt, assumed that someone knows what it means. More and more people suffering from schizophrenia, depressive illnesses and other mental handicaps have been discharged from hospitals, not cured but symptom-treated and labelled 'relieved'. More and more of the mentally subnormal have been placed under statutory supervision in the community. (p. 105)

Titmuss's concern was that the reduced reliance on hospitals would not be balanced by a major expansion of community-based services. In the following year, the then Minister of Health, Enoch Powell, took the 'policy' of community care one stage further with his 1962 Hospital Plan, which launched an official closure programme for large mental health and mental handicap hospitals and their replacement by a network of services to be provided in the community by local health and welfare services.

Although the origins of the phrase are obscure, it is clear that the term 'community care' was initially used to refer to a policy shift away from hospitals and towards community-based provision for 'mentally handicapped' people and for people with mental health problems. However, it soon began to be used in reference to the provision of services for elderly people and for physically disabled people. For example, the Chief Welfare Officer at the Ministry of Health was claiming in 1964 that with regard to older people:

> the true centre of the picture so far as geriatric services are concerned really has shifted, or is rapidly shifting, to care in the community supported by domiciliary services, and the important thing is to remember that residential homes are in fact a vital and most important part of community service. (Aves, 1964, p. 12)

The context of this quotation was government concern about the cost of long-term hospital care for frail elderly people. The Chief Welfare Officer was justifying a move to a cheaper form of institutional care (local authority residential care) by referring to it as a community service.

However, residential care in the 1970s was itself being seen by many as an overly expensive form of provision, which consumed resources that would be better employed funding non-institutional services such as home care, day care and sheltered housing (Bosanquet, 1978). *A Happier Old Age*, a discussion document produced by the then Labour Government (Department of Health and Social Security, 1978a) called for a major expansion of such services to keep the majority of frail elderly people out of expensive local authority residential care.

In the 1980s the definition of community care seemed to have been tightened by central government yet again. The White Paper response, *Growing Older*, to the discussion document was produced by a Conservative rather than a Labour government. It argued that:

> whatever level of public expenditure proves practicable and however it is distributed, the primary sources of support and care for elderly people are informal and voluntary ... It is the role of public authorities to sustain and, where necessary, develop – but never to displace – such support and care. Care in the community must increasingly mean by the community. (Department of Health and Social Security, 1981, p. 3)

The overall message was that community care (that is, informal care) needed to be maximised, partly because it was cheaper than care based on state-provided domiciliary services. By this definition, community care becomes what Abrams (1977, p. 151) called 'the provision of help, support and protection to others by lay members of societies acting in everyday domestic and occupational settings'.

In the past, therefore, the term 'community care' has been used to argue for changes in service emphasis. The positive virtues of community care have been juxtaposed against expensive, rigid and bureaucratic alternatives, such as hospitals, care homes and sometimes even domiciliary services. However, the 1989 White Paper *Caring for People* (Department of Health, 1989a) took a very different approach by referring to the full spectrum of care and services received by certain groups as being what it meant by community care:

> community care means providing the right level of intervention and support to enable people to achieve maximum independence and control over their own lives. For this aim to become a reality, the development of a wide range of services provided in a variety of settings is essential. These services form part of a spectrum of care, ranging from domiciliary support provided to people in their own homes, strengthened by the availability of respite care and day care for those with more intensive care needs, through sheltered housing, group homes and hostels where increasing levels of care are available, to residential care and nursing homes and long-stay

hospital care for those for whom other forms of care are no longer enough. (p. 9)

The White Paper explains that its focus is mainly upon the role of the statutory and independent sectors but that 'the reality is that most care is provided by family, friends and neighbours' (ibid.). The statutory and independent sectors are seen as responsible for providing social care (including housing), health care and appropriate social security benefits. This book takes a similarly broad view of what is meant by the term 'community care'. It thus considers not only informal support by unpaid carers but also the provision of the full spectrum of institutional and non-institutional services by the public, private and voluntary sectors.

A final definitional complication has emerged in recent years because of the growing use of the term 'social care' rather than 'community care' by the government. Thus, 2005 saw the publication of a Green Paper on Adult Social Care (Department of Health, 2005a) rather than on community care or adult community care. Rather like Titmuss's search for the origins of community care, we have not been able to trace the first 'official' use of the term 'social care' let alone a clear rationale from government for it being preferred over 'community care'. In other words, what did 'community care' do wrong? Although, there is no definitive answer to this question there is a strong suspicion that the driver relates to the lead agency role of social services in community care (see Chapter 3). By using the term 'social care', this apparent policy commitment can be sidestepped rather than officially reversed. A good example of this was *Shifting the Balance of Power within the NHS: Securing Delivery* (Department of Health, 2001h) which stressed the growing centrality of primary care trusts in health care policy. This policy document stresses how this includes their pivotal role in social care which requires them to drive forward 'joint work with local government and other partners' (p. 5). Interestingly, the government has not lost all interest in the positive power of the word 'community'. Thus, the 2006 health and social care White Paper was called *Our Health, Our Care, Our Say* but was also subtitled *A New Direction for Community Services* (Department of Health, 2006a).

One of the biggest ironies in the community care versus social care debate is that the actual legislation, which empowers local authorities to deliver and/or fund services such as care homes, day centres and home care, flows from a patchwork of different acts spread over the last 60 years. Thus, the National Assistance Act 1948 remains the main piece of legislation which defines the role of local authorities with regard to residential care.

In practical terms, the primary focus of the fourth edition of this book remains adult social care services, what used to be called 'community care'. This means that health care and especially health services have a key role in subsequent chapters, but mainly in terms of their implications for adult social care services.

Who are the users? Who are the carers?

This book follows the broad definition of the 1989 White Paper *Caring for People: Community Care in the Next Decade and Beyond* in terms of defining who are the potential users of community care services:

> many people need some extra help and support at some stage in their lives, as a result of illness or temporary disability. Some people, as a result of the effects of old age, of mental illness including dementia, of mental handicap or physical disability or sensory impairment, have a continuing need for care on a longer-term basis. People with drug and alcohol related disorders, people with multiple handicaps and people with progressive illnesses such as AIDS or multiple sclerosis may also need community care at some time. (Department of Health, 1989a, p. 10)

The emphasis of this book is equally broad although it concentrates most of its comments on the traditional main client groups, namely frail older people, physically disabled people, people with mental health problems and people with learning difficulties. However, it does this with a recognition that client groups are really bureaucratic and/or medical labels which rarely reflect how service users and carers perceive their personal assistance needs. Such labels have a number of negative consequences. First, they have the effect of dividing service users against each other in the scramble for resources rather than facilitating and coming together to campaign for the appropriate resourcing for health and welfare systems (see Chapter 7).

Second, they fail to recognise that many people cut across traditional client boundaries. For instance, physically disabled people become old as do people with learning difficulties. Many older people experience the physical problems of later life but significant numbers will also have mental health problems (Care Services Improvement Partnership, 2005) such as dementia (Hofman *et al.*, 1991; Woods, 2005; Alzheimer's Society, 2007) or depression (Fiske and Jones, 2005). The danger is that social services will respond to only some aspects of the support needs of such individuals and this will be determined by the client focus of their social work team (Rummery, 2002). Both Walker *et al.* (1996) in their study of older people with learning difficulties in the community and Beattie *et al.* (2004; 2005) in their study of marginalised groups in dementia care found this tendency of some to fall between traditionally defined services. The people in the Walker *et al.* study were falling 'between services for people with learning difficulties and those for older people' (p. 56). In a similar way, Beattie *et al.* (2005) found that service commissioners and providers struggled to deliver adequate services for younger people with dementia and for people with dementia from minority ethnic groups. As one manager put it, 'they don't quite fit the way we organise our services' (p. 67).

Third, much service provision, especially in areas such as supported housing, has traditionally targeted narrowly defined groups such as drug abusers, homeless people or people with mental health problems (Foord and Simic, 2005). People in need of accommodation and support are thus encouraged to define themselves as drug abusers, homeless people or people with mental health problems rather than as individuals who might face all three challenges. The requirements of many people cut across such narrow administrative categories but they still feel obliged to present themselves as having one particular dominant need if they want to get help. Client group categories encourage service-led rather than user-driven community care provision. Chapter 6 explores whether the *Supporting People* initiative (Department of Transport, Local Government and the Regions, 2001b) is achieving a genuine break from the limitations of this past approach.

In terms of actual numbers of service users, the clearest information is available for those over 65 as a result of the work of the

Royal Commission on Long Term Care (Sutherland Report, 1999a) with its associated Research Volume 1 (1999b) and from the Wanless Review (2006) on *Securing Good Care for Older People* which also commissioned its own research (Jagger *et al.*, 2006). Table 1.1 draws upon the Royal Commission to show that in the late 1990s about 600,000 older people were receiving home care funded through a local authority while just over 480,000 were in care homes of one kind or another. Figure 1.1 is drawn from the Wanless Review and profiles the use of community-based services in England for 2004–2005.

However, it needs to be remembered that those 'known' to the community care system are only a small percentage of those with support needs or those providing informal caring services. The Office of Population Censuses and Surveys (OPCS) research in

TABLE 1.1   *Number of people in the UK receiving long-term care services by type of service and funding*

	Number of recipients	
(a) Domiciliary care		
Home care	610,000	
Community nursing	530,000	
Day care	260,000	
Private help	670,000	
Meals	240,000	
(b) Institutional care		*Total*
Residential care		
Publicly financed	205,000	
Privately financed	83,750	288,750
Nursing home care		
Publicly financed	115,000	
Privately financed	42,500	157,500
Hospital	34,000	34,000
All institutional residents		480,250

Source: Sutherland Report (1999a) p. 9.

FIGURE 1.1   *Numbers of people aged 65 and over receiving community-based services during the year 2004/05*

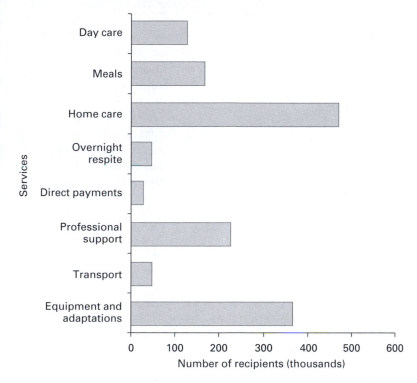

Source: Wanless Review (2006) p. 50.

the mid-1980s is still often quoted on the prevalence, range and severity of disability in Britain. The researchers distinguished 13 different types of disability based on the international classification of impairments, disabilities and handicaps used by the World Health Organization (see Table 1.2). They also developed a classification system for severity of disability which could be used to classify people with different numbers and types of disabilities. The severity of disability in each of the 13 areas was established for each individual and the three highest scores were then combined so that people could be allocated to an overall severity category. Category one was for the least severe and category ten was for the most severe.

TABLE 1.2   *Estimate of numbers of disabled adults in Great
Britain with different types of disability (thousands)*

Type of disability	In private households	In establishments	Total population
Locomotion	4,005	327	4,332
Reaching and stretching	1,083	147	1,230
Dexterity	1,572	165	1,737
Seeing	1,384	284	1,668
Hearing	2,365	223	2,588
Personal care	2,129	354	2,483
Continence	957	185	1,142
Communication	989	213	1,202
Behaviour	1,172	175	1,347
Intellectual functioning	1,182	293	1,475
Consciousness	188	41	229
Eating, drinking, digesting	210	66	276
Disfigurement	391	*	*

* Data not provided.
Source: Martin *et al.* (1988) p. 25.

It was estimated that six million adults in Great Britain had
one or more impairments, of which one million were assigned to
the lowest severity category. Smaller numbers were identified in
each successive category, with 200,000 in category ten. As one
might expect, elderly people dominated the two highest categories. The Sutherland Report (1999b) also looked at the issue of
dependency in later life. Drawing upon the concept of activities
of daily living, it was 'estimated that 2,470,000 (28%) of the
elderly household population have some level of dependency' of
which 606,000 (7%) faced difficulties sufficiently severe to mean
they could not complete some of these activities without the
assistance of another person (p. 6). Jagger *et al.* (2006) forecast
future disability levels under changing patterns of disease for the
Wanless Review (2006) and Table 1.3 sets out the initial 2005
figures used in this modelling work.

TABLE 1.3   *The age-specific prevalence of disease in 2005*

	Percentage (N in thousands)			Percentage (N in thousands)	
Stroke			**Coronary heart disease**		
65–74 years	5.4	(238)	65–74 years	19.9	(877)
75–84 years	8.8	(268)	75–84 years	23.3	(709)
85+ years	9.5	(95)	85+ years	22.1	(222)
TOTAL	7.1	(601)	TOTAL	21.4	(1,808)
Arthritis			**Mild cognitive impairment**		
65–74 years	48.1	(2,116)	65–74 years	15.4	(676)
75–84 years	55.0	(1,677)	75–84 years	27.7	(844)
85+ years	55.8	(561)	85+ years	28.5	(286)
TOTAL	51.5	(4,354)	TOTAL	21.4	(1,807)
Moderate cognitive impairment					
65–74 years	3.1	(136)			
75–84 years	10.7	(326)			
85+ years	36.2	(364)			
TOTAL	9.8	(827)			

Source: Based on Jagger *et al.* (2006) p. 25.

There have also been prevalence estimates with regard to people with learning difficulties. Drawing upon a range of epidemiological sources, the 2001 White Paper estimated there were 210,000 people with severe and profound learning difficulties (Department of Health, 2001a) of which 65,000 were children and young people, 120,000 were adults of working age and 35,000 were older people. With regard to people with mental health problems, the National Service Framework (NSF) document noted that one-quarter of routine GP consultations were for people with a mental health problem and that around 90 per cent of mental health care is provided solely by primary care (Department of Health, 1999b). The most common mental health problems are depression, eating disorders and anxiety disorders. The NSF pointed out that in any one year one woman in 15 and one man in 30 will be affected by depression and 4,000 suicides are attributed to this cause.

Finally, there is a need to profile the extent to which people with support needs receive help from informal carers. Estimates of the number of informal carers have traditionally been drawn from the regularly repeated General Household Survey (GHS), enabling Maher and Green (2002) to use the 2000 survey to estimate that there were about six–eight million adult carers in five million households. However, the 2001 census did ask individuals for the first time about their caring activities. This has allowed Lloyd (2006b) to point out that 'of the 5.2 million carers identified ... 68 per cent (3.56 million) provide care for up to 19 hours a week, 11 per cent (0.57 million) 20–49 hours a week and 21 per cent (1.09 million) for 50 hours a week or more, over half of whom are aged over 55 and 225,000 of whom state that they are not in good health' (p. 947). Research increasingly distinguishes between 'informal helping' and 'heavily involved' caring with only the latter likely to lead to any request for public support. Pickard (1999), in her review of research on the 1995 GHS, explains how 'most of the indicators suggest that there were between one and three-quarters and two million heavily involved carers at this time' (p. 18). Phillipson *et al.* (2001), in revisiting three classic community studies in England, compared the present situation for older residents with regard to informal care and social support to the 1950s. They concluded that close kin remained pivotal but that neighbours and friends were playing a growing role in informal helping.

However, it needs to be remembered that there is no agreed methodology for translating prevalence figures for dependency, illness or caring into the need for community care provision. Feminist commentators have long argued that the real need for state-provided services has been suppressed by the encouragement of women to take on this role by government as a mechanism for controlling public expenditure (Finch and Groves, 1983; Dalley, 1996). In a similar vein, disability rights theorists have pointed out how prevalence data stress personal inadequacy requiring a care response when the real problem may be poverty or environmental barriers (Oliver, 1990). For example, Abberley (1991) argued that many of those defined as having major locomotion difficulties in the OPCS disability surveys may simply be disadvantaged by societal failure to build accessible environments. Much of the need for individual community care support would disappear for many if such discrimination was tackled. Chapter 7 explores such critiques of community care policy and practice in more detail.

Introducing social care services

The last section looked at the most important stakeholders in any community care system, namely service users and informal carers. However, there is also a need to introduce the reader to local authority social care services and some of the other actors and organisations which influence their attempts to fund, coordinate and deliver care provision.

The starting point has to be to stress the complexity and variety of social services throughout the United Kingdom and what Challis (1990, p. 2) called 'the dazzling array of problematic characteristics which they exhibit', including accountability to elected members, the wide range of responsibilities, the variety of staff employed and high media interest. However, the exact organisational nature of a social services department has never been precisely defined in law when compared to many NHS agencies and hence there has been a long history of organisational variation (Means *et al.*, 2002). Before the 1990 reforms individual departments might split their activities by such categories as client group (childcare services and adult services), geography (north and south of the authority) and function (domiciliary services and residential care), and these dimensions could be combined in a variety of complex ways. In more recent years at least three new sources of organisational complexity have emerged. First, the community care reforms introduced by the 1990 Act encouraged social services authorities to split their functions between those with a purchaser/assessor focus and those concerned with direct service provision (see Chapter 3). Second, local authorities increasingly combined all or some of their social services functions with other statutory responsibilities such as housing or education (Hill, 2000a). Finally, local authorities and health services have pursued a variety of options for establishing joint commissioning and provider functions for particular client groups (Chapter 5) to a point where some have queried the very future of a local authority role in the provision of social care (Glendinning and Means, 2002).

New Labour's policy of devolved government for Scotland,

Wales and Northern Ireland has further promoted diversity in the organisation and funding of social services across the UK. In England and Wales, during the 1990s, children's and adults' services had become increasingly separate within the generic 'Seebohm' social services departments created in 1971. This trend was confirmed by the Children's Act 2004, which removed the duty from local authorities to appoint a Director of Social Services. Henceforth a Director of Adult Social Services (DASS) would be responsible for organising social care in each local authority (Department of Health, 2005a). The situation in Wales is different with councils retaining a single social services director responsible for adult and children's services, a policy confirmed in a new ten-year plan for social services in Wales (Welsh Assembly Government, 2007). The picture in Scotland is also one of organisational variety, though there is also less evidence of separation between adults' and children's services compared with England. Devolution has resulted in an increased level of funding for social services, in comparison to England and Wales, and a much greater emphasis on development of the social work profession and the wider social care workforce (Community Care, 2006b). Northern Ireland has had a system of joint health and social services boards, responsible for planning, purchasing and commissioning services from community and acute health care trusts dating back to the 1970s and 1980s. Widely seen as a useful model for service integration, this too is scheduled to change. From April 2008, there will be a single health and social services authority which will commission services from just five health and social services trusts. Although the purpose of the reorganisation is to reduce bureaucracy, it has also been criticised as a potentially damaging cost-cutting measure (Callaghan, 2006).

The first three editions of *Community Care: Policy and Practice* were primarily about England and Wales with occasional references to other parts of the UK. The fourth edition is mainly the story of community care in England although divergent developments in Wales and Scotland are drawn upon as appropriate. This is especially true of Chapter 9 which addresses the crucial issue of 'where next?' for community care and whether the present enthusiasm for markets is an English only phenomenon.

Whilst the history of community care policy over the years is mainly a domestic story, influences from outside the UK can at times be discerned. The expansion of case management under the Older Americans Act 1965, was used extensively by Davies and Challis (1986) in developing their long-term model for community care in Britain (see Chapter 8). Their work was central to the debate in the 1980s on the development of care in the community and the role of care managers. The flow of ideas on user empowerment came in part from groups of disabled activists drawing lessons from innovative practices in the USA, such as the Center of Independent Living movement or the People First forum of people with learning difficulties. The UK Royal Commission on Long Term Care (Sutherland Report, 1999b) drew on practices in other post-industrial societies in reaching its conclusions. For example, the development of a national carers' strategy in Australia was highlighted. More specifically, the idea of laying 'delayed discharge' fines on local authorities came from Scandinavia (see Pedersen, 1998). As a member state of the European Union, legislation on such matters as working conditions in the labour market have impacted on organisations providing social care services. The enlargement of the EU in 2004 has resulted in the availability of workers with relatively low wage expectations to be employed by care agencies in Britain. More broadly, the designation of special years, such as the 2003 European Year of People with Disabilities, and the publication of a wide range of social care and social policy documents by the European Commission, tend to affect the climate of domestic debate within member states. Whilst influences on policy from outside the UK should not be exaggerated, neither should they be ignored (see Chapter 8).

Variations in organisational form have long been matched by variations in the range and depth of services provided. For example, a mid-1980s study by the Audit Commission (1985) on services for elderly people in seven different authorities found wide differences, both in terms of residential care places per thousand elderly people and in terms of expenditure on domiciliary services. The following chapters will show how implementation of the community care reforms and the modernisation agenda have done little to reduce such variation despite the growing emphasis by government on performance indicators and league tables.

Such organisational and service variation is partly a reflection

FIGURE 1.2   *Pressures upon local authority committees
with responsibility for social care services*

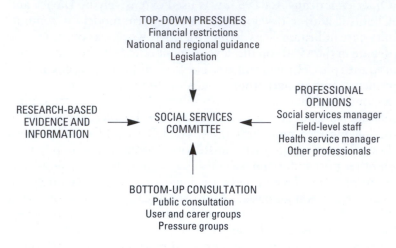

of the fact that social services are embedded in local government
where councillors from different political parties may have
opposing views about what kinds of services should be provided
and how best they should be delivered (Clough, 1990; Means *et
al.*, 2002). These debates have in the past been played out in the
formal policy-making system of the full social services committee
but also through more informal meetings and contacts which
ensure that many decisions are made prior to full committee
meetings (Hill, 2000b). Changes in local government arrangements, such as cabinets and scrutiny committees, have not less-
ened the force of this comment. Tensions between social services
directors and members are common, partly because of the
myriad of pressures which have to be faced and balanced (see
Figure 1.2). Many of these are top-down pressures from central
government, flowing from such factors as the strengths and
weaknesses of the legislation and Treasury-driven financial
restrictions as well as the service frameworks, practice guidance
and performance indicators issued by the Department of Health
(Hill, 2000b).

Chapters 3 and 4 illustrate how an important element of this
pressure is the growing emphasis on audit and inspection
through both the Commission for Social Care Inspection (CSCI)

and the Audit Commission which is a quango with a remit to improve the economy, efficiency and effectiveness of the work of local authorities and the health service. A critical inspection report or a poor rating for services can easily imperil directors responsible for social care services.

Against this, councillors have to struggle with a range of professional opinions and advice from social services managers, health managers and others about the direction that community care policy should take in their authority. Both local professionals and those responsible for central government guidance are likely to make reference to research and audit-based evidence to justify their views. Authoritative sources now include not only the Audit Commission but also the Social Care Institute for Excellence (SCIE), a key element of the government's strategy to encourage evidence-based personal social services (Department of Health, 1998a). Finally, members see themselves as the conduit for the views of local people in terms of public consultation, a role they are expected to strengthen as a part of local government reform (Deputy Prime Minister, 1998). In addition, professional staff are also increasingly organising consultation meetings with service users and carers which are now seen as central to 'Best Value' scrutiny to achieve service improvements (Department of the Environment, Transport and the Regions, 1998) while the disability movement continues to call for fundamental changes in the way professionals engage with the consumers of their service (see Chapter 7).

The impact of these conflicting and ever-strengthening pressures is a central focus of this book. There is a need to understand to what extent they help to improve the quality of services available to those with community care needs or whether the end result is moving close to organisational chaos.

Chapter 2

From Institutions to Care in the Community: The History of Neglect

This chapter discusses the historical development of social care and health provision for older people and for people with physical impairments, learning difficulties and mental health problems. The response to the perceived needs of all these groups was overwhelmingly institutional in the nineteenth and early twentieth centuries. Current services for these groups carry this institutional legacy, and present community care policies are, at least in part, an attempt to shake off that legacy. The history of community care services is highly complex. Therefore tackling this theme in one chapter of a textbook risks the danger of oversimplifying events and issues. No attempt will be made to provide a detailed history for all services since such accounts exist elsewhere for most of the main care groups. Rather the focus will be on the extent of service neglect in terms of priority for resources and in terms of the quality of what has been provided from the resources made available. In the 1950s and 1960s, critics of this neglect often referred to the 'Cinderella services' or the 'Cinderella groups'. In terms of priority for resources, they were always waiting for a fairy godmother to arrive and get them to the ball. The second half of the chapter goes on to explore the main explanations which have been put forward to account for this neglect.

The inclusion of this chapter is based on the strong belief that a knowledge and understanding of community care history is of practical value to busy social care managers, field-level staff and students, as well as of interest to the community care academic. Those struggling with contemporary policy issues can be supported through a grasp of the way the current situation came about. More specifically, this chapter will help an understanding of two crucial issues. First, the changing needs of the labour market and the economy often shapes the availability and form of public services for the main community care groups and this continues to be the case (see also Chapter 9). Second, neglected services are usually run by neglected staff for low status clients. This creates situations in which the service user may be open to abuse especially if they are frail or physically disabled, and especially if they have mental health problems or learning disabilities. The 2006 exposé of abuse in homes for people with learning disabilities in first Cornwall and then in Sutton and Merton underlines this point (McCormack, 2007b; Healthcare Commission, 2007). Equally, this culture of neglect means that the closure of institutions has rarely been followed by their replacement with high quality community based services and the implications of this flow throughout this book.

The long history of neglect: services for older people and physically impaired people

Through much of the Victorian period, there was little recognition of a social group, definable as elderly people, who needed special provision because of their age. Elderly people, and especially elderly men, were expected to work until they died. Those elderly people who were unable to support themselves in the community through the labour market or with the help of relatives were often forced to enter the workhouse, where no distinction was made between them and other paupers. As Cole and Edwards (2005) point out, 'institutionalisation in the dreaded workhouse increased between the mid and late 19th century for both men and women' so that 'by 1901, almost 10 per cent of English men and 6 per cent of women aged 75 and over were in the workhouse' (p. 233). The stereotype of the workhouse is one of brutality, although research suggests that regimes were often more neglectful in terms of boredom and regimentation rather than anything else (Crowther, 1981) and that there was also considerable local variation in practice (Digby, 1978).

However, a variety of pressures began to change the role of the Poor Law in meeting the needs of older people from the late Victorian period onwards. Technological changes were seen as forcing older workers out of the labour market through no fault of their own and into dependence upon Poor Law indoor and outdoor relief. As Macnicol (2006) explains, 'the overwhelming weight of contemporary testimony in Britain and the USA from the 1890s onwards indicates a growing concern from a wide spectrum of political opinion that capitalism appeared to be entering a significant, new phase and was dispensing with the labour of older males' (p. 41). In parallel with these economic pressures, social researchers such as Charles Booth were chronicling the extent of poverty in old age and calling for the establishment of a national system of old age pensions.

The complex system of contributory and non-contributory pension arrangements which emerged through the legislation of 1908, 1925, 1940 and 1948 resulted in the gradual removal of older people from the labour market and the social construction of the concept of retirement (Phillipson, 1982). However, the state pension provided only the most basic of incomes so that poverty remained the outcome for most of those unable to work so that 'men, especially, often ended their lives in workhouses or other institutions' (Thane, 2005b, p. 273). Meanwhile, workhouse provision for older people was itself undergoing change with separate medical provision for the 'chronic sick' gradually emerging as well as a more general segregation of older people from other inmates in some institutions. Major organisational change of the Poor Law system was introduced by the Local Government Act 1929, through which the best Poor Law hospitals were retitled 'public health hospitals' and became the responsibility of local authority health committees, and hence no longer part of the Poor Law system. However, these hospitals were almost entirely focused on the acute sick, rather than medical provision for older people, who were usually seen as chronic cases.

The remaining medical provision together with other workhouse provision also ceased to be the responsibility of the 62 Poor Law boards, and was transferred to 145 counties and county boroughs, each of which was required to establish a public assistance committee. The workhouse was retitled the public assistance institution (PAI). However, the 1929 Act made little attempt to abolish the taint of pauperism. For example, entry to a PAI meant that the new elderly 'inmate' was disqualified from receiving a pension unless he or she was admitted specifically for medical treatment and even then pension rights were lost after three months. Equally, the principle of family responsibility for destitute people was maintained. The Poor Law Act 1930 stated:

> It should be the duty of the father, grandfather, mother, grandmother, husband or child, of a poor, old, blind, lame or impotent person, or other poor person, not able to work, if possessed of sufficient means, to relieve and maintain that person not able to work.

In other words, an application for relief involved an assessment of the means of near relatives, who were also expected to make a contribution to those in institutional care.

Restrictive regulations remained in force about different elements of the institutional regime such as clothing, the retention of personal possessions, visiting rights and the ability to take days out. As Roberts (1970, p. 26) put it, most elderly inmates continued to sleep 'in large dormitories, sat on hard chairs, looked out on cabbage patches diversified by concrete, were separated by sex and, except on one day a week, could not pass the gates without permission'. Disquiet about this situation developed in the late 1930s. For example, Matthews (undated) called for more colour to be brought into the lives of elderly people in institutions 'through contact with visitors from the outside world, by providing occupations as well as entertainments and by introducing more variety into their food, clothing and surroundings' (p. 13). A campaign emerged calling for the introduction of pocket money for inmates. Some public assistance committees developed small homes with more liberal regimes, although they were usually reserved for 'women of the more gentle type' or men of 'the merit class' (quoted in Means and Smith, 1998a, p. 19).

A more detailed picture of life in the medical and non-medical parts of public assistance institutions emerged during and just after the Second World War. It was a portrait of extensive neglect (Titmuss, 1976; Means and Smith, 1998b, Chapters 2 and 3). With regard to the so-called 'elderly chronic sick', there seems to have been a shortage of both beds and high quality care. Writing in the late 1940s, McEwan and Laverty (1949) argued that the 1929 Act had a disastrous impact upon people with long-term health care needs since 'many of the new and aspiring municipal hospitals got rid of their undesirable chronic sick ... sending them to Public Assistance Institutions to upgrade their own medical services' (p. 9). This placed added pressure upon the medical wards of public assistance institutions, many of which could not cope with the increased demand for beds, and so elderly patients often had to be 'housed' elsewhere in the institutions. For example, in Bradford:

> In the Public Assistance Hospitals (The Park and Thornton View) ... patients are discharged or returned from the chronic sick wards to the ambulant or 'house' section ... In The Park, where the chronic sick wards were overcrowded, the most fit (but often frail) patients had to be sent to the ambulant wards to make room for admissions to the hospital section. There was, in consequence, a proportion of sick or disabled people in the ambulant section, where they had to remain, often confined to bed, there being no room for them in hospital. (p. 8)

The overall situation was further worsened by the creation of a 300,000 bed Emergency Medical Service at the outbreak of the Second World War since this involved the discharge of 140,000 patients in just two days. Many of the reserved beds were in PAIs and one commentator of the time claimed that:

> the people who fared worst of all were the chronically sick, the bedridden, the paralysed, the aged, people suffering from advanced cancer or from tuberculosis who were discharged in their hundreds from public institutions to their own homes, where they could get little, if any, care, where in all too many cases they were regarded as an intolerable burden on their relatives, and even to houses from which all their relatives had been evacuated to the country. (Morris, 1940, p. 189)

As the war progressed, further problems emerged. Many elderly patients who remained in PAI hospitals were in danger from bombing raids but there was government reluctance to move them. The ability to manage outside the hospital was undermined by the disruptions of war and so 'thousands who had formerly been nursed at home were clamouring for admission to hospitals when families were split up, when homes were damaged or destroyed, and when the nightly trek to the shelter became a part of normal life for Londoners' (Titmuss, 1976, p. 448). Some of these problems eased, but the extent to which such hospitals continued to fail to offer effective treatment to their 'chronic sick' patients was underlined by the government hospital surveys of the 1940s. Ten survey teams were appointed in 1941, some by the Minister of Health and some in conjunction with the Nuffield Provincial Hospitals Trust, to cover both voluntary and public hospitals. The aim of the surveys was to gather information about existing hospital facilities as a basis for future planning for a possible National Health Service. The findings were drawn together in *The Domesday Book of the Hospital Services* which stressed how the surveys outlined the haphazard growth and lack of planning within existing hospital services. *The Domesday Book* showed how care for the 'chronic sick' received the bitterest comments from the investigators:

> All are agreed that 'the reproach of the masses of undiagnosed and untreated cases of chronic type which litter our Public Assistance Institutions must be removed'. Without proper classification and investigation, at present young children and senile dements are 'banded together' in these institutions, along with many elderly patients whom earlier diagnosis and treatment might have enabled to return to their homes ... 'The great essential is that every patient should be thoroughly examined and treated with a view to restoration to a maximum degree of activity. Only if treatment is unsuccessful or is clearly useless, should he be regarded as chronically sick', and 'even then [he] should be subject to periodic review'. (Nuffield Provincial Hospitals Trust, 1946, p. 16)

All the investigators called for hospital services and accommodation to be completely divorced from public assistance institutions.

The subsequent establishment of the National Health Service in 1946 did bring the PAI hospitals under the same administrative system as other types of hospital provision. *The Domesday Book* did generate government awareness of the cost of blocked hospital beds from the failure both to tackle the acute illnesses of elderly patients and to provide them with appropriate rehabilitation services. Elements of the medical profession also began to argue the need to develop the specialism of geriatric medicine so as to transform the quality of medical care available to elderly patients (Thane, 2005a). There is not the space in this chapter to trace the development of hospital-based geriatric medicine after the Second World War. However, it remained a low-status route for medical graduates and a low priority for health care expenditure (Martin, 1995). Some impressive initiatives did emerge but many elderly people were classified as non-curable and placed in long-stay annexes and supervised by visiting GPs. Martin has argued that these annexes were little better than the overcrowded chronic wards of the inter-war years.

The Second World War also had a negative impact on the ability of elderly people to remain in their own homes even when they had no major health problems. Support from children was reduced. Others were made homeless as a result of bombing raids. One consequence was that 'respectable' elderly people were being pushed towards PAIs, as were many elderly people definable as war victims or casualties. Many felt that regimes of PAIs and their continued association with pauperism were inappropriate for such people. A campaign around these issues emerged in spring 1943 as a result of a letter which appeared in the *Manchester Guardian*. The letter was entitled 'A Workhouse Visit' and spoke of 'a frail, sensitive, refined old woman' of 84 who was forced to live in the regime described in the following extract:

> But down each side of the ward were ten beds, facing one another. Between each bed and its neighbour was a small locker and a straight-backed, wooden uncushioned chair. On each chair sat an old woman in workhouse dress, upright, unoccupied. No library books or wireless. Central heating, but no open fire. No easy chairs. No pictures on the walls ... There were three exceptions to the upright old women. None was allowed to lie on her bed at any time throughout the day, although breakfast is at 7 a.m., but these three, unable any longer to endure their physical and mental weariness, had crashed forward, face downwards, on to their immaculate bedspreads and were asleep. (Quoted in Samson, 1944, p. 47)

The subsequent Nuffield survey committee on the problems of ageing and the care of old people, which was chaired by Seebohm Rowntree, indicated that poor conditions and restrictive regimes were not unusual:

Day-rooms in such institutions are usually large and cheerless with wooden Windsor armchairs placed around the walls. Floors are mainly bare boards with brick floors in lavatories, bathrooms, kitchens and corridors. In large urban areas such institutions may accommodate as many as 1,500 residents of various types, including more than a thousand aged persons. (Rowntree, 1980, p. 64)

The survey committee confirmed that rules in these large institutions were often harsh or harshly administered, while apathy was widespread among the residents.

The National Assistance Act 1948 was presented to Parliament as the solution to these problems. Section 21 of the Act stated that 'it should be the duty of every local authority ... to provide residential accommodation for persons who are by reasons of age, infirmity or any other circumstances in need of care and attention which is not otherwise available to them'. Townsend (1964) argued in *The Last Refuge* that changing the names of PAIs to residential homes and transferring responsibility for running them from public assistance committees to health/welfare committees had achieved little. This is perhaps a little unfair. The old system of family responsibility for maintenance was abolished and users were now perceived as residents who contributed to their keep through their pension, although they were allowed to retain five shillings for pocket money (Means, 2001). However, in many respects, the tradition of neglect continued. For example, Townsend (1964) reported that ex-PAIs 'accounted for just over half the accommodation used by county and county borough councils, for just under half the residents and for probably over three-fifths of the old people actually admitted in the course of a year' (p. 190). With regard to the 39 former PAIs visited by Townsend, 57 per cent of the accommodation was in rooms with at least ten beds. Basic amenities such as handbasins, toilets and baths were not only insufficient, but were often difficult to reach, badly distributed and of poor quality. With regard to staff, Townsend found that many were middle-aged and elderly persons who had given 'a lifetime's service under the old Poor Law as well as the new administration' (p. 39). Townsend felt:

it would be idle to pretend that many of them were imbued with the more progressive standards of personal care encouraged by the Ministry of Health, geriatricians, social workers and others since the war ... Some were unsuitable, by any standards, for the tasks they performed, men and women with authoritarian attitudes inherited from Poor Law days who provoked resentment and even terror among infirm people. (p. 39)

In conclusion, Townsend argued that the main shortcoming was not the failure to improve the quality of residential buildings and staff, but rather the failure to develop community-based services so as to reduce the need for people to enter institutional care.

The legislative power to provide social care services in the community was very slow to develop and is a further indication of neglect, especially towards elderly people. Section 29 of the National Assistance Act 1948 did empower local authorities 'to promote the welfare of persons who are blind, deaf or dumb and others, who are substantially and permanently handicapped by illness, injury or congenital deformity'. Nevertheless, it remained *ultra vires* for local authorities to develop preventive services for most frail elderly people, with the exception of home care, where legal empowerment was provided through the National Health Service Act 1946. Under the 1948 Act, local authorities could not develop their own meals-on-wheels services, chiropody facilities, laundry services, visiting schemes or counselling services for elderly people, a situation which led Parker (1965) to remark:

The concern to maintain and foster family life evident in the Children Act was completely lacking in the National Assistance Act. The latter made no attempt to provide any sort of substitute family life for old people who could no longer be supported by their own relatives. Institutional provision was accepted without question. (p. 106)

The belief of the legislators behind the 1948 Act was that domiciliary services were an 'extra frill' and so could be left to voluntary organisations, such as old people's welfare committees (now Age Concern), the Women's (Royal) Voluntary Service and the Red Cross to develop. A complex patchwork of visiting services, day centres, meals services and chiropody did emerge but much of this provision was not easily available or was unevenly spread geographically, despite attempts by central government to develop the planning role of local authorities (Sumner and Smith, 1969). For example, Harris (1961) carried out a survey of 453 meals-on-wheels schemes and found that 40 per cent had difficulties finding enough volunteers, 40 per cent of recipients received a meal on only one day a week and 162 schemes closed completely for part of the year.

However, legislative change to empower local authorities occurred very slowly despite growing research evidence of the paucity of services being provided through the voluntary sector (Means and Smith, 1998b, Chapter 6). The National Assistance (Amendment) Act 1962 allowed local authorities to provide meals services directly for the first time, whereas previously they could only provide a grant to enable a voluntary organisation to do so. The Health Services and Public Health Act 1968 gave local authorities the general power to promote the welfare of elderly people, while the National Health Service Act 1977 made home care a mandatory responsibility rather than a discretionary power as had hitherto been the case. The implementation of the 1968 Act was delayed until April 1971 to coincide with the creation of unified social services departments. These new departments were soon dominated by childcare concerns, especially after the death of Maria Colwell in January 1973 (Parton, 1991). Research studies confirmed that social services departments maintained client group hierarchies with elderly people at the bottom so that elderly clients were usually allocated to unqualified staff on the grounds that intervention was perceived as likely to be routine and unglamorous (Bowl, 1986). Hopes of a major expansion of domiciliary services were further hit by the first tremors on the public expenditure front in the mid-1970s with the oil crisis. Increasingly, debate shifted away from the need for overall increases in social care expenditure towards arguments about the need for a shift of priorities between domiciliary and residential provision (Means *et al.*, 2002).

In terms of the historical development of health and welfare services for physically disabled people, several authors have also stressed the negative impact of industrial and economic change by claiming that 'with the Industrial Revolution and the advent of machinery designed to be operated by the able-bodied, disabled people were progressively excluded from the workplace' (Drake, 1996, p. 150). Thus, the combination of new work patterns and the breakdown of traditional community support systems imposed dependency upon many disabled people and made them heavily reliant upon welfare services. This was not very different from the experience of elderly people. Large numbers of physically disabled people were forced to live in institutions.

At first glance, Section 29 of the National Assistance Act 1948 seemed to ensure that people with physical, visual and sensory impairments were not neglected in the post-war period especially when compared with frail elderly people, since this section gave local authorities the power to develop domiciliary services for these groups. However, this was largely illusory, for reasons pointed out by Eyden in the mid-1960s:

> It is clear ... that if local authorities implement to the full this legislation in close co-operation with voluntary organisations, all groups of the handicapped or their families should have a comprehensive service to which they can turn to meet any of their specialized needs. Unfortunately, this has not been the case. The duty of providing services was continued under the National Assistance Act only for the blind. Guidance to local authorities on the provision of welfare services for other classes of handicapped persons was issued by the Ministry of Health in Circular 32/51 in August 1951, and local authorities were invited to submit schemes and their subsequent implementation was not made compulsory until 1960 ... As a result, the development of services for the deaf and other categories of handicapped persons over the past sixteen years has been patchy and inadequate. (Eyden, 1965, p. 171)

Even the 1960 deadline had little meaning since local authorities were able to offer minimal provision yet still meet the requirements of the Act. This situation meant that the main community-based service available to physically disabled people and their families was the home care service (Topliss, 1979).

These inadequacies led Alf Morris MP to introduce a private member's bill designed to compel local authorities to develop comprehensive welfare and support services for disabled people and this subsequently became the Chronically Sick and Disabled Persons Act 1970. This Act imposed duties but it was not paralleled by the allocation of sufficient extra resources to local authorities. Topliss claims that 'this has meant that the claims of the disabled have had to compete with the claims on the local authority budget of all other sections of the community' and that 'the sort of massive reallocation of expenditure needed to implement the ... Act fully, in the absence of special earmarked funds, has apparently proved politically impossible for local authorities' (p. 114).

On residential care for physically disabled people, the National Assistance Act 1948 did make reference to the specific needs of younger physically disabled people as being different from those of frail elderly people. However, most local authorities continued to place physically disabled people in residential homes for older people. Only a minority of local authorities developed separate homes in the 1950s and 1960s, despite the growing awareness that the overall number of younger disabled people had increased because of a number of factors, including the war, the 1950s polio epidemic and increased life expectancy from medical advances. Detailed figures in the balance of provision are difficult to come by, although Leat (1988, p. 206) shows that in 1972 'there were 8,000 younger people in homes also housing elderly people although more than half of these younger people were in their early sixties'. She also draws upon a survey by Harrison (1986) to show that by the mid-1980s only 54 of the 115 local authorities in England and Wales had set up homes catering specifically for younger physically disabled people, but she points out that many of the others may have been making use of specialist voluntary and private homes. By far the most influential of these independent sector providers of residential care was Cheshire Homes, which was founded in 1948 and developed the concept of a 'family home' which claimed to meet the needs of younger physically disabled people.

The most detailed survey of residential provision in the early post-war period was carried out by Miller and Gwynne (1972) who revealed many of the same inadequacies found by Townsend (1964) for elderly people, but with the added concern that many of those surveyed were being offered residential care as their only accommodation option for the whole of their adult life course and not just for the last part of it. They lamented that 'by the very fact of committing people to institutions of this type, society is defining them as, in effect, socially dead' because 'society has effectively washed its hands of the inmates as significant social beings' (p. 89). By the early 1980s, some of these 'inmates' had decided to organise their own housing and support solutions outside such residential institutions. Integrated living and independent living models began to emerge (Wagner Committee, 1988). However, most commentators point out that this was the response of disabled people to the neglect they had received from able-bodied professionals and policy-makers in terms of developing service responses, which enable disabled people to be fully integrated within society (Finkelstein, 1993).

Services for people with mental health problems and learning difficulties

Having looked at the development of provision for elderly and physically impaired people, it is now appropriate to consider the growth of services for people with mental health problems and learning difficulties. Does the same pattern of neglect emerge? Several authors have charted the growth of asylums for 'lunatics' (people with mental health problems) and 'idiots' (people with learning difficulties) from a community care perspective (see, for example, Malin *et al.*, 1980; Murphy, 1991; Jones, 1993; Dale and Melling, 2007), while others have studied asylums from a more general sociological interest in madness (Scull, 1993). More recently, Bartlett and Wright (1999) have produced a detailed account of the care in the community from 1750 to 2000 which has always existed outside the walls of the asylum.

Murphy (1991) has argued that the growth of the lunatic asylum from the late 1840s onwards was initially a development to be welcomed, since previous workhouse provision was failing to cope. She argues that the social reformers had a vision of a therapeutic community in which 'insanity ... might be healed by a gentle system of rewards and punishments, amusements, occupation and kindly but firm discipline' (p. 34) although she accepts that the reality proved far inferior to the vision. Others have been far less sanguine. Scull (1993) saw the asylums as a mechanism by which the community and individual families could shed their responsibilities for troublesome and unwanted people. Certainly the legislative framework was draconian up to 1930, since admission depended on certification as 'a lunatic, an idiot or a person of unsound mind', which involved an order to be detained by a judicial authority. As Parker (1988, p. 12) points out:

Such a requirement imposed a stigma additional to any that was associated with being in an asylum. Not only was admission dependent upon certification, but the order for commitment carried with it the prospect of its irrevocability. De-certification and release were not easily obtained.

The majority of such inmates were also certified as paupers unless they or their relatives could pay privately for their detention.

The numbers of people with mental health problems detained in asylums (renamed mental health hospitals in 1930) grew spectacularly. Gibbons (1988, p. 161) talks of a situation where:

> by 1890 there were sixty-six county and borough asylums in England and Wales with an average 802 inmates and 86,067 officially certified cases of insanity in England and Wales, more than four times as many as forty-five years earlier. By 1930 there were nearly 120,000 patients in public asylums and by 1954 at the peak in numbers, there were over 148,000.

Gibbons sums up this situation as being one in which there were 'ever larger numbers of chronic cases in institutions of increasing size, with ever fewer therapeutic pretensions' (p. 160). Scull (1993) argues forcibly that such growth reflected how these 'warehouses of the unwanted' covered a disparate collection of individuals whom the community were keen to be rid of, such as the alcohol-dependent with *delirium tremens*, people with epilepsy, women depressed and exhausted by multiple pregnancies and older people with dementia.

Pearce (2007) presents a rather more subtle picture, arguing that the Mental Treatment Act 1930 was an attempt to reduce the stigma of the asylum and the Poor Law through the renaming of asylums as mental health hospitals and through the introduction of new classes of voluntary and temporary patient. He argues that this encouraged more people to come forward at an earlier stage of their mental health problems and also stimulated more innovative treatments. However, he also points out that the 1930 Act was also associated with the rapid expansion of what he calls 'the unpleasant and more hazardous shock therapies' (p. 128).

In many respects, the situation was just as depressing for people with learning difficulties in the pre-war period as it was for those with mental health problems. The term 'neglect' is probably misleading since services for this group have often been influenced by moral panics about the need to protect the genetic stock of the country by discouraging those of 'low' intelligence from 'breeding'. Gladstone (1996) indicates that the Victorian period was often a period of optimism about the potential for training and educating people with learning difficulties, even if this was often in the context of their removal to an institution under the Idiots Act 1886.

More specifically, optimism about the potential of asylums to help those with learning difficulties was undermined by the new science of genetics with its tendency to perceive 'mental defectives' as less than human. Most geneticists believed that intelligence was innate. They were alarmed by high birth rates amongst the poorest and by implication the least intelligent members of society, since such a trend could undermine the overall genetic stock of the nation and hence the capacity to remain a dominant colonial power. Mental defectiveness was seen as genetically inherited and hence the segregation of 'mental defectives' from the rest of society was essential. Such 'mental defectives' were also seen as undermining the therapeutic role of the asylum for the mentally ill and hence their removal from mixed asylums was seen as essential by many reformers (Dale, 2007).

Several authors have charted how this led to calls for the establishment of farm and industrial colonies, together with the prohibition of marriages involving those labelled as 'moral defectives' who were seen as often on the borderline of 'mental defectiveness' (Malin *et al.*, 1980, Chapter 4; Abbott and Sapsford, 1987). Such views had a major impact upon the thinking of the 1908 Royal Commission on the Care and Control of the Feeble-Minded and on the legislative details of the Mental Deficiency Act 1913. This Act made reference to idiots, imbeciles and the feeble-minded, categories based on the extent of the learning difficulty, while the term 'moral imbecile' was introduced to cover what was seen as a more generalized social problem group whose low intelligence made them prone to 'loose morals'. Section 2 of the Act specified the circumstances under which a 'defective' from these groups might be dealt with by being sent to an institution or placed under guardianship:

- At the insistence of his parent or guardian;
- If in addition to being a defective he was a person (i) who was found neglected, abandoned, or without visible means of support, or cruelly treated or ... in need of care or training which could not be provided in his home; or (ii) who was found guilty of any criminal offence, or who was ordered to be sent to an approved school; or (iii) who was undergoing imprisonment, or was in an approved school; or (iv) who was an habitual drunkard; or (v) who had been found incapable of receiving education at school, or that by reason of a disability of mind required supervision after leaving school. (quoted in Malin *et al.*, 1980, p. 41)

Once a person had been admitted to an institution on these grounds, the Board of Control was in a position to block the discharge of anyone they considered unfit to live in the community. Certain safeguards were built into this draconian system. Parents and guardians needed two medical certificates, one of which had to be approved for such purposes by the local health authority or the Minister of Health. Section 2(b), quoted above, used the phrase 'in addition to being a defective'. However, in practice, it was relatively easy to place any person with learning disability in an institution using this Act, while others experiencing social difficulties such as homelessness were equally vulnerable irrespective of their mental abilities. Once they were committed, 'the term "certification" had a permanence about it, probably enhanced by the prevailing views of invariance of intellectual abilities and certainly compounded by the essentially subjective nature of the definitions of the Act' (Malin *et al.*, 1980, p. 42).

Ryan and Thomas (1980, p. 107) summed up the overall national situation in the following way:

This Act established the basis of a separate and unified service, which would exclude mental defective people from other welfare and social agencies as well as from the general education system.

However Dale's (2007) detailed work in Devon has alerted us to significant local variations with that county, offering an approach with a much stronger role for lay professionals and for community liaison than suggested by Ryan and Thomas. What is clear is that the total number of 'defectives' under the care and control of the mental deficiency legislation rose rapidly. Figures supplied by Tredgold (1952) and quoted by Malin *et al.* (1980, p. 43) show that numbers rose from 12,000 in 1920 to 90,000 by 1939. Most of them were placed in large isolated 'colonies', whose regime was outlined in the Report of the Mental Deficiency Committee (1929):

> The modern institution, generally a large one, preferably built on a colony plan, takes defectives of all grades of defect and all ages. All, of course, are probably classified according to their mental capacity and age. The Local Mental Deficiency Authority has to provide for all grades of defect, all types of case and all ages, and an institution that cannot, or will not, take this case for one reason and that case for another is of no use to the Authority. An institution which takes all types and ages is economical because the high-grade patients do the work and make everything necessary, not only for themselves, but also for the lower grade. In an institution taking only lower grades, the whole of the work has to be done by paid staff, in one taking only high grades the output of work is greater than is required for the institution itself and there is difficulty in disposing of it. In the all-grade institution, on the other hand, the high-grade patients are the skilled workmen of the colony, those who do all the higher processes of manufacture, those on whom there is a considerable measure of responsibility; the medium-grade patients are the labourers, who do the more simple routine work in the training shops and about the institution; the rest of the lower-grade patients fetch and carry or do the very simple work. (Quoted in Malin *et al.*, 1980, p. 43)

How was the situation changed for people with learning difficulties and mental health problems by the establishment of a National Health Service and other related reforms? The National Health Service saw provision for those with mental health problems and learning difficulties brought more into mainstream health care provision. Asylums were redesignated as hospitals and became the responsibility of regional hospital boards. Local authorities became responsible for the following range of services under Section 28 of the National Health Service Act 1946:

- the initial care and removal to hospital of persons dealt with under the Lunacy and Mental Treatment Acts;
- the ascertainment and (where necessary) removal to institutions of mental defectives, and the supervision, guardianship, training and occupation of those in the community, under the Mental Deficiency Acts;
- the prevention, care and after-care of all types of patients, so far as this was not otherwise provided for.

However, the first two were statutory responsibilities, while the third represented a permissive power. Local authorities showed little enthusiasm for using their permissive powers and in 1958/59 overall local authority expenditure on people with mental health problems was only £4.1 million (Goodwin, 1990, p. 68).

Expenditure on hospital-based provision was not much more impressive. Drawing upon a number of sources, Goodwin (1990, p. 67) found that in the early 1950s, mental and mental deficiency hospitals contained 40 per cent of in-patient beds in the NHS but received only 20 per cent of the hospital budget. He also pointed out that the average cost of treating a mentally distressed in-patient was £3 15s. 11d. in 1950/51 compared with £4 13s. 11d. in 1959/60 (at 1950/51 prices) but that far more dramatic price rises had occurred for other groups in the same period. For example, the cost of in-patient maternity care rose from £6 9s. 5d. to £16 11s. 3d. Goodwin claims 'these figures clearly underline why the mental health services have earned the tag of a "Cinderella" service' (p. 67).

At first glance, the Cinderella tag appears to have been removed as a result of the Royal Commission on Mental Illness and Mental Deficiency which sat from 1954 to 1957, and the subsequent Mental Health Act 1959. The latter reformed the legislative framework of constraint and envisaged the development of a complex infrastructure of local authority-provided services such as hostels, day care, social work support and sheltered employment schemes.

However, not only did these services largely fail to materialise (Welshman, 1999), but in 1961, Enoch Powell, the then Minister of Health, informed the annual conference of the National Association for Mental Health that:

I have intimated to the hospital authorities who will be producing the constituent elements of the plan that in fifteen years time, there may be needed not more than half as many places in hospitals for mental illness as there are today. (Quoted in Jones, 1993, p. 160)

As a result, Murphy (1991, p. 60) describes 1962–90 as 'the disaster years' for people with mental health problems. She explains that 'by 1974 there were 60,000 fewer residents in large mental hospitals than there had been in 1954, but very few services at all existed in the community', while Payne (1999) points out how this situation encouraged the 'revolving door' syndrome of admission, discharge and readmission for those with enduring mental health problems. In a similar vein, Atkinson (1988) notes the failure of local authorities to develop services for children and adults with learning difficulties. She indicates that 'a few residential homes, or hostels, appeared here and there' while 'local authorities developed some training facilities in the community and appointed Mental Welfare Officers to make routine visits to the family homes' (p. 128). Provision remained based on hospitals. Institutional and treatment regimes remained controversial. For people with mental health problems, the emphasis was now on treatment not custody. However, the introduction of anti-psychotic drugs and new treatments such as ECT were seen to raise major issues about civil liberties. There were also numerous exposés of physical and mental cruelty by staff on patients. Such practices with regard to psycho-geriatric patients were outlined by Robb (1967) in *Sans Everything: A Case to Answer,* while Morris (1969) in *Put Away* provided evidence of the generally poor conditions in many long-stay mental handicap hospitals. Against this, Jones (1972) lamented how the popular press of the late 1960s began to exaggerate such stories and to imply that the worst abuses were the norm rather than the exception.

Governments continued to take initiatives in the 1970s to promote community-based provision and to reduce hospital provision for both people with learning difficulties (*Better Services for the Mentally Handicapped,* Department of Health and Social Security, 1971) and for people with mental health problems (*Better Services for the Mentally Ill,* Department of Health and Social Security, 1975). Yet the pivotal report of the

Audit Commission (1986), *Making a Reality of Community Care*, found limited movement on the hospital front and virtually no progress in terms of developing adequate community services. Both groups continued to be treated as a low priority for service developments.

As a result it is impossible to be certain about the overall standard of provision and how this varied in the 40 year period from the establishment of the National Health Service in 1946 to the publication of *Making a Reality of Community Care* (Audit Commission, 1986). However, Frank Thomas's diary of everyday life in the ward of a large mental handicap hospital in the late 1970s perhaps captures how 'patients' become treated as less than fully human through mundane everyday actions rather than through spectacular examples of abuse. Here are two examples:

1.   Tea mixed with milk and sugar to save time, mess and trouble. How many lumps, say when with the milk? You must be joking. (Thomas, 1980, p. 35)
2.   Bad habit I picked up from the other nurses. Fitting out someone for his trip to the workshop and muttering 'That'll do', as if the guy's appearance meant nothing to him, just a neat reproduction of my own preferences or lack of them. Not asking the guy if he was all right, whether it'll do. If a person is not allowed a say in what he looks like, then what is the point? Haircuts en masse – short back and sides, no one is allowed to refuse. Choice of raincoat from a communal pile, communal underwear and socks. Communal combs and brushes. One tube of toothpaste and a couple of tooth mugs for twenty-five patients. (p. 43)

Throughout this section on the long history of neglect of community care services for all the main care groups, one cannot but be struck by the continuity of the images of institutional regimes over the last hundred years, and the persistent failure to develop alternative community-based systems of provision.

Explanations of neglect

How can we explain the long history of neglect of services for these 'Cinderella' groups? This chapter makes no pretence that there is a single simple answer to this question, but rather identifies a number of strands. Four different explanations will be addressed. First, we will look at the political economy approach which explains social policy developments (or lack of them) by reference to the changing needs of the capitalist mode of production. Second, the complex role of institutions in social control will be considered. Third, we will outline the central concern of governments to encourage informal care and the knock-on consequences of this for the neglect of community-based services. The fourth and final explanation looks at cultural stereotypes about ageing and disability.

The political economy perspective

The main tenets of the political economy approach to disability have been clearly summarised by Oliver (1990):

> Changes in the organisation of work from a rural-based, cooperative system where individuals contributed what they could to the production process, to an urban, factory-based one organised around the individual waged labourer, had profound consequences ... As a result of this, disabled people came to be regarded as a social and educational problem and more and more were segregated in institutions of all kinds including workhouses, asylums, colonies and special schools, and out of the mainstream of social life. (p. 28)

Oliver points out that this is a major simplification of some highly complex processes but stresses that the key insight is the need to search for linkages between changes in public policy and changes in the sphere of production. Such linkages have also been identified with regard to older people by Cole and Edwards (2005), Macnicol (2006) and Phillipson (1982) amongst others. Also, in a similar vein, Scull (1993) argues that the asylum became a convenient dumping ground for a wide range of individuals who could not cope in the community and hence contribute to the economy.

Perhaps the clearest example of this relationship concerns the emergence of a system of retirement pensions in the early twentieth century as part of a process of rationalising the removal of elderly people from the labour market during a period of high unemployment (Phillipson, 1982). The effect of such initiatives has been to minimise opportunities for elderly and disabled people in the labour market and this has ensured their 'structural dependency' on the state (Townsend, 1981; 2006). At the same time, elderly people form a reserve army of labour which can be drawn back into work during periods of labour shortage. Research has provided graphic illustrations of the way retirement from work was painted as encouraging physical decline and death in the labour market shortage years of the 1950s so as to draw older people back into employment (Phillipson, 1982). Against this, in the recession years of the 1980s, older workers were encouraged to make way for younger workers by retiring as early as possible. In a similar way, it could be argued that Conservative Governments in the 1980s encouraged disabled people on to invalidity benefit so as to reduce unemployment rates, only to reverse this trend when their primary concern switched from unemployment to levels of social security expenditure, a policy emphasis very much reinforced by Labour Governments since 1997. Structured dependency has taken a number of forms. First, it has involved dependence on state benefits which keep many elderly and disabled people trapped within poverty (Oliver, 1996; Tregaskis, 2002; Townsend, 2006). Second, it has encouraged an outlook in which health and community care services for disabled people are seen as a low resource priority compared with service developments for children, since the latter have a clear future role in production and reproduction. During the Second World War there was early support for the evacuation of children and mothers from areas under threat from bombing raids, but a great reluctance to extend this provision to frail elderly people because they were not, in the government jargon of the day, 'potential effectives' (Means and Smith, 1998b, Chapter 2). Equally, the overall cost of providing health and social care services for elderly and disabled people can be seen as a public expenditure burden which inhibits economic growth. Such concerns have appeared in official reports. For example, *The Rising Tide* from the Health Advisory Service (1983) explained that the number of people with dementia would rise rapidly because of the growth of the very old and that 'the flood is likely to overwhelm the entire health care system' (p. 1). Godsell (2002) has argued how a key driver for deinstitutionalisation was the high cost of specialist hospital-based care rather than the limitations of such provision.

There are several criticisms which can be levelled at the political economy approach, although, in fairness to most of its proponents, they recognise that its value lies in providing a very broad grasp of the link between changes in the means of production and changes in public policy (Phillipson, 1998). In Chapter 1, it was shown how some people misuse history to manufacture a fictitious golden past based on mythical values. Prior to the Industrial Revolution, all frail elderly people were *not* supported in the 'bosom' of their extended families, local villages did *not* 'support' every person with a learning difficulty, and appropriate work was *not* found for all those with physical impairments and mental health problems. However, this is recognised by Oliver (1990, p. 28), who indicates that the Industrial Revolution had a major impact on disabled people but that it is impossible 'to assess whether these changes affected the quality of the experience of disability negatively or positively, largely because history is silent on the experience of disability'.

Another linked criticism is the argument that the emergence of state benefits represented a major 'gain' for elderly and disabled people compared with their previous reliance on the workhouse, Poor Law relief, the family and low-paid employment (P. Johnson, 1987). Pensions are provided as a right. They protect elderly people from the vagaries of the labour market and hence provide many of them with the option of a fairly comfortable retirement which they are likely to prefer to continued employment in unattractive work. However, such views can be challenged on the grounds that they deflect attention away from the extent of benefit-based poverty amongst elderly and disabled people and that the only group who have been offered real choice are 'that minority of (middle-class) retirees who are beneficiaries of final salary pension schemes' (Macnicol, 2006, p. 43). They can also be challenged on the grounds that many elderly and disabled people wish to work. Indeed, Oliver (1996) quotes from the fundamental principles of disability as laid out by the Union of the Physically Impaired Against Segregation which included the need to fight for jobs rather than improved benefits. This is because 'in the final analysis the particular form of poverty principally associated with physical impairment is caused by our exclusion from the ability to earn an income on a par with our able-bodied peers, due to the way employment is organised' (p. 23).

A third criticism is that the concept of structured dependency can easily drift into an acceptance of structural determinism which treats elderly and disabled people as 'cultural dopes' who lack any autonomy or capacity for self-determination (Gilleard and Higgs, 2000). It is crucial to recognise the frequent imbalance of power between elderly and disabled people and the providers of state services. However, the consequent 'dependency' should not be perceived as a static, determined phenomenon, but rather recognised as a component of social processes in which elderly and disabled people continue to struggle to influence the form of their lives even in situations where they have only limited power (Tulle and Mooney, 2002). Walker (2005), however, has pointed out that the political economy perspective does not deny the importance of agency but rather stresses the inequality of resources generated through neo-liberal economic policies and the consequences of this for the denial of opportunities for many. He also argues that the globalisation of these neo-liberal policies makes it even more important than in the past to commit to a political economy perspective.

Institutions and service neglect

There is a rich and complex literature on institutions and their role in social control. A frequent theme in the literature on institutions is that many were designed to impose stigma upon residents, and that one function of the institution was to provide a warning to others. Here are two quotations reflecting this perspective:

> Residential homes for the elderly serve functions for the wider society and not only for their inmates. While accommodating only a tiny percentage of the elderly population, they symbolise the dependence of the elderly and legitimate their lack of access to equality of status. (Townsend, 1986, p. 32)

> The workhouse represented the ultimate sanction. The fact that comparatively few people came to be admitted did not detract from the power of its negative image, an image that was sustained by the accounts that circulated about the harsh treatment and separation of families that admission entailed. The success of 'less eligibility' in deterring the able-bodied and

others from seeking relief relied heavily on the currency of such images. (Parker, 1988, p. 9)

From this perspective, neglect within institutions can be understood in terms of the need to generate a negative image to those outside their walls. This negative image, in turn, helps to persuade people into accepting the lack of sufficient public expenditure on benefits, health care services and social care services which would enable people to remain in the community with comfort. Instead, the choice is between discomfort in the community, and discomfort and stigma in the institution.

Not everyone has been satisfied with this approach to understanding institutions. Jones and Fowles (1984) argue that the classic literature on 'total institutions', 'institutional neurosis' and 'carceral power' associated with Goffman (1968), Foucault (1967) and others contained 'sweeping statements, massive generalisations, and some fairly shoddy reasoning; but also disturbing insight, sound scholarship and lively argument' (p. 1). Not all institutional regimes are totally oppressive, and this was true of workhouses (Digby, 1978) as well as of more recent institutions. Not all institutions have a negative impact upon potential users as argued, for example, by Oldman and Quilgars (1999) with regard to care homes for older people. Jones (1993) has argued that the rundown of mental health hospitals has itself been a form of neglect with negative consequences for many with severe mental health problems. Nevertheless, the critical literature on institutions does provide insights into the neglect of health and social care services for elderly and disabled people.

Finally, it is quite clear that the increasing cost of institutional provision has been a factor in the growing emphasis of governments in both the UK and other countries in arguing for a need to switch resources from institutional provision to the development of care in the community (Godsell, 2002; Leichsenring and Alaszewski, 2004). What had started as a low-cost form of provision had become an increasingly expensive response to the needs of disabled people. However, to understand the slow government response to the growing criticisms of institutions on grounds of both cost and quality of care, it is necessary to consider the politics of informal care.

Informal care and service neglect

Most disabled people have always lived in the community rather than in institutions, and the majority of them have received enormous support from their families and relatives, and in particular from female kin (Phillipson *et al.*, 2001). There is an extensive literature which argues that the reluctance of government to fund the development of domiciliary services springs from a fear that such services will undermine the willingness of families (that is, female kin) to continue their caring role. This would have the effect of both increasing public expenditure and undermining the family as an institution (Means and Smith, 1998b).

Detailed information about the extent of informal care and the pressures that this places upon carers has been available for a long time. For example, Sheldon (1948) studied 600 elderly people from Wolverhampton and found that the management of illness was carried out by wives and daughters, so that 'whereas the wives do most of the nursing of the men, the strain when the mother is ill is yet to fall on the daughter, who may have to stay at home as much to run the household as to nurse her mother' (p. 164). Sheldon felt the burden upon such women needed to be shared with the rest of the community through the establishment of a national home help service. Sheldon's findings were subsequently backed up by a number of other studies, which emphasised not only the willingness of families to care but also the costs this imposed upon them (Townsend, 1957; Shanas *et al.*, 1968).

However, such evidence was being generated at a time of concern that the welfare state reforms of the 1940s might undermine the willingness of families to carry out their traditional obligations, one of which was to provide care and support for disabled members. Thompson (1949) was involved in the surveys of chronic sick patients after the NHS reforms and he argued that:

> the power of the group-maintaining instincts will suffer if the provision of a home, the training of children, and the care of disabled members are no longer the ambition of a family but the duty of a local or central authority. (p. 250)

Ten years later, a consultant physician from a geriatric unit was putting forward a similar argument:

The feeling that the State ought to solve every inconvenient domestic situation is merely another factor in producing a snowball expansion on demands in the National Health (and Welfare) Service. Close observation on domestic strains makes one thing very clear. This is that where an old person has a family who have a sound feeling of moral responsibility, serious problems do not arise, however much difficulty may be met. (Rudd, 1958, p. 348)

From such a perspective it was essential for the state to avoid the development of domiciliary services if families were not, in turn, to avoid their domestic responsibilities towards elderly and disabled people. The failure to expand home care services and the heavy reliance upon the voluntary sector for the provision of other domiciliary services is a consequence of this point of view.

Such views were heavily challenged by those involved in research on caring:

The health and welfare services for the aged, as presently developing, are a necessary concomitant of social organization, and therefore, possibly of economic growth. The services do not undermine self-help, because they are concentrated overwhelmingly among those who have neither the capacities nor the resources to undertake the relevant functions alone. Nor, broadly, do the services conflict with the interest of the family as a social institution, because they tend to reach people who lack a family or whose family resources are slender, or they provide specialized services the family is not equipped or qualified to undertake. (Townsend, 1968, p. 129)

Rather than being restricted from a fear of undermining the family, domiciliary services needed to be rapidly expanded to support families and help the isolated.

This argument was gradually accepted by central government. However, this was achieved by emphasising the capacity of domiciliary services to persuade family members to continue to care for disabled relatives rather than their capacity to offer such members real choices about whether or not to continue such care. Moroney (1976) put the argument for more services quite bluntly:

By not offering support, existing social policy might actually force many families to give up this function prematurely, given the evidence of the severe strain many families are experiencing. If this were to happen, the family and the state would not be sharing the responsibility through an interdependent relationship and it is conceivable that eventually the social welfare system would be pressured with demands to provide even greater amounts of care, to become the family for more and more elderly persons. (p. 59)

In this respect, service neglect continues to the present day. All governments assume that if you care about someone you should be willing to care for them (Dalley, 1996).

This has always been the assumption about frail elders but it is also now the basis of policy with regard to people with learning difficulties and mental health problems. The family is assumed to exist and expected to cope. Informal carers may be offered more support from the state than was once the case and this is a positive development where both the service user and informal carer wish the latter to take on the primary caring responsibilities. However, there is little sign of policies emerging which enable service users and family members to make choices about who should carry out such personal assistance roles. In this respect, Morris (2002) asserts that disabled people have a right not to be made dependent upon family members and other close relatives in order to have such needs met.

Cultural stereotypes about ageing and disability

Most Western societies possess negative stereotypes about old age and disability (Phillipson, 1998). Wilson (1991) has argued that most Western views of the life course are pyramidal, in which 'ageing is seen as an inevitable or irreversible slide downwards into dependency' (p. 43). Or as Johnson (1990) put it:

Dependency is one of the words closely associated in the public mind with old age. The image of older people becoming like children – dependent on able-bodied adults – and the loss of mental faculties, are other stereotypes which have wide currency. Even my children, long schooled in the rejection of ageism, like to remind me of the epigram 'old professors never die, they only lose their faculties'. (p. 209)

Similarly negative images and stereotypes are often associated with the term 'disability'. Morris (1990, p. 22), for example, bluntly states that 'just as the issue for black people is racism rather than being black so the issue for disabled people is the fear and hostility that our physical difference and limitations raise for non-disabled people'. Barnes (1996), although sympathetic to this view, points out that not all societies and cultures are universally hostile to disabled people. However, 'the importance and desirability of bodily perfection is endemic to western culture' (p. 56), resulting in the oppression of disabled people through such mechanisms as genetic engineering, prenatal screening, denial of medical treatments, misrepresentation in the media, and institutional discrimination in education, employment, housing, welfare and leisure.

Such everyday cultural attitudes to elderly and disabled people will be part of the assumptive worlds of many of those who develop community care policies and by many of those who deliver community care services. Certainly, Rowlings (1981) has argued that this helps to explain the oft-remarked reluctance of social workers to develop their careers in community care rather than childcare:

> Old age confronts us not just with death (which is inevitable) but with decline (which is probable, at least to some degree) ... It is the prospect of loss in old age – impairment in mental and/or physical function, loss of spouse and family and loss of independence – which is more frightening to contemplate than loss of life itself ... Social workers may well be faced with clients whose experience of and response to ageing represent those very aspects of old age which they, the social workers, fear most for their future selves. (pp. 25–6)

Although this quotation is from a book on *Social Work with Elderly People*, similar comments could be made about the fear of many professionals about working with physically impaired people and people with learning difficulties and mental health problems.

Such fear may provide a partial explanation of service neglect, especially if combined with an appreciation of the low status of work with these groups rather than in childcare (for social workers) or acute medicine (for doctors). Neglect can also result from pessimism about what can be achieved in terms of improving lives through health and social care intervention. This pessimism has deep roots. Haber (1983), for example, found in her study of medical models of growing old in the late nineteenth and early twentieth centuries that:

> most European clinicians seemed to imply that illness and old age were inseparably intertwined, if not quite synonymous. At best the division between the two was extremely subjective. A large proportion of the diseases of old age are attributed to natural intractable changes in the organism. (p. 62)

The term 'chronic sick' sums up this attitude of mind within the medical profession. Illness in old age was chronic, inevitable and barely treatable since 'the organic difficulties that increased with age made the hope of corrective treatment illusory' (p. 72).

However, such arguments do have their limitations. First, to say that older people and disabled people are oppressed by the negative stereotypes generated by the young and non-disabled does little to help us understand how such stereotypes emerge from a complex interplay of cultural, political, economic and social factors. For example, how do such stereotypes relate to the process of removal from the labour force associated with the Industrial Revolution? Are these stereotypes and their implications the same for disabled men as for disabled women and are negative attitudes to frail elderly people connected not just to issues of age but also to the fact that the majority of them are women rather than men. Second, authors such as Gilleard and Higgs (2005) have stressed how older people (and disabled people) play a key role in consumer society and hence are centrally involved in the construction of their own identity through their chosen lifestyles.

Concluding comments

The focus of this chapter has been upon the neglect of services for elderly and disabled people and the different ways in which this can be explained. However, as we warned at the outset, there is a real danger that a compressed chapter on the complex history of services is likely to oversimplify policy developments. More specifically, the thematic focus on neglect risks obscuring the fact that social care and health provision for these groups have achieved a high visibility on political and policy agendas from time to time.

At least three main strands to such periodic increased interest can be identified. First, wars can generate concern about the quality of health and welfare provision for members of the armed forces and/or civilians. For example, the emergence of blind welfare legislation in 1920 was a response to the perceived needs of blind and partially sighted ex-servicemen from the First World War. With regard to civilians, this chapter has illustrated the lack of priority allocated to older people in terms of evacuation places and with regard to access to health care services. However, the second half of the Second World War saw the debate on reconstruction driven by the Beveridge Report (1942). This period saw elderly citizens being increasingly defined as war victims and deserving of state support. This helps to explain the *Manchester Guardian* campaign about workhouse conditions in the 1940s (see earlier discussion) as well as the emergence of home care and meals-on-wheels services for older people in the same period.

Second, the ideology of family and family care means that there are great sensitivities about the 'abandonment' of elderly and disabled people to the state, especially if this is low-quality provision where staff abuse inmates. The history of institutional provision is one of periodic scandals, taken up by pressure groups and the media, and then responded to with campaigning energy by politicians. However, such energy rarely lasts and the Cinderella groups return to being the concern of the committed few at the margins of political and policy influence. Despite this periodic determination to improve and humanise institutional regimes, one is struck by the continuity of the institutional descriptions in this chapter from the Victorian period to the present day. This tradition of scandals about individuals in institutions is now in the process of being transformed into media stories of people being abandoned in the community with inadequate support services. For example, the early 1990s saw high profile coverage of a young man with mental health problems who was mauled by a lion after entering its cage at London Zoo (Jones, 1993, pp. 228–34). In the mid-1990s there was enormous press interest in the killings of Jonathan Zito and Jonathan Newby by people with severe mental health problems (Timmins, 1996). More recently, deaths caused by people with severe mental health problems such as Michael Stone (Simic, 2005) have further helped to generate the fierceness of the debate about the arguments 'for' and 'against' compulsory detention and treatment (Department of Health, 2000e; Pilgrim, 2007) (see also Chapter 5).

Third, policy-makers raise the visibility of community care debates when they become concerned about the cost of existing, usually institutional, provision because of demographic and other trends. This became the case in the mid-1980s when concern grew about both the projected growth in the 'old old' (those over 75 years), the mushrooming cost of social security payments to residential and nursing homes, and the failure to run down expensive mental health and mental handicap hospitals. The development of disquiet about this situation and how this eventually fed into *Caring for People*, the 1989 White Paper on community care, is the initial focus of the next chapter. A central concern of the rest of the book is whether or not the Cinderella tag of service neglect has become outdated.

Chapter 3

Implementing the Community Care Reforms

The focus of the last chapter was on the historical neglect of service provision for older and disabled people and for people with mental health problems and learning difficulties. By the late 1980s the pressures for reform had built up and the then Conservative government commissioned Sir Roy Griffiths to review the funding and organisation of community care. His report, *Community Care: An Agenda for Action* (Griffiths Report, 1988), proposed a radical strategy for reform that reflected the government's commitment to increasing choice and efficiency through the development of welfare markets. There would be an increased role for the private and voluntary sectors in residential and domiciliary services, but with social services authorities assuming the lead role in purchasing and organising care. His recommendations fed into the White Paper *Caring for People* (Department of Health, 1989a) and the National Health Service and Community Care Act 1990.

This and the following chapter look at the development of community care policy and practice since the implementation in April 1993 of the main community care changes required by the 1990 Act. This chapter looks at the implementation of the reforms by social services departments in their new lead agency role. It starts with a discussion of the White Paper. It moves on to consider the political and organisational context within which social services authorities were operating in the mid-1990s, as any judgement about their performance needs to be set against an awareness of the difficult climate they faced in this period, since key elements of the modernisation agenda for social services are based on a critique of their community care performance (see next two chapters). Implementation required fundamental changes in practice as well as in the organisation of care. Evidence from research is used to examine the most significant of these changes in detail: the introduction of care management and assessment and the development of the mixed economy of care. This is followed by consideration of three issues that have assumed increasing importance in the period since 1993: the shifts and uncertainties in care provision; tensions within the reforms for service users and carers and the growing emphasis on audit and inspection. The chapter ends with an assessment of the strengths and weaknesses of the reforms inherited by the Labour Government elected in 1997. Chapter 4 takes the analysis one stage further by outlining the main community care changes brought in by Labour governments since 1997 as part of their modernisation agenda. It explores the impact of these changes on the quality and effectiveness of services.

The community care reforms

The Griffiths Report was published in March 1988 and yet the White Paper on community care did not appear until November 1989. During that period, central government examined several alternatives to the proposals made by Griffiths, but in the end decided that none of them were implementable. The White Paper therefore followed the main recommendations of the Griffiths Report, but with some notable exceptions.

Despite the reported reluctance of several cabinet ministers, social services authorities were given the lead agency role and it was stressed that the government 'endorses Sir Roy's vision of authorities as arrangers and purchasers of care services rather than as monopolistic providers' (Department of Health, 1989a, p. 17). The White Paper went on to list the main responsibilities for this lead agency role:

- carrying out an appropriate assessment of an individual's need for social care (including residential and nursing home care), in collaboration as necessary with medical, nursing and other caring agencies, before deciding what services should be provided;
- designing packages of services tailored to meet the assessed needs of individuals and their carers. The appointment of a 'case manager' may facilitate this;

- securing the delivery of services, not simply by acting as direct providers, but by developing their purchasing and contracting role to become 'enabling authorities'. (p. 17)

The implied critique of past approaches was that they involved slotting people into a limited number of inflexible and traditional services which often did not meet their needs or which were organised to meet the requirements of service providers rather than service users and carers. Now, at the operational level, social services authorities were to develop case management (soon to be called care management) as a way to deliver needs-led rather than service-led systems of assessment and care delivery. At the strategic level, social services were to be responsible for producing community care plans based on an assessment of need for the whole community. These plans were to be consistent with the plans of health authorities and other relevant agencies, and were to be submitted on an annual basis to the Social Services Inspectorate of the Department of Health. They were to be the basis for developing a wide spectrum of services, many of them contracted out, which could be drawn on as appropriate by care managers. Care managers would be responsible for client assessment and then for delivering flexible packages of care for individual clients. The White Paper was quite clear that such packages should 'make use wherever possible of services from voluntary, "not for profit" and private providers insofar as this represents a cost-effective care choice' (p. 22). In other words, social services authorities were expected 'to take all reasonable steps to secure diversity of provision' (p. 22) and 'in particular, they should consider how they will encourage diversification into the non-residential care sector' (p. 23).

The White Paper indicated that 'the government ... favours giving local authorities an opportunity to make greater use of service specifications, agency agreements and contracts in an evolutionary way' (p. 23) as the best way to achieve such a mixed economy of care. It also suggested that this required local authorities to separate their purchaser functions from their provider functions. Through this mechanism, purchasing staff within social services could be encouraged to assess objectively the contribution of 'in-house' service providers, such as the home care service, against what the independent sector might be able to provide.

The position of social services as purchasers of social care would be secured through a new funding structure for those seeking public support for residential and nursing home care. Local authorities would take over responsibility for the financial support of people with low incomes and resources in private and voluntary homes, over and above their entitlement to general social security benefits. This was to be funded primarily through a transfer of money, currently used as payment for such residents in private and voluntary residential care, from the social security budget to local authorities. Local authorities would have discretion to use this money to fund domiciliary services, to reduce the need for so many people to enter residential care.

Most of these proposals were very close to those of the Griffiths Report. However, the White Paper did not propose a Minister of Community Care and it did not offer a new system of earmarked funds for social care along the lines advocated by Griffiths. Apart from a limited scheme to fund community services for those with severe mental health problems and another to fund alcohol and drug services, the extra funds to meet the increased social care responsibilities of local authorities were to be channelled through the revenue support grant system. In the years since implementation the lack of earmarked funding for social care has remained controversial.

Two other important changes were announced in the White Paper. Local authorities were required to establish procedures for receiving comments and complaints from service users and a new system of inspection was to be developed for residential care in all sectors. Each authority would have an inspection unit 'at arm's-length' from the management of services and accountable to the Director of Social Services.

The NHS and Community Care Act was passed by Parliament in the summer of 1990, only for the government to announce major delays in the implementation timetable. Proposals on the inspection of residential homes, the new complaints procedure and the earmarked mental health grant proceeded as scheduled on 1 April 1991, but community care plans did not become a statutory requirement until 12 months later and the new funding regime was not introduced until April 1993.

The history of neglect associated with social care services in England and Wales was described in the previous chapter. As a result, social services authorities were not only being asked to implement a complex reform package, but were doing this in a context where existing service provision was often woefully inadequate. They were soon warned by the Audit Commission (1992) that they faced 'a cascade of change' with the clear implication that they risked being swept away if the pace and timing of changes were not thought through by individual departments. Social Services were being asked to tackle this massive implementation challenge in the mid-1990s in a context of considerable uncertainty in terms of national politics, financial stringency, dependency upon others and organisational uncertainty as already outlined in Chapter 1.

Political uncertainty seemed initially to have been overcome with the return of a Conservative Government after the 1992 general election. The possibility of a Labour Government, less committed to the development of social care markets, had encouraged some Labour-controlled local authorities to delay their thinking on future structures until the outcome of the election was known. However, the result did little to resolve or reduce overall tensions between central and local government. In many Labour and Liberal Democrat authorities, in particular, these tensions created an immensely stressful climate for senior managers as they attempted to respond to the often conflicting advice and instructions from central government and from local politicians (Hoyes *et al.*, 1994). Uncertainty continued right through to the 1997 general election, fuelled by the early and extensive lead for the Labour Party in national opinion polls combined with their ambiguity about which elements of the reforms they would change.

Closely linked to political uncertainty was the issue of *financial stringency*, both in terms of local government finance overall and community care funds in particular. The funding system for community care was highly complex (Lunt *et al.*, 1996), with the money available to social services drawing upon such diverse elements as the revenue support grant, the council tax, specific grants and income generated through charges. All of these components were mediated through the budgetary process of individual authorities to produce an agreed budget for each new financial year. The squeeze from central government on all forms of public expenditure in this period meant that local authorities often had to cut services, withdraw grants, increase service charges or freeze posts in order to stay within agreed budgets.

The third area of pressure concerned *dependence upon others* in that social services could only be successful in implementing the community care reforms with the cooperation of a wide range of other organisations with local purchasing and providing responsibilities. This included both health agencies (health authorities and trusts) and housing agencies (housing associations, housing authorities). It also included a dependence on the rules and regulations of the social security and housing benefit systems in terms of the financial viability of various housing and support arrangements (hostels, sheltered housing, group homes) for service users (Griffiths, 1997a).

This links into the final area of pressure, namely *organisational uncertainty*. A review of local government boundaries was initiated in the early 1990s with an initial emphasis from central government on the desirability of abolishing those authorities which were seen as somehow artificial entities (for example 'newer' counties such as Avon, Cleveland and Humberside), together with the need to extend the number of single-tier arrangements whereby all local authority services are provided by a single unit of administration (unitary authorities). In Wales, 22 unitary authorities were established in April 1996 out of the previous eight county councils and 37 districts. Local government reorganisation (LGR) in England, completed in 1998, involved a wider mix of new unitary authorities, in urban and rural areas, with the retention of some two-tier counties and districts.

The resultant disruption to social services was enormous. Each new unitary authority had to appoint a new Director of Social Services (or equivalent) and management team which in turn needed to review with councillors the most appropriate approach of the new authority to the implementation of the community care reforms. Craig and Manthorpe's research on the impact of LGR on community care suggested that 'the process of transition' generated 'uncertainty, political tension, service planning blight and disruption to working arrangements' (1996, p. 32). This was not only amongst social services staff but also within those voluntary agencies whose very survival depended upon grants and contracts from social services.

Developing care management and assessment

The White Paper stressed that a primary objective of the community care reforms was 'to make proper assessment of need and

good case management the cornerstone of high quality care'
(Department of Health, 1989a, p. 5).

Subsequent policy guidance outlined the three stages of a
proper care management system, namely:

- assessment of the circumstances of the user, including any
  support required by carers;
- negotiation of a care package in agreement with users, carers
  and relevant agencies, designed to meet identified need
  within available resources;
- implementation and monitoring of the agreed package,
  together with a review of outcomes and any necessary revision
  of services provided. (Department of Health, 1990, p. 24)

By identifying individual needs and securing services to meet
those needs, the new system of assessment and care management
would achieve no less than six major objectives:

- ensuring that the resources available (including resources
  transferred from the social security system) are used in the
  most effective way to meet individual care needs;
- restoring and maintaining independence by enabling people
  to live in the community wherever possible;
- working to prevent or to minimise the effects of disability
  and illness in people of all ages;
- treating those who need services with respect and providing
  equal opportunities for all;
- promoting individual choice and self-determination, and
  building on existing strengths and care resources;
- promoting partnership between users, carers and service
  providers in all sectors, together with organisations of and
  for each group. (Department of Health, 1990, p. 23)

So far, it might appear that care management is like 'mum's
apple pie', an uncontroversial positive development for users,
carers and professionals alike. However, the implementation of
care management strategies proved far from straightforward and
continued to generate concerns, as well as improvements, for all
three groups. To appreciate some of the reasons for this, we need
to understand the background and some of the disputes about
the way care management should be organised, whom it should
be aimed at and what it might be able to achieve.

The approach of the Department of Health to care management was heavily influenced by the research findings of the
Personal Social Services Research Unit (PSSRU) at the University
of Kent in their evaluation of care management pilot projects in
Thanet (Kent) and Gateshead (Davies and Challis, 1986; Challis
et al., 1988). Both were aimed at frail elderly people at risk of
entering residential or nursing home care. The emphasis was on
giving social workers with considerable experience of work with
elderly people, and with smaller caseloads than usual, access to a
decentralised budget. This money could be used to bring in a
variety of services not normally available through the social
services system. Just under 100 frail elderly people were
supported through this care management service in Thanet and
their experiences were compared to a matched group receiving
services in the conventional way from a neighbouring area in
Kent. The results were overwhelmingly positive (as they were in
the subsequent Gateshead experiment). The probability of death
within one year and of admission to long-term care within one
year was halved and the probability of continuing to live at home
was doubled. Informal carers felt less exploited and more
supported, while perceptions of well-being on the part of service
users were improved. All of this was achieved at lower cost than
if residential care had been the main option.

However, at least three complications arose in interpreting
these results in terms of their general implications for the
reform of community care in England and Wales. First, queries
were raised about the robustness of the methodology in terms
of whether or not too many problematic clients were filtered
out from the experimental group. Fisher (1990–91) pointed out
that 110 of the originally identified cases were excluded by
using criteria such as clients keen to enter care, carers being
unwilling to share care and so on, leading him to suggest that
some key practice dilemmas were not addressed. A second
linked point was whether or not 'success' with frail elderly
people wishing to avoid residential care could be translated into
'success' for a much wider range of elderly people and also for
the other main user groups. Indeed, the PSSRU research team
have warned repeatedly that this is an approach which can
benefit certain types of users in certain types of situations,
rather than an approach which should be applied to all users, or
even to all users with the most complex needs. Hence, their

justification for screening large numbers of elderly people from their original samples is that they have known all along that care management cannot keep everyone in the community and out of residential care at low-cost and within tolerable levels of burden for carers. Therefore, Davies (1992, p. 20) is unapologetic about the fact that the Thanet experiment was based on the principle of offering 'case-managed care for selected users', who were essentially people who were 'at high risk of *inappropriate* and *avoidable* admissions to institutions for long-term care' (our emphasis).

The third complication facing local authorities as they considered their care management implementation strategy was that available care management models were much wider than just the Thanet/Gateshead approach. One reason for this was that the Department of Health and Social Security (DHSS) established in 1983 28 pilot 'care in the community' projects designed to help long-stay hospital residents move to community settings. These pilot projects covered people with learning difficulties, mental health problems and physical impairments as well as people with age-related problems. Cambridge (1992) stressed the enormous variety of service delivery arrangements which emerged from this initiative with one key dimension of variation being whether the care management pilots were based in social services, in a health setting or within multidisciplinary teams. Also, several of the models chosen stressed the need for care managers to act as advocates or brokers on behalf of clients. They should not be constrained by the resource dilemmas of the statutory agencies, but rather should be based in independent or semi-independent organisations.

Thus, local authorities found themselves facing considerable uncertainty and disagreement about what care management was and how it might be able to help within the new community care arrangements. Was care management something to be applied to all clients, all clients with complex needs or clients in very specific situations? Should care managers be located inside or outside social services? Are they advocates on behalf of clients, rationers on behalf of social services, or both? Should assessment be carried out just by social workers, or also by other professional groups such as home care organisers, community nurses and occupational therapists? Further policy guidance, on assessment and care management, only confirmed the complexity of the choices facing local authorities (Department of Health/Social Services Inspectorate, 1991a, b and c).

The full extent of the implementation challenge was perhaps best summarised by the Audit Commission's (1992) report on *Community Care: Managing the Cascade of Change*. This report opened by outlining how, under previous systems, the user was expected to fit in with existing service requirements, and the service received was often more dependent on which professional received the initial request for help rather than on actual needs, even for people in very similar situations. Hence, an occupational therapist referral would be assessed as requiring an occupational therapy service, whilst the same person, if referred to home care, might be defined as requiring a home help. However, the simple decision to place user and carer needs first had sparked off a cascade of change. The central point was not only the scale of change required, but also the order in which the changes might have to be tackled. Key strategic decisions had to be made about how to create an internal split within social services between purchasers and providers and how to stimulate a mixed economy of care. These decisions then had to be underpinned by new and appropriate financial, structural and procedural arrangements. Social services authorities also needed to develop new assessment systems which were needs-driven and which were acceptable to a wide range of agencies. Decisions had to be made about who would be a priority for services in the light of scarce resource levels. And thought would have to be given as to how wide a range of staff within and outside social services might perform the role of care manager. All this had to be tackled before a needs-led assessment and care management system could be put into operation. As the Audit Commission (1992) explained, 'a process of change has been set in motion which will turn organisations upside down' (p. 19).

Under these circumstances, it is perhaps not surprising that most authorities took some considerable time to establish assessment and care management systems. Early research by Hoyes *et al.* (1994) into the initial approach by four authorities found wide variations in the resultant systems, which were often closely linked to different approaches to the implementation of an internal purchaser–provider split. For example, the split could be at district level, with the purchasing function allocated to care management teams as distinct from provider units, or at team level, with team members retaining a mixture of purchaser and provider functions. A similar spread of approaches to the development of care management was identified by Lewis and Glennerster (1996) from their study of five local authorities. The feasibility of applying care management to all client groups and the difficulties in meshing care management into the broader purchasing and enabling strategy of each of the authorities studied were among the major problems reported.

It was not only managers who faced significant challenges. Front-line staff also had to adapt to new ways of working although most welcomed the opportunity to work with service users in ways that were more responsive to their needs. From the earliest days of implementation, examples of creative and flexible responses to the needs of service users were in evidence:

> A young [disabled] woman ... had been enabled to take part in swimming, relaxation and Tai Chi groups, using local facilities and volunteers where necessary. This reflected the authority's aim to move from a model of day provision dominated by more traditional, statutory day centres. These activities had become such a part of this woman's life that she no longer regarded them as part of her package. (Hoyes *et al.*, 1994, p. 19)

This kind of imaginative care package depended not only on well-designed care management systems but on the development of assessment skills in care managers. A growing consensus began to emerge on what the benchmarks of good assessment practice needed to be (see Box 3.1). However, it was one thing to agree these benchmarks but another to create an environment in which they could flourish.

Good assessment, as defined in Box 3.1, requires highly developed communications and interpersonal skills and a capacity for reflective practice. However, evidence from research suggests that although good practice exists, the way in which assessment and care management systems have been implemented may have restricted the use and development of such skills.

From the earliest days two contrasting approaches to care management were apparent (Challis, 1993). An *administrative* approach rests on an interpretation of the core care management tasks as essentially administrative activities. Potentially, different

BOX 3.1   Benchmarks for assessment practice

1. Empower both the user and carer – inform fully, clarify their understanding of the situation and of the role of the assessor before going ahead;

2. involve, rather than just inform, the user and carer, make them feel that they are full partners in the assessment;

3. shed their 'professional' perspective – have an open mind and be prepared to learn;

4. start from where the user and carer are, establish their existing level of knowledge and what hopes and expectations they have;

5. be interested in the user and carer as people;

6. establish a suitable environment for the assessment, which ensures there is privacy, quiet and sufficient time;

7. take time – build trust and rapport, and overcome the brief visitor syndrome; this will usually take more than one visit;

8. be sensitive, imaginative and creative in responding – users and carers may not know what is possible, or available. For carers in particular, guilt and reticence may have to be overcome;

9. avoid value judgements whenever possible – if such judgements are needed, make them explicit;

10. consider social, emotional, relationship needs, as well as just practical needs and difficulties. Pay particular attention to the quality of the relationship between user and carer;

11. listen to and value the user's and carer's expertise or opinions, even if these run counter to the assessor's own values;

12. present honest, realistic service options, identifying advantages and disadvantages and providing an indication of any delay or limitations in service delivery;

13. not make assessment a 'battle' in which users and carers feel they have to fight for services;

14. balance all perspectives; and

15. clarify understanding at the end of the assessment, agree objectives and the nature of the review process.

Source: Nolan and Caldock (1996) pp. 83–4.

individuals, employed in a variety of roles, may take responsibility at different stages of the process. A *clinical* approach emphasises human relations skills and assumes the involvement of a single care manager throughout. From the outset local authorities tended towards an administrative approach, with care managers spending increasing time on administrative tasks at the expense of direct contact with service users and with the balance shifting firmly away from counselling (Lewis and Glennerster, 1996). A longitudinal study of care management in ten local authorities found that only one in three care managers, interviewed in relation to individual cases, reported time spent on counselling and that counselling was most likely when a principal informal carer was involved (Bauld *et al.*, 2000). An in-depth study of care management in two teams (Postle, 2001a) found that care managers employed a variety of strategies to cope with the changed nature of their work, with the result that different approaches to care management coexisted within the teams. Some practitioners seemed willing to follow procedural methods of working and had adapted to a client processing role. Others tried, with some success, to incorporate social work skills into the care management task, whilst others again were confused or demoralised about their role.

The trend towards an administrative approach to care management may have accelerated in recent years. Research by Ware *et al.* (2003) in seven local authorities found a process that is increasingly fragmented into four main elements: initial screening and assessment; devising and arranging care services; service provision; and review (p. 420). With different staff responsible for each stage of the process in four of the authorities, there was a perception amongst practitioners, as well as users and carers, of a discontinuous or episodic process rather than one that is coordinated, integrated and continuous. Providing a highly personalised service and continuing contact between care manager and service user, through the ongoing cycle of assessment, care planning, monitoring and review, presents substantial challenges in circumstances where high caseloads and high staff turnover are the norm (Balloch and McLean, 2000; Henwood, 2001).

Faced with continuing financial stringency and organisational turbulence, it is scarcely surprising that local authorities have focussed on the administrative aspects of the care management task (Rummery, 2002). Care management systems were soon dominated by debates about which types of client should be a priority for a care package, as social services authorities sought to target scarce resources by bureaucratic means. Eligibility criteria and priority matrices abounded as devices for defining ever more narrowly the number of people likely to receive services. The twin concepts of risk and dependency were widely used to determine eligibility and to create priority bands, the significance of which often differed between authorities. The end result of this was a growing perception of access to care as a 'postcode lottery' and a proliferation of highly complex assessment forms in which 'criteria that define those needing care with sufficient precision to limit expenditure in a predictable way may well be too complicated for people to understand or operate on a day-to-day basis' (Audit Commission, 1996, p. 11).

Such forms have generated much ill will amongst those expected to use them, especially when linked to the collection of information about the personal resources of clients in order to estimate service charges. Field-level staff have felt care management has meant more paperwork and more bureaucracy or, as one third-tier manager told Lewis and Glennerster (1996):

> I think people have felt weighed down by paperwork ... and they feel the department wants to turn them into administrators and financial processors. All the emphasis is on filling out forms, and a lot of staff are saying 'That isn't what I was trained to do ...' (p. 140)

The emphasis on form filling has also impacted on interactions with service users and carers. Richards (2000) found that the process of completing assessment forms could help all the parties involved to develop a clear picture of the difficulties to be addressed. However, there was also a real danger that structuring the interview around an assessment schedule could distort the process of communication and impede the development of understanding. By pre-determining the areas of investigation and focussing on routine information required by the agency, this approach to assessment risked marginalising the concerns of users and carers. Time and energy could be wasted through exhaustive questioning that ultimately failed to capture the subtlety and complexity of individual needs.

BOX 3.2　Review of care management by the Department of Health

- There is continuing acknowledgement by SSDs [social services departments] that older people usually prefer to remain in their own homes as long as is feasible;
- assessment has become more needs-led, but assessment arrangements need to match the complexity and needs of individual cases better than they do;
- while there is a more planned approach to the care of older people, often care plans are not sufficiently focussed on outcomes nor agreed by users;
- many SSDs continue to give insufficient attention to monitoring and reviewing cases;
- older people and family carers feel more involved in assessment and care planning;
- despite considerable investment in public information, many leaflets do not reach the public and users, and some are not particularly helpful.

Source:　Warburton and McCracken (1999) p. 28.

Another factor frustrating the development of a creative user-centred care management system was the lack of computer-based information systems to underpin the purchasing of complex care packages and their subsequent monitoring. There was much talk of the contract economy and spot purchasing, but the harsh reality was that numerous social services authorities developed care management systems based on the devolved purchase of services with completely inadequate IT and information system back-up (Bovell *et al.*, 1997; Postle, 2001a). Inadequate IT systems also continue to pose substantial barriers to the exchange of information between agencies (Department of Health/Social Services Inspectorate, 2000).

Despite these problems, by the end of the 1990s the view of the Department of Health was that progress had been made with regard to care management and older/disabled people (see Box 3.2). However, there was much less satisfaction with regard to people with mental health problems relating to the parallel/overlapping system of the care programme approach (CPA)

(Department of Health/Social Services Inspectorate, 1995, 1999). Shaw (2000) explains how the care programme approach was introduced in 1991 and required social services authorities and health to collaborate in a new coordinated framework of care. Chapter 5 looks in more detail at attempts to mesh this with the care management system.

Closely linked to care management and assessment was the need for social services authorities to develop a mixed economy of care, in which providers from the voluntary and private sectors would play a much greater role. The next section takes a detailed look at how this challenge was addressed.

Developing a mixed economy of care

Another key objective of the community care reforms was to increase the range of services available and to widen consumer choice (Department of Health, 1989a). As a first step towards this, social services departments were advised to separate their purchasing and providing functions, as explained in the subsequent policy guidance (Department of Health, 1990).

In practical terms in developing the enabling role authorities will need to distinguish between aspects of work in SSDs concerned with

- the assessment of individuals' needs, the arrangement and purchase of services to meet them;
- direct service provision. It will be important that this distinction is reflected within the SSD's management structure at both the 'macro' level (involving plans to meet strategic priorities as a whole) and at the 'micro' level (where services are being arranged for individuals). (Department of Health, 1990, pp. 37–8)

It can be argued that the purpose of this proposed split was twofold. First, it would ensure equality of treatment for alternative suppliers and the authorities' own services in terms of the identification of service costs. Second, it would increase the fairness of consumer choice, since the care manager would feel distanced from in-house provision and hence under no pressure to recommend its take-up in preference to those services available from alternative suppliers.

The restructuring that this implied was tackled in different ways and with varying degrees of enthusiasm by local authorities. Nevertheless, the end result was a devolving of purchasing power down social services departments so that team managers and/or care managers were now the most likely staff to make purchasing decisions both from internal/in-house providers and from external independent sector providers of social care services (Wistow *et al.*, 1996; Challis *et al.*, 2001).

By the late 1990s attention increasingly focussed on the further development of the commissioning role of local authorities. In part this was a consequence of the steady withdrawal by local authorities from their role as direct service providers, with some authorities ceasing in-house provision altogether in particular services (Knapp *et al.*, 2001). However, it also reflected the recognition that local authorities were not simply purchasers of care, but were also charged with the strategic role of planning and developing resources in the most effective way to meet the needs identified in their communities.

Caring for People (Department of Health, 1989a) placed emphasis on the need for local authorities to develop their lead agency role by stimulating markets in social care through maximising the service delivery role of the voluntary and private sectors. As we saw in Chapter 2, a mixed economy of care had always existed but the inherited market structure varied enormously between residential and day and domiciliary services and between authorities and geographical areas. Thus social services departments faced very different starting points with regard to the further development of social care markets in their areas.

The social security system had funded a major growth in the private residential and nursing home sector in the 1980s. This provision was unevenly distributed with a concentration in seaside resorts (Audit Commission, 1986). However, if future services were to be based on individual packages of care for people in their own homes, domiciliary and day services were bound to assume greater importance. The independent market in these services was far less developed in nearly all authorities, with voluntary sector organisations playing a significant role as providers, usually with the aid of grants from the local authority or through joint finance monies. Table 3.1 illustrates not only the extent of social services funding of non-statutory organisations in the late 1980s, but also the great variation in the extent of that

TABLE 3.1 *Local authority social services department funding of non-statutory organisations as percentage of total expenditure, 1988–89[1]*

	General contributions to voluntary organisations			Contracts with private and voluntary organisations		
	ELD[2]	MH/LD[3]	ALL[4]	ELD[2]	MH/LD[3]	ALL[4]
Inner London mean	2.6	1.1	3.2	7.1	27.2	8.0
Outer London mean	0.6	1.0	1.1	5.0	16.9	7.1
Metropolitan district mean	0.3	0.7	1.1	1.4	4.1	3.0
Shire county mean	0.8	1.5	1.4	2.8	10.0	3.8
All authorities mean	0.8	1.1	1.4	3.2	11.2	4.6

Notes:
1. Allocations expressed as percentages of relevant total client group expenditure.
2. Services for elderly people.
3. Services for people with mental health problems or learning disabilities.
4. All personal social services.
Source: Taken from Knapp *et al.* (1993) p. 8.

funding between different local authorities and between different user groups.

The role of social services departments as a purchaser of social care services substantially increased with the transfer of funding from social security. To ensure that this money was used to develop the independent sector, and not simply to support or increase local authority provision, the government stipulated that 85 per cent of the funding was to be used in that sector.

However, stimulating new and diversified markets proved to be difficult. The voluntary sector expressed fears about losing autonomy and flexibility and about compromising its advocacy and campaigning roles. Smaller groups in particular did not always feel up to the demands of bidding for and fulfilling contracts (Deakin, 1995; Taylor *et al.*, 1995; Means *et al.*, 2002). The government recognised the need for authorities to continue to provide core grant funding to voluntary organisations to underpin administrative infrastructure and development work, but it was questionable whether social services authorities would choose to spend their limited resources on this rather than the purchase of particular services. Diversification from residential provision appeared to be a logical step for many suppliers, especially if demand was shrinking. However, it would not necessarily be a straightforward move for small, or even larger, organisations whose experience was limited to providing care in an institutional setting (Wistow *et al.*, 1996).

If a local authority was to stimulate a market, it would need to do more than contract out its own residential care. Interventions required on the supply side included help with business development grants; subsidies and credit for start-up and working capital; training; and licensing and regulation. Local authorities could attempt to influence the market by the way in which they related to service providers. For example, to what extent were local authorities willing to draw upon the rhetoric of user-centred services and the mixed economy to support the growth of voluntary organisations 'where services are provided for minorities by minorities' (Atkin, 1996, p. 150)? For conventional markets to operate efficiently, perfect competition required that there should be neither a monopoly (one or few providers) nor a monopsony (one or few purchasers). It was likely that in some areas, for some services, the social services department would be the only purchaser. Whilst this might make it easier for the authority to dictate terms, it might also deter potential providers from entering a market where they would be dependent on a single buyer. On the other hand, if an authority, for the sake of administrative convenience or economy, chose to enter into block contracts with one or two providers, they risked squeezing out other smaller providers and could find themselves faced with a monopoly and in a very weak position. Authorities needed to consider to what extent they were able and would wish to guard against these situations by, for example, operating care management systems which devolved responsibility and resources to many purchasers, and by encouraging many suppliers by undertaking the interventionist strategies of the kind described above.

Research by Wistow *et al.* monitoring progress in 25 local authorities, suggests that authorities soon gained confidence in terms of their individual purchasing strategies (Wistow *et al.*, 1996, Chapters 4 and 5). However, their information about both need and supply was patchy. On the need side, key gaps tended to include the lack of work on projected future need across client groups and the paucity of information on client groups other than older people. On the supply side, much more was known about residential and nursing home care provision compared with the providers of other services. More recent findings from authorities participating in the same monitoring project suggest that gaps in information about needs and services persist. For instance, care managers reported difficulties in recording unmet need so that this information was not available to guide the development and commissioning of new services. There were also indications that processes for contracting with independent sector providers at the local authority level fail to take account of care managers' local knowledge and experience (Ware *et al.*, 2003).

Shifts and uncertainties in care provision

Since the early 1990s and implementation of the community care reforms, there have been substantial shifts in the provision of care services. As local authorities increasingly contracted out their home care work to the independent sector there was a mushrooming of small agencies. By 2005, the independent sector was providing 73 per cent of home care contact hours compared with 2 per cent in 1992 (Commission for Social Care Inspection (CSCI), 2006a, p. 4). A survey of independent sector providers of home care services, affiliated to the United Kingdom Homecare Association (UKHCA), gives an insight into this rapidly expanding market. Replies were received from 266 organisations or 26 per cent of the membership, the vast majority of whom were small recently established for-profit organisations:

> Sixty per cent of organisations are providing services to less than 100 clients and just five per cent had more than 500 clients on their books. Only 4 per cent of respondents were providing more than 25,000 hours of service per month and 74 per cent fewer than 5,000 hours. Around 6 per cent of providers had been in business for less than one year, 23 per cent for between one and two years and just 10 per cent for more than ten years. (Young and Wistow, 1996, p. 18)

Most of these small providers found such business to be sporadic with no clear flow of cases and that small profit margins were being offered for working with often complex cases. The resultant high turnover of staff risked undermining the quality of provision and caused many of these providers to be pessimistic about the future of their organisations. A decade later large numbers of home care agencies were continuing to enter and leave a sector which still gave the appearance of a 'cottage industry' with a plethora of small providers delivering an average of 500 hours care a week (CSCI, 2006a, p. 4). Nevertheless, a trend towards consolidation is also noted as local authorities have moved towards purchasing from fewer providers through a process of competitive tendering.

Growth in demand for domiciliary services has been accompanied by increasing difficulties in the market for residential care. By 2005, 90 per cent of all residential care home places for adults were in the independent sector (CSCI, 2006b), but this had not been an expanding market for some years. From 1998 onwards there is clear evidence of a rising number of closures, with 141 nursing homes closing that year and 215 closing in 1999 (Player and Pollock, 2001). The trend towards closure has been sustained with 142 homes registered to care for older people closing in 2005–6 (CSCI, 2006b, p. 34). In part the problems are

attributed to falling occupancy rates. A survey of private residential homes in Devon found that in 1994 a majority (84 per
cent) of the proprietors claimed that they had had no vacancies
immediately before the local authorities took over the purchasing of care. By 1997 only 25 per cent claimed to have no vacancies and a further 25 per cent of proprietors claimed that their
homes were barely breaking even or were operating at a loss
(Andrews and Phillips, 2000). Another important factor has
been the pressure on local authorities, the main purchaser of residential care, to control expenditure by severely restricting the
prices paid to care homes. At the same time, care home owners
have faced increased costs associated with the implementation of
national directives and policies such as the national minimum
standards (see Chapter 4); the national minimum wage and the
European working time directive (Netten *et al.*, 2005). A survey
by Netten *et al.* of residential care home inspectors suggests that
homes are much more likely to close for financial reasons than
because poor care standards have enforced closure (p. 326).

Local authority commissioning arrangements have also
created problems for both domiciliary and residential care
providers in the independent sector. The emphasis of many
authorities on placing purchasing decision at the level of the care
manager, and their team managers, encourages a system of spot
contracts or purchase which may be user-centred but typically
the provider bears the financial risk if places are unoccupied.
This can easily undermine the financial viability of small
providers. Agreements from social services to block purchase
services from established providers give greater financial security, but providers may then find themselves committed to taking
costly high dependency residents at a fixed fee. On the whole,
commissioning arrangements are such that the provider bears all
the risk (Netten *et al.*, 2005, p. 335).

Future directions within the market have remained unclear.
The Commission for Social Care Inspection has detected growing sophistication in local authority approaches to contracting.
Different types of contracting arrangements offering greater
security for providers, whilst retaining some flexibility, are
emerging. For example, there is the use of additional spot
contracts with providers who also have block contracts (CSCI,
2006b). Nevertheless, to the dismay of providers, the use of spot
contracts in residential care has remained high at 76.3 per cent in

2006, an increase of 2.7 per cent on the previous year. The opposite trend is apparent in home care provision where block contracts were used in 32 per cent of cases in 2005–06, an increase of 5 per cent on the previous year (CSCI, 2006a, p. 83).

The trend towards consolidation amongst home care providers is mirrored in the residential care sector, where there has been a substantial increase in ownership by large for-profit companies. This is particularly the case in nursing home provision where the average unit size is larger and therefore greater economies of scale can be achieved (Holden, 2002). Laing and Saper (1999) have argued that consolidation of the independent sector is inevitable since 'only larger scale operators will be able to offer local authorities the systems, management skills and financial strength that local authorities will increasingly require' (p. 100). However, the involvement of large corporations in the care market has meant massive movements in care home ownership as companies have been successfully bought and sold in international financial markets (Drakeford, 2006). As Drakeford observes, this trend towards monopoly providers delivering care in increasingly large units is at odds with the vision of individualised, customer focussed services promised by the community care reforms. The substantial rise in the numbers of people using direct payments in England, up from 14,000 in 2004 to 32,000 in 2006 (CSCI, 2006b, p. 23) and the introduction of individual budgets (Department of Health, 2005a) (see Chapter 4), may revitalise the vision of personalized care, at least for users who are purchasing domiciliary and other community-based services. Whilst large numbers of direct payment clients would be likely to employ their carer(s), others might spot purchase the required help from a myriad of small providers.

The introduction of direct payment schemes is described in the next section, which also considers the ambiguous position of service users and carers within the community care reforms.

Service users and carers: an emerging agenda

A central objective of the reforms, emphasised throughout the White Paper, was to improve choice and independence for service users and carers. This was to be achieved through the provision of:

- services that respond flexibly and sensitively to the needs of individuals and their carers;
- services that allow a range of options for consumers;
- services that intervene no more than is necessary to foster independence;
- services that concentrate on those with the greatest needs. (Department of Health, 1989a, p. 4)

Further legislation intended to strengthen the position of service users and carers followed soon after implementation of the NHS and Community Care Act. The Carers (Recognition of Services) Act 1995, passed as a result of a private member's bill, received wide political backing. It gave a right to a separate assessment for people providing informal care on a regular basis to ill, elderly or disabled friends or relatives who were seeking help from social services departments. The latter were required to take the results of the assessment into account when deciding what services to provide to the person being cared for. The White Paper had acknowledged 'that the great bulk of community care is provided by friends, family and neighbours' and 'that carers need help and support if they are to continue to carry out their role' (Department of Health, 1989a, p. 4). The proponents of the Carers Act argued that this required a right to a separate assessment so as (i) to recognise the pivotal role of carers in many care packages; (ii) to encourage social services to think about carers' support needs; and (iii) to discourage social services from exploiting carers, especially where they are young.

A more radical step was the Community Care (Direct Payments) Act 1996. This gave physically disabled people and people with learning difficulties, below the age of 65, the possibility of receiving a payment to arrange their own care services rather than receiving services arranged for them by the local authority. Previously, such direct payment, personal assistance or independent living schemes were legal only if social services gave a grant for a third party (usually a well established voluntary organisation) to run such schemes on behalf of others. This private member's bill was advocated by the British Council of Organisations of Disabled People and the Independent Living Movement because it would enable many more people to arrange their own personal assistance, employ their own workers and manage their own care. It received cautious government support because it was seen as consistent with their self-help/mixed economy philosophy so long as it was not extended to older people which might 'open the floodgates' in terms of public expenditure (House of Lords Library, 1995). Direct payments were eventually extended to older people by the Labour Government, from February 2000.

Neither of these legislative measures addressed the fundamental contradictions within the reforms, which became increasingly obvious as implementation proceeded. Choice and independence for service users were a central objective of the reforms, yet this represented only part of the government's agenda. More pressing concerns were the spiralling costs of care provision and its consequence for public expenditure, which had provided the impetus for reform. As the policy guidance made clear, provision was to be targeted on those in greatest need with what counted as need defined by the local authorities (Department of Health/Social Services Inspectorate, 1991b). The way in which local authorities went about this difficult task had profound consequences for service users and carers and for those seeking access to services.

Across all user groups, priority for services has been given to individuals with complex needs who are considered at risk of admission to residential care. In the period since the reforms clear evidence of such targeting has emerged. For example, in 1992 the average number of contact hours a week for households receiving home help/home care services was 3.2. By 2005 this had more than trebled to an average of 10.1 hours whilst the number of households receiving home help/care in 2005, approximately 354,500, had declined from a figure of 500,000 in 1992 (CSCI, 2006d, p. 22).

This suggests that a growing number of individuals have been able to stay in their own homes, instead of entering residential care. This is indeed confirmed by the research findings from Bauld *et al.* (2000) in a 'before' and 'after' the community care reforms study of 419 service users. They concluded that the reforms resulted 'in scarce resources being targeted more effectively than hitherto towards those older people with the greatest need and there is clear evidence that this resulted in tangible benefits' (p. 388). However, this increase in intensive care packages, which typically involve help with personal care, has been accompanied by a withdrawal of low-level support services, mainly help with housework and shopping, to those deemed at only medium or low risk (Raynes *et al.*, 2001; Help the Aged, 2002). As a consequence, this latter group may be left to struggle on alone, or become increasingly dependent on family members and other informal carers, with a reduced quality of life. Research by Clark *et al.* (1998) reveals the importance of domestic help, especially for older women whose self-esteem is often closely linked to the appearance of their home:

> Well you go down if you let the house go down, don't you? If you're not troubled about the house, you're not troubled about yourself are you? No you must keep overall plimsoll line, dear, keep yourself up regardless. (Mrs George, 82 years, quoted in Clark *et al.*, 1998, p. 19)

Left without support, older people may face increased risks to their physical and mental well-being and thus to their ability to remain in their own homes:

> Mrs Smith, a widow aged 81, became tearful as she explained that her curtains 'were filthy'. Following a fall two weeks before our first meeting no housework had been done. She explained to the researcher during the second visit that the curtains 'have never been that colour in my life' and that before her fall, they had been 'religiously done'. She used to, she said, 'drag the steps upstairs', stepping from them onto a blanket box under the window to change her nets: 'It took a time but I did it'. (Clark *et al.*, 1998, p. 27)

The priority given to personal care needs has meant that other needs may be ignored or met with only a limited service response. Social contact and company, for example, may be perceived by service users as central to their quality of life but be rated as wants rather than needs by social services (Vernon and Qureshi, 2000). The social needs of older service users and people with learning disabilities have been addressed through segregated day centre provision rather than through individual support that is tailored to their needs and preferences. When individual support for social activities is available this may transform the quality of life of younger and older disabled people:

> I've a very good social life now ... I go for drinks, go to friends' houses, they come to me, go out to have a bite and I have a

mobile phone so I can phone my PA for her to be here when I want to come back. (Vernon and Qureshi, 2000, p. 264)

When people are denied access to particular services, or to services in general, they have no choice. But the extent to which choice increased for those in receipt of services was also unclear. The number of care providers, particularly of domiciliary services, substantially increased with the growth of the independent sector. However, from the perspective of service users and carers, choice is about much more than just the range of service providers. Accessing and organising services is likely to involve not only major decisions, for example whether a person with learning disabilities should move into independent accommodation or an older person into residential care, but also numerous micro-level choices. Box 3.3 illustrates the potential dimensions of choice at each stage in the assessment and care management process.

Hardy *et al.* (1999) investigated the parameters and types of choice for older service users in four local authorities. Care managers, service users and carers were interviewed for the study, which also explored the extent to which users and carers perceived themselves as 'able to make genuinely informed choices at each stage of the process' (p. 487). Their findings suggest that the scope for choice was exceedingly limited:

> Even if encouraged to participate in their assessment, domiciliary care users and carers were being restricted to choosing from an increasingly limited range of options; and those with the most complex needs often felt under pressure to enter residential care because it was 'too expensive' to maintain them in their own home. (p. 488)

They concluded that although the growth of provider numbers represented an increase in choice, in practice this was more significant for purchasers than for service users and carers. The latter were more concerned with the day-to-day workings of their care package than with who provided it and, at this level, there was no guarantee that users would automatically receive either the provider, the care worker or the service of their choice. It is also extremely difficult for service users to exercise choice if they have difficulty in understanding the process and when

BOX 3.3   Dimensions of choice in the assessment and care management process

Assessment and definition of needs

Choices about what services

- choice between residential or nursing care and remaining at home with domiciliary support;
- choice over the type and range of support provided within the categories of residential, nursing or domiciliary care.

Care planning and implementation

Choices about what services and when to receive them

- choice over the timing, duration and components of the care package;
- choice over level and method of client contribution for different elements of formal support.

Choices about from whom to receive services

- choice between local authority 'in-house' provision and the independent sector (including voluntary, not-for-profit and private sector organizations);
- choice between individual providers of residential, nursing or domiciliary care;
- choice of care worker to deliver the different elements of the care package;
- choice over the balance between formal and informal support (paid and unpaid).

Monitoring and review

Choices about what, when and from whom to receive services

- choice over the nature of the response to changing user and carer needs;
- choice in terms of when and how the case is reviewed.

Note: Assessment and care management is not the strictly linear process implied here.
Source: Hardy *et al.* (1999) p. 485.

professionals behave in a disempowering way. Although the majority of users and carers interviewed for this study were satisfied with the outcome of the assessment, this did not necessarily mean that they had defined their own needs or been asked if the package offered was what they thought they needed. Older people in crisis situations are particularly likely to be marginalised in the assessment process if the care manager fails to establish the problem as perceived by the older person and their preferred solutions (Richards, 2000).

Rigorous targeting does not necessarily mean that all those with high levels of need receive services. Concerns have continued to emerge about particular groups who may fall through the net. Sometimes the problem relates to the way in which need is defined. For example, people with learning disabilities may be denied access to care management if access is dependent on having additional needs such as physical disability or a mental health problem (Cambridge *et al.*, 2005). Failures in joint working between health and social services and between primary health care teams and specialist services are another factor, as illustrated by the findings of a study of provision for people with Parkinson's disease. Despite having complex needs which made them obvious candidates for community care services, only 9 per cent of respondents with the disease were certain that they had had a community care assessment (M. Lloyd, 2000). Lloyd reports high levels of unmet need amongst users and carers, with only a minority referred to social services by their neurologist or general practitioner.

Besides access and choice, another issue of growing importance for service users and carers was the quality and reliability of service provision. How did the government and local authorities respond to the challenge of monitoring and regulating the proliferation of services provided by diverse organisations within the private and voluntary sectors?

The growth of inspection and regulation

Increasing concerns about care standards in the years prior to the community care reforms had led to the growing involvement of central government agencies in reviewing and inspecting performance at local level. From 1985 the national Social Services Inspectorate (SSI) became responsible for a national programme of inspections to evaluate the quality of services. This was supplemented in 1996 with a system of joint reviews conducted by the SSI with the Audit Commission over a seven-year cycle (later reduced to five years). Besides assessing performance and identifying how services might be improved, these reviews were intended to help local authorities achieve better value for money.

As part of the implementation of the reforms, local authorities were required to establish inspection units, 'at arm's-length' from the commissioning and management of services. These were responsible for the registration and inspection of care homes in both the independent and statutory sectors. Responsibility for the registration and inspection of nursing homes lay with local health authorities. Significant weaknesses in these arrangements, including evidence of inconsistency between local authorities, and between local and health authorities, in the application of their regulatory regimes, were soon identified in *Moving Forward*, a consultation document from the Department of Health (1995e). There were also concerns, despite the 'arm's-length' arrangement, about a potential conflict of interest between the regulatory and service commissioning roles of local authorities. Also, the burgeoning number of day and domiciliary care providers lay outside the regulatory framework. The Burgner Report (1996) that followed recommended a fundamental revision of the entire framework for the regulation and inspection of care services. After the defeat of the Conservative Government in 1997, it was New Labour that embarked on this task as part of its modernisation agenda (see Chapter 4).

To understand these developments it is helpful to locate the community care reforms within the wider process of welfare restructuring, begun under Conservative governments in the 1980s. This has involved significant changes in the role of the state, as the delegation of responsibilities for direct welfare provision to private and voluntary organisations led to a substantial growth in the mechanisms for regulation and control over an increasingly fragmented welfare sector (Clarke and Newman, 1997; Hood *et al.*, 2000). The implications of this have been far-reaching with the move to regulation through contracting, monitoring and inspection seen as symptomatic of wider cultural changes and the development of *an audit society*, in which accountability is achieved through constant checking and verification (Power, 1997).

Strengths and weaknesses of the reforms

Despite the many changes in local authority social services in the wake of the community care reforms, by May 1997 and the election of a Labour Government it was clear that there had been at best only partial success in meeting the aims set out in the 1989 White Paper, *Caring for People*. The underlying objective of the reforms, to cap public expenditure on independent sector residential and nursing home care, had been achieved with the establishment of a needs-based yet cash-limited system. Local authorities had transformed themselves into commissioners and purchasers of care with decreasing involvement in direct care provision; and there was continuing growth in the independent sector provision of day and domiciliary services. For some users at least there was increased choice. Funding and services were now available to support frail older people in their homes as an alternative to residential care. Younger people with severe disabilities could now access a wider range of services and, through direct payments schemes, exercise greater control over the organisation and delivery of support. However, concerns about the organisation and quality of care continued to appear in the media and were confirmed in reports by the Social Services Inspectorate and the newly established joint review teams, and by organisations representing users and carers (Frazer and Glick, 2000; Social Policy Ageing Information Network, 2001). A wide range of difficulties could be identified.

There have been continuing problems with the funding arrangements for community care. The local authorities have consistently argued that the system is undermined by chronic underfunding and is liable to collapse, especially in winter months when demand increases. Independent sector providers complain that the level of fees paid by local authorities make it impossible to provide high quality care and threaten their businesses with closure. Social services routinely spend more on care costs than the amount allocated to them by central government through the standard spending assessment. This has consequences for their ability to develop and improve their services and for the resourcing of other local services. By 2000–01 local authorities were spending on average 8.9 per cent more than allowed for by the standard spending assessment and typically entered the following financial year with their budget overspent

(Social Policy Ageing Information Network, 2001, p. 15). Also, the decision to channel the funding for community care through the revenue support grant system, rather than to create earmarked funding as proposed by the Griffiths Report, has meant that councils can divert money intended for community care into services where the priority and pressures for improvement are greater.

Whatever the reasons for the funding problems, the lack of resources for social care has increased the emphasis on rationing and targeting. Inevitably, therefore, the pressures on care managers to restrict access to services, in their role as gatekeepers for the local authority, make it more difficult for them to promote individual choice and self-determination (Rummery, 2002). The need for advocacy that is independent of the local authority, albeit in limited circumstances, is recognised in the policy guidance (Department of Health/Social Services Inspectorate, 1991c) but with little acknowledgement of the fundamental contradictions in the care management role (Richards, 1994). From the user perspective, the priority given to risk and to particular types of need, such as the need for personal care, in the framing of eligibility criteria may mean that they have little choice in deciding which of their needs are met.

The restructuring of social services was intended to achieve a system of care that put the needs of services users and carers first. However, in responding to this fundamental shift in thinking, authorities concentrated from the outset on developing structures and procedures (Lewis and Glennerster, 1996). Much less attention was paid to processes and outcomes and to how these are experienced by practitioners and by service users. A growing number of research studies have revealed the difficulties faced by users and carers when gaining access to services and in making sense of the systems and procedures they encounter and the information they receive (Rummery and Glendinning, 1999; Richards, 2000; Vernon and Qureshi, 2000). There is also continuing evidence that efforts are focused on the critical phases of the care management process, assessment and care planning, with a relative neglect of monitoring and review. The longitudinal study of care management by Bauld *et al.* (2000) found that only 60 per cent of cases were reviewed within the timescale of the study.

Workforce issues have been a further cause for concern. The

lack of formal training for much of the social care workforce has raised doubts about its capacity to deliver high quality care. The problem is compounded by difficulties in recruiting staff in both the statutory and independent sectors. These difficulties are attributed to the low rates of pay for work that is often challenging and demanding. Low morale and high staff turnover have been reported not only amongst basic-grade staff but also amongst managers in all sectors (Hadley and Clough, 1996; Andrews and Phillips, 2000).

The progress, or otherwise, of successive Labour governments in addressing the challenges in each of these areas is examined in Chapter 4 and subsequent chapters.

Conclusion

This chapter has looked at the strategy for the reform of community care set out in the 1989 White Paper *Caring for People* and at the way in which these reforms were implemented by social services. As the lead agency for community care, departments were expected to develop a needs-based system of care in which their role was to be commissioners and purchasers of care rather than direct providers. This involved the development of care management systems, promoting a mixed economy of social care and introducing purchaser–provider splits. By the end of the 1990s it seemed that they had been only partially successful in their task, given the growing concern about the quality of services and about the failures in interagency working, particularly in the relationship with health. These issues are explored in depth in the next two chapters.

Chapter 4

Community Care and the Modernisation Agenda

The last chapter focused on the reforms of the 1990s and the implementation challenge facing local authorities as the lead agency for community care. Continuing upheaval and uncertainty followed the election of a Labour Government in May 1997. The incoming government planned to 'lay the foundations of a modern welfare state in pensions and community care' (Labour Party, 1997) but gave little indication of an alternative vision for community care to set against the market-orientated approach of its predecessors. Nevertheless, by the time Labour was returned for a third term, in May 2005, significant changes affecting all the agencies involved in community care were in place and further reforms were promised. This chapter stays with the local authorities in England to look at the development of a complex and interlocking set of reforms, intended to transform the regulatory framework for social care and to improve performance in every sector. The following chapter moves the story forward by exploring the impact of health care reform on community care policies and practice.

This chapter begins by locating these reforms within the context of a wider New Labour agenda for 'modernising' government and public services, an agenda which includes a significant increase in the involvement of central government in the management and delivery of services. This is followed by an overview of the White Paper *Modernising Social Services* (Department of Health, 1998a) as a starting point for Labour's programme of reform in social care. Different elements in this programme are examined, beginning with the cluster of initiatives intended to raise standards and improve consistency in care services and to protect vulnerable groups. These include: *Fair Access to Care*; the Commission for Social Care Inspection; National Minimum Standards; and the *No Secrets* guidance. The standards and skills of the workforce are addressed through the creation of the General Social Care Council (GSCC), working in conjunction with Skills for Care and the Social Care Institute for Excellence (SCIE). Measures to improve services for specific groups include a White Paper on learning disability, *Valuing People* (Department of Health, 2001a), and strategies for carers (Department of Health, 1999d) and disabled people (Prime Minister's Strategy Unit, 2005). The chapter moves on to consider the future direction of adult social care as proposed in the Green Paper *Independence, Well-being and Choice* (Department of Health, 2005a) and the subsequent White Paper *Our Health, Our Care, Our Say* (Department of Health, 2006a). It ends with a brief assessment of the progress and impact of the reforms.

Modernising government: changing structures and improving performance

New Labour came to power with an ambitious programme for modernising government and public services, the overall aims of which were set out in a White Paper *Modernising Government* (Cabinet Office, 1999):

- ensuring that policy is more *joined up and strategic*;
- making sure that *public service users*, not providers, are the focus, by matching services more closely to people's lives;
- delivering public services that are *high quality and efficient*. (p. 6, emphasis in original)

Note that issues of interdepartmental and interagency working are now seen as central to public sector reform. Tackling them requires the development of new ways of working and a willingness to collaborate in every area of policy-making and implementation at all levels of government and the public services. Acknowledging the complexity of this task and the challenge of raising standards overall, *Modernising Government* outlines principles to guide the process of reform. These have become hallmarks of the New Labour approach to modernisation, for much of its period in office, and distinguish it not only from its Conservative predecessors but also from previous Labour administrations. These principles include:

- a focus on outcomes to enable working across organisation structures;
- the promotion of partnership between different areas of government and with the voluntary and private sectors;
- greater use of evidence and research;
- consultation with service users;
- the use of targets and performance monitoring to secure quality and continuous improvement in public services;
- additional investment to be conditional on improved results;
- a greater valuing of public services by developing skills and rewarding results;
- the development of information technology throughout government. (Cabinet Office, 1999)

The caveat 'for much of its period in office' is applicable because, as the next chapter will show, frustration with the slow pace of reform in health care has caused New Labour to turn back to quasi-market-driven reforms.

Local authorities were an early target for reform. Proposals to increase their efficiency and accountability by reforming council decision-making structures had already emerged in another White Paper *Modern Local Government: In Touch with the People* (Deputy Prime Minister, 1998). Streamlined arrangements, such as executive cabinets and executive mayors, which draw a clear distinction between executive responsibilities and the other roles of elected members, would replace the existing committee system. In the case of social services, the social services committee would be replaced by a named councillor, or councillors, with executive responsibilities for social services and for monitoring the performance of the Director of Social Services and his or her staff. Non-executive or 'backbench' councillors would be responsible for holding both the executive and senior officers to account through arrangements such as social services scrutiny committees (Department of Health, 1998a, pp. 120–3).

Many local authorities were already engaged in organisational restructuring, partly as a consequence of the reorganisation of local government in the mid-1990s and the creation of small unitary authorities (see Chapter 3). In addition the Seebohm model of a social services department was increasingly giving way to alternative models in which social services were combined with other functions such as housing and health (Hill,

2000a). A growing number of councils had also separated adult services from childcare services (see Chapter 1).

Another significant element in the local government White Paper was the introduction of Best Value, a performance regime extending to every aspect of local authority activity including social services. Local authorities would have a duty to achieve 'continuous improvements in both the quality and cost of services' and to 'deliver services to clear standards – covering both cost and quality – by the most effective, economic and efficient means available' (Deputy Prime Minister, 1998, p. 50). Compliance with Best Value would be monitored through a process of internal review and through external inspections by the Audit Commission and by service-specific inspectorates. Further pressure on local authorities to improve efficiency followed the publication in 2004 of the review into public sector efficiency by Sir Peter Gershon. This identified scope for savings through innovation in service delivery, investment in technology and rationalization of administration (Gershon, 2004). The accompanying three-year spending review (HM Treasury, 2004), set targets for sustainable efficiency gains in the administration of public services, with local councils in England expected to save £6.45 billion, or the equivalent of 2.5 per cent of their budgets in 2005–06 and 2006–07, and with further savings expected in subsequent years. An added complication is that individual government departments are also given annual efficiency targets. For the Department of Health the overall target is £6.5 billion by 2007–08, of which £685 million is for savings in adult social care (Department of Health, 2005d). This means that although it is left to individual councils to decide where efficiency savings are made, they face the difficult task of relating general targets set at a local level to the more specific targets at a national level (Valios, 2005).

A system designed to provide an overall assessment of each council's performance was introduced after a further local government White Paper *Strong Local Leadership: Quality Public Services* (Department of Transport, Local Government and the Regions, 2001a). Comprehensive performance assessment (CPA) combines performance indicator data and data from service-based inspections and reviews to categorise local authorities according to their performance overall. At the time of writing, councils may be assigned to one of five categories, ranging from 4 stars (the best) to 0 stars (the worst). High performing councils are rewarded with extra freedoms, such as reduced revenue ring-fencing and a lighter inspection regime, whilst poor performers face intervention measures and the possibility that other bodies may be brought in to run their services (Audit Commission, 2005a; 2006). In addition, the Department of Health introduced a system of star ratings for social services as a further incentive to councils to improve in this key function. These annual league tables, the first of which was published in May 2002, are also intended to provide easily accessible information for local people to compare the performance of their services with those of other authorities. The rating system is based on a range of data including self-assessment, performance indicator data and evidence from service inspections (Commission for Social Care Inspection, 2006a). From 2006 separate star ratings have been awarded for adults' and children's care services.

Modernising Social Services – the White Paper

After the Labour victory in the general election of May 1997 the new government's intentions for social care remained unclear. Would it broadly continue the policies of its Conservative predecessor or choose a path of radical reform? Specific commitments in the Labour manifesto (Labour Party, 1997) included the introduction of a long-term care charter, an independent inspection and registration service for residential and domiciliary care and a Royal Commission on the funding of long-term care (see Chapter 5), but there was no indication of any overall strategy for social care.

What soon became clear was that the reform of social care would be closely linked to the reform of the health service. A White Paper, *The New NHS* (Department of Health, 1997), published within months of the election, signalled the government's intention for a closer integration between health and social care through proposals that included the involvement of social services in primary care groups (see Chapter 5).

A year later, in November 1998, the White Paper *Modernising Social Services* (Department of Health, 1998a) finally appeared. It provided the first clear indication of how the New Labour reform agenda would be pursued within the context of social care services. In his foreword, the Secretary of State makes the government's aspirations plain:

> We are determined to have a system of health and social care which is convenient to use, can respond quickly to emergencies and provides top quality services. We haven't got that at present. (Department of Health, 1998a, p. 2)

The White Paper begins by identifying six areas of difficulty:

- *Protection*: the lack of effective safeguards to protect children and vulnerable adults from neglect and abuse;
- *Coordination*: the failure of various agencies to work together to support people in need;
- *Inflexibility*: provision that suits social services rather than the needs of the individual and that may increase dependency and exclusion;
- *Clarity of role*: a lack of clear objectives and standards has meant that no one has a clear understanding of which services are or should be provided, or what standards can reasonably be expected;
- *Consistency*: a problem of inconsistency in the quality of and access to services between and even within areas and perceived unfairness in the operation of charging policies;
- *Inefficiency*: evidence from joint reviews that there are wide variations in costs between similar authorities providing the same services in the same parts of the country. (pp. 5–7)

The clear implication of this is that, despite a decade of reform, little progress had been made in tackling many of the problems identified in the Griffiths Report (1988) and elsewhere (see Chapter 2). So who or what is responsible? The White Paper attributes part of the blame to the social services themselves, on the basis of evidence from SSI inspections and from joint reviews. However, they are not solely responsible as 'the law and the central framework within which social services operate' are also flawed (p. 7). Stephen Mitchell, the civil servant with overall responsibility for the production of the White Paper, explains the problem as follows:

> The Conservative governments of the 1980s and 1990s never really succeeded in providing an overall policy and strategy

for the personal social services, in which the role of local authorities could be clearly, and positively, located. This lack of a clear strategy with which all concerned in central and local government could identify, was compounded by continuing evidence (not least from Social Services Inspectorate reports) of serious deficiencies in the quality, effectiveness and efficiency of social services. (Mitchell, 2000, p. 182)

He acknowledges that the major policy implementation challenges of the 1990s, the community care reforms and the reform of childcare services following the Children Act 1989, were, for the most part, successfully tackled. But, in doing so, he highlights the active role taken by the Department of Health in 'prescribing, monitoring and supporting the implementation' (p. 182).

Accordingly, the proposals for reform in the White Paper involve a significant increase in the mechanisms for directing and controlling the social services at a national level. The problems in social services, it stated, require a new approach, one that contrasts with the previous government's 'devotion to privatisation of care provision' which 'put dogma before users' interests and threatened a fragmentation of vital services' (Department of Health, 1998a, p. 8). The White Paper is equally clear that there can be no return to earlier times and the monolithic model of service provision where 'users were expected to accommodate themselves to the services that existed' (p. 8). Instead, the reforms should focus on the quality of services and their outcomes for users and carers, not on who provides the service. This 'third way for social care' is to be based on seven key principles as a foundation for high quality effective services:

- Care should be provided to people in a way that supports their independence and respects their dignity. People should be able to receive the care they need without their life having to be taken over by the social services system.
- Services should meet each individual's specific needs, pulling together social services, health, housing, education or any others needed. And people should have a say in what services they get and how they are delivered.
- Care services should be organised, accessed, provided and financed in a fair, open and consistent way in every part of the country.

- Children who for whatever reason need to be looked after by local authorities should get a decent start in life, with the same opportunities to make a success of their lives as any child. In particular they should be assured of a decent education.
- Every person – child or adult – should be safeguarded against abuse, neglect or poor treatment whilst receiving care. Where abuse does take place, the system should take firm action to put a stop to it.
- People who receive social services should have an assurance that the staff they deal with are sufficiently trained and skilled for the work they are doing. And staff themselves should feel included within a framework which recognises their commitment, assures high quality training standards and oversees standards of practice.
- People should be able to have confidence in their local social services, knowing that they work to clear and acceptable standards, and that if those standards are not met, action can be taken to improve things. (pp. 8–9)

It is interesting to compare these principles with the objectives for service delivery set out a decade earlier in *Caring for People*:

- to promote the development of domiciliary, day and respite services to enable people to live in their own homes wherever feasible and sensible;
- to ensure that service providers make practical support for carers a high priority;
- to make proper assessment of need and good case management the cornerstone of high-quality care;
- to promote the development of a flourishing independent sector alongside good quality public services;
- to clarify the responsibilities of agencies and so make it easier to hold them to account for their performance;
- to secure better value for taxpayers' money by introducing a new funding structure for social care. (Department of Health, 1989a, p. 5)

There is considerable overlap here. Both are concerned with promoting independence, ensuring that services are responsive to the needs of individual users and with holding agencies to account for their performance. However, where *Caring for*

People promotes the role of the independent sector, *Modernising Social Services* emphasises the protection of vulnerable service users, consistency in provision and in access to services, and the need to raise standards and to monitor them more effectively.

The Labour Government's proposals for change were complex and engage with the details of service provision at an operational level to a far greater extent than in the earlier Conservative White Paper. The most significant of these proposals, and their subsequent implementation, are considered here under three main headings: improving standards and protection; improving the workforce; and improving services for specific groups.

Improving standards and protection

Variations between local authorities in the quality and efficiency of care provision and in access to services are seen, in the White Paper, as symptomatic of the fundamental lack of clarity about the role and expectations of the social services, as described earlier by Mitchell. Ten years before, Sir Roy Griffiths had reached similar conclusions in his report on the state of community care when he observed:

> the imperative is that policy and resources should come into reasonable relationship so that we are clear about what community care services are trying to achieve and so that leadership and direction to those providing service can be given. (Griffiths, 1988, p. iv)

Echoes of Griffiths appear in the White Paper's call for a more prescriptive approach that provides direction to local authorities and requires explicit linkage between national and local policies. It is to be achieved through the creation of a coherent framework for social services, which will establish service objectives and an expectation of the outcomes they are to deliver, set targets for performance, provide resources to support change and include effective systems to monitor and manage performance (p. 109).

Central to this process is the introduction of a new performance assessment framework for the social services. The framework, which comprises a series of performance indicators, is

---

BOX 4.1   Examples of adult services performance indicators for 2006–07

All Adults
AO/B12   Cost of intensive social care for adults and older people

Older People
AO/C32   Older people helped to live at home (BVPI54)

Adults aged 18–64
AO/C73   Adults aged 18 to 64 or over admitted to residential/ nursing care during the year

Physically disabled and sensorily impaired adults aged under 65
AO/C29   Adults with physical disabilities helped to live at home

Adults with learning disabilities aged under 65
AO/C30   Adults with learning disabilities helped to live at home

Adults with mental health problems aged under 65
AO/C31   Adults with mental health problems helped to live at home

NHS interface indicators
AO/D41   Delayed transfers of care

Source: Commission for Social Care Inspection (2007).

---

revised annually in line with changing objectives and after consultation with interested parties, as the selection of indicators and targets and the ways in which they are defined and measured, may be contested. The framework for adult services for 2006–07 contained 24 performance indicators, examples of which are shown in Box 4.1.

Two further initiatives, the Long Term Care Charter and *Fair Access to Care*, are intended to clarify expectations of social care provision and to reduce disparities in access to services, as a result of differing eligibility criteria in local authorities.

The Long Term Care Charter and Fair Access to Care

The Long Term Care Charter was published under the title *Better Care, Higher Standards* (Department of Health, 1999e). Its purpose is 'to set out more clearly at national level what people – both users and carers – can expect if they need support from health, housing and social services; and also what individuals' own responsibilities are in their dealings with the agencies' (Department of Health, 1998a, p. 32). Local authorities and health services were then required to develop local *Better Care, Higher Standards* charters, following the principles and values set out in the national charter, in partnership with users, carers and the independent sector.

A more significant development was *Fair Access to Care (FACS)*, published guidance for local authorities on the principles to follow when devising and applying eligibility criteria and other procedures relating to access. At its centre is a framework for determining eligibility, which councils are directed to use. The framework is divided into four bands, critical, substantial, moderate and low, 'which describe the seriousness of the risk to independence or other consequence if needs are not addressed' (Department of Health, 2003a, p. 4). Within each band the risk to independence is broadly defined to include not only physical safety and well-being but a range of factors seen as essential to maintaining independence over time, such as employment and the fulfilment of family and social roles and responsibilities. Any impression that this implies an extension in service provision is short-lived. It is firmly stated that there are only limited resource consequences as, for the most part, the guidance only confirms and consolidates the earlier policy guidance that accompanied the community care reforms (Department of Health, 1990; Department of Health/Social Services Inspectorate, 1991a; 1991b). It should also be noted that *Fair Access to Care* may reduce but not abolish differences between local authorities in determining access to care, for when 'setting their eligibility criteria councils should take account of their resources, local expectations and local costs' (p. 5). Consequently one local authority may undertake to provide services for people with 'critical' or 'substantial' needs, whilst another provides only for those whose needs are deemed as 'critical'. Specific difficulties in implementing FACS have emerged in mental health settings where the health-led care programme approach (CPA), with its own eligibility criteria, runs in parallel with care management (see Chapter 5). Evidence from research suggests a spectrum of interpretations amongst practitioners ranging from attempts to integrate FACS and CPA criteria to the belief that FACS and CPA criteria are concerned with quite different things (Cestari *et al.*, 2006).

The initiatives described so far focus on three of the areas of difficulty in the organisation and provision of care identified in *Modernising Social Services*: clarity of role, consistency and inefficiency. Another area of concern was protection and specifically the problem of safeguarding children and vulnerable adults who are receiving care services from neglect and abuse.

A shifting regulatory landscape

The Labour Government had come to power in 1997 committed to establishing an independent inspection and registration service for residential and domiciliary care (Labour Party, 1997). This would replace the existing 'at arms-length' local authority inspection units criticised in the Burgner Report (see Chapter 3).

Modernising Social Services proposed the creation of eight Regional Commissions for care standards based on the boundaries of the NHS and Social Care Regions (Department of Health, 1998a, pp. 67–9). This proposal was later modified and a single body with a network of regional and area offices, the National Care Standards Commission, was established under the Care Standards Act 2000. It started work on 1 April 2002 but within a month the government had announced that the newly established Commission would be merged with the Social Services Inspectorate to form the Commission for Social Care Inspection (CSCI). This surprise decision went some way to meeting the demands of local authorities for a rationalisation of the inspectorate regime (Brown, 2002). The primary function of the new Commission would be to promote involvement in every sector of social care. It started work in April 2004 with responsibilities that include:

- registration and inspection of social care services against national minimum standards and taking enforcement action when services do not meet minimum standards;
- assessing the performance of local council social services through the collection of qualitative and quantitative inspection and review evidence;
- publishing performance ratings of local council social services;

- reporting annually to parliament on the state of social care and advising ministers and policy-makers;
- assessing use of resources and appropriateness of services;
- investigating complaints about council services and care providers. (Adapted from CSCI (2004))

The announcement, in March 2005, that this new Commission was to be merged with the Healthcare Commission and Mental Health Act Commission in 2008, to reduce duplication amongst inspectorates, fuelled concerns that the social care perspective was being subordinated to that of health (Samuel, 2005a). In advance of this merger the scope of CSCI's responsibilities was reduced with the transfer of its remit for the regulation and inspection of children's services to the Office for Standards in Education, Children's Services and Skills (OFSTED) from April 2007.

Another proposal in *Modernising Social Services* was the introduction of national minimum standards for care services, as a basis for regulation and inspection (Department of Health, 1998a, pp. 78–9). The first set of standards to appear proved the most controversial. *Fit for the Future? National Required Standards for Residential and Nursing Homes for Older People* (Department of Health, 1999c), drafted by the Centre for Policy on Ageing, was generally welcomed by social services, health authorities and organisations representing service users, but greeted with consternation by care home owners (Department of Health, 2001b). In response to their concerns, the deadline for reaching many of the standards was extended by five years to April 2007 (Department of Health, 2001c). Despite this concession, the National Care Homes Association and other provider organisations continued to argue that implementation of the minimum standards for room size and for staffing ratios would force many homes to close unless there was a significant increase in the fees paid by local authorities (Revans, 2001a). Faced with continuing care home closures, the government responded the following year, with amended proposals, which exempted care homes open before April 2002 from meeting some of the environmental standards, including those for room size (Department of Health, 2002). Subsequently, the government announced a review of the regulations for inspection and of the minimum standards for adult care homes, to reduce bureaucracy for better providers and to target attention on failing homes (Hayes, 2004). A report by a government task force had found evidence that an over-prescriptive approach to standards and regulation not only created problems for providers but also reduced choice and independence for older people (Better Regulation Task Force, 2004).

Encouragement for different agencies to work together to protect vulnerable adults from abuse came with the publication of *No Secrets* (Department of Health, 2000f). This provided statutory guidance to local authorities on the development and implementation of interagency policies and procedures for preventing and dealing with the abuse of vulnerable adults in private households as well as in residential settings. A further significant step was the introduction of the Protection of Vulnerable Adults (POVA) scheme in 2004. This is intended to protect vulnerable adults aged 18 years and over in care settings in England and Wales. All social care employers are required to check potential employees or volunteers for work with vulnerable adults against a POVA list, operated at the time of its introduction by the Department for Education and Skills (DfES). Employers are also required to refer to the list any person considered guilty of harming, or placing at risk of harm, a vulnerable adult, so that he or she is effectively barred from work with vulnerable adults unless his or her name is removed from the list (Department of Health, website).

Improving the workforce

Improving the quality of social care depends crucially on the quality of the workforce and *Modernising Social Services* devoted a whole chapter to this issue. It identified three serious problems in a workforce numbering around one million people, two-thirds of whom were working in the independent sector:

- 80 per cent of this large workforce which works directly with very vulnerable people have no recognised qualifications or training;
- there are no national mechanisms to set and enforce standards of practice and conduct;
- the standards and suitability of some education and training in social care do not enjoy general confidence. (Department of Health, 1998a, pp. 84–5)

The General Social Care Council and Skills for Care

The strategy for tackling these problems has two main elements. The first was the creation of a new regulatory body, a General Social Care Council (GSCC) and equivalent bodies in Scotland, Wales and Northern Ireland. Formally an independent statutory body, the Council members are appointed by the Secretary of State with a lay person as chair. Although all key interests are to be represented, service users and lay people form a majority on the Council (Department of Health, 1998a, p. 86), an indication of the government's concern to avoid any perception of the Council as a self-regulating professional body.

The GSCC has three main areas of responsibility. First, it is responsible for setting conduct and practice standards for all social care staff. Enforceable standards of conduct and practice are published as codes, which staff are required to sign up to as a condition of their employment. Second, the Council has responsibility for registering members of the social care workforce, beginning with qualified and student social workers and eventually covering all groups. Breaches of codes of conduct and practice may lead to suspension from the register and to deregistration. Finally, the Council became the regulatory body for social work education in place of the Central Council for Education and Training in Social Work (CCETSW), which had undertaken this role since 1971. The GSCC became fully operational in October 2001.

The responsibility for developing and promoting training throughout the social care workforce was given to another body, the Training Organisation for the Personal Social Services (TOPSS), renamed Skills for Care in 2005. With its equivalent bodies in Scotland, Wales and Northern Ireland, Skills for Care acts as the strategic workforce development body for adult social care working in close conjunction with employers, service users and carers. Its functions include:

- developing national standards and a qualification framework for the social care sector;
- collecting skills data and researching issues affecting carers and people who use care services;
- creating a national workforce development strategy;
- building employer-led regional support networks to liaise with health, local government and education at local,

regional and national levels. (Adapted from Skills for Care website, 'Who We Are and What We Do')

A Quality Strategy for Social Care

The proposals in the White Paper left pressing concerns unresolved. In particular *Modernising Social Services* had little to say about the future of social work and social work training, as distinct from other aspects of social care. Academics and practitioners had long argued that the standard two-year qualifying programme did not prepare student social workers adequately for the demands and increasing complexity of their role (Orme, 2001a). A related issue – the widespread concern of academics and practitioners about the failure of research to influence policy and the development of practice – had also been neglected. Although *Modernising Social Services* emphasised the importance of practice that is based 'on the best evidence of what works for clients' and that is 'responsive to new ideas from research' (p. 93), there were no specific suggestions for how this might be fostered. Most glaring of all, the White Paper had also failed to mention the growing crisis in recruitment for training courses and to jobs in all areas of social care, particularly in London and other inner cities (Douglas, 1998).

The government returned to the problem of the social care workforce with the publication, two years later, of *A Quality Strategy for Social Care* (Department of Health, 2000a). This proposed further reforms to address shortcomings in training, inconsistencies in practice and other workforce-related issues. Its centrepiece was the announcement of the creation of a Social Care Institute for Excellence (SCIE), which would address the perceived lack of reliable evidence about what works best in social care by:

- establishing and developing a rigorous knowledge base founded on the views and experiences of users, research evidence, Social Services Inspectorate and Audit Commission reports and the experiences of managers and practitioners;
- producing authoritative and accessible guidelines on effective social care practice and service delivery;
- ensuring dissemination through creative partnerships across the diverse range of organisations involved in the research,

monitoring, regulation, commissioning and provision of social care. (Department of Health, 2000b)

Established as an independent not-for-profit organisation, SCIE started work in October 2001. Despite the continuing shortage of research in key areas and of funding for research programmes in social care at a national level, it has maintained a steady output of knowledge reviews, practice guides and other research-based publications. However, uncertainties about its future direction and its relations with government have been apparent, most notably when plans to transfer responsibility for the Care Services Improvement Partnership to SCIE were abandoned. This cluster of health and social care programmes would have significantly expanded SCIE and increased its funding (Samuel, 2005b).

A Quality Strategy for Social Care also addressed the concerns of the social work profession about its future with the statement that:

social work has a specific contribution to make to the government's modernising agenda, with its emphasis on rights and responsibilities, citizenship and participation. (p. 37)

Views were sought on how best to proceed with the reform of social work education and it was announced, in March 2001, that the basic social work qualification would be upgraded to a three-year honours degree, with integrated academic and practice learning. This would be followed by a probationary year in employment prior to full registration with the GSCC. The changes came into effect from the start of the academic year 2003–04.

Improving the quality of practice and addressing the continuing crisis in recruitment and retention in the wider social care workforce would require action on various fronts. A requirement that 50 per cent of care staff in all care establishments should be qualified to NVQ2 by 2005 was included in the National Minimum Standards document, although for domiciliary care the deadline was extended to 2008 (Department of Health, 2003b). However, progress towards developing an agreed strategy for further action, with resources to match, has been slow. *Options for Excellence*, a joint review of the social care and social work workforce was completed in 2006 (Department of Health/Department for Education and Skills, 2006). Highlighting the need to increase support for social workers and to promote continuing professional development, it lacked any specific funding commitments. Its publication was followed by the announcement of a further review into the roles and tasks of social work as a profession, led by the General Social Care Council with the involvement of users and carers and other social care bodies (Gillen, 2006). This would mirror similar reviews in Scotland (Scottish Executive, 2006) and Wales (Association of Directors of Social Services/Cymru, 2005) and is due to report in late 2007.

Improving services for specific groups

Modernising Social Services announced an extension of the direct payment scheme to people aged 65 and over (p. 18). Otherwise, the White Paper contained little that was targeted at specific groups, as these initiatives were to follow. The Health White Paper, *The New NHS* (Department of Health, 1997), had already announced the development of national service frameworks which would set national standards and define service models for specific services, for example mental health, or care groups, for example older people. These frameworks, each with associated performance targets, brought a further increase in the level of monitoring for both health and social services (see Chapter 5).

A National Strategy for Carers

The Carers (Recognition of Services) Act 1995 had given carers the right to request a separate assessment of their needs, but no right to services independent of those provided to the user (see Chapter 3). In response to pressure from carers' organisations and research evidence on the contributions of carers, the demands of the caring role and the patchy implementation of the 1995 Act (Arksey, 2002), the government published its National Strategy for Carers (Department of Health, 1999d). The strategy was developed in consultation with carers and has three main elements (pp. 5–7). First, it should increase the *information* available for and about carers. Second, it should provide more *support* for carers, through services provided by the NHS, housing and other agencies. Third, it should *care* for carers by meeting their health care and training needs, and enable them to have services in their own right including respite breaks. Help for carers who were in employment or who wished to undertake employment was an important theme.

Legislation soon followed. The Carers and Disabled Children Act (2000) gave carers rights to assessment and services that are not dependent on any assessment or services provided to the person they support and made them eligible for direct payments. Subsequently, the Carers (Equal Opportunities) Act 2004, first introduced as a private member's bill in response to campaigning by carers' organisations, increased the duties and powers of local authorities. These included the duty, in the context of assessment, to consider carers' needs in relation to employment and leisure and powers to enlist the help of other agencies in supporting carers.

The Commission for Social Care Inspection focussed specifically on the state of support for unpaid carers in its second annual report on the state of social care in England (CSCI, 2006b). The findings suggested that councils had increased the number of carer assessments and the number of carers receiving services in their own right had also increased (p. 106). However, the extent of progress still to be made is illustrated by a survey of carers for people with learning disabilities, only 46 per cent of whom claimed that they had been told of their right to an assessment of their own needs (p. 92). Councils were also beginning to respond to the requirements of the 2004 Act. Nevertheless, the emphasis still appeared to be on supporting carers in their caring role, rather than on increasing their life chances by reducing social exclusion. The financial pressures on councils, and the consequent tightening of eligibility criteria, are seen as a significant factor in the failure to address the needs of carers more fully (p. 106).

Valuing People: A New Strategy for Learning Disability for the 21st Century

The publication in March 2001 of *Valuing People* (Department of Health, 2001a), a White Paper on services for people with learning disabilities, was seen as long overdue. In the 30 years since the last White Paper, *Better Services for the Mentally Handicapped* (Department of Health and Social Security, 1971), the context within which people with learning disabilities live their lives had changed dramatically. In addition to the changes brought about by the closure of large long-stay institutions and the development of services in the community, the growth of the disability rights movement had led to a general questioning of the position of people with learning disabilities in society by service users and their families and by service providers (see Chapter 7).

Valuing People takes as its starting point the position of people with learning disabilities as 'amongst the most vulnerable and excluded in Britain today' (p. 14). Most lack independence and choice throughout their lives and their views are rarely heard. The extent of the consultation process which informed the White Paper signalled the importance of challenging that exclusion at every level. Service users and carers served alongside policy-makers and service providers on working groups and contributed through other consultative processes. Their views were presented in the White Paper itself and in three reports published alongside it (Department of Health, 2001d; 2001e; 2001f).

The White Paper identified a wide range of problems affecting people with learning disabilities and carers. They include:

- poorly coordinated services for **families with disabled children especially for those with severely disabled children;**
- poor planning for **young disabled people at the point of transition into adulthood;**
- insufficient support for **carers, particularly for those caring for people with complex needs;**
- people with learning disabilities often have little **choice or control** over many aspects of their lives;
- substantial **health care** needs of people with learning disabilities are often unmet;
- **housing choice** is limited;
- **day services** are often not tailored to the needs and abilities of the individual;
- limited opportunities for **employment;**
- the needs of **people from minority ethnic communities** are often overlooked;

- **inconsistency in expenditure and service delivery;**
- few examples of real **partnership** between health and social care or involving people with learning disabilities and carers. (Department of Health 2001a, pp. 2–3, emphasis in original)

Addressing these problems requires radical change, but of a kind that is consistent with the government's wider modernisation agenda. Echoing *Modernising Social Services,* the proposals in *Valuing People* are intended to:

- tackle social exclusion and achieve better life chances;
- ensure value for money from the large public investment in learning disability services;
- reduce variation and promote consistency and equity of services across the country;
- promote effective partnership working at all levels to ensure a really person-centred approach to delivering quality services;
- drive up standards by encouraging an evidence-based approach to service provision and practice. (p. 22)

As in the 1998 White Paper, *Valuing People* is explicit about the principles, four in number, on which the proposals are based. People with learning disabilities are to have enforceable *civil and legal rights* in order to eradicate discrimination and to ensure the full protection of the law. They will be supported in exercising these rights by the Disability Rights Commission established in April 2000 (see Chapter 7). Second, the aim of services for people with learning disabilities will be to promote *independence* rather than dependence. Third, people with learning disabilities, including those with severe and profound disabilities, should be enabled to make *choices* and express preferences in daily living. Finally, they should be able to use mainstream services and be fully *included* in their local community (pp. 23–4).

Valuing People sets out 11 national objectives for services for people with learning disabilities, the purpose of which is to provide a clear direction for local agencies and to achieve greater consistency and equity in services (p. 26). The first eight focus on outcomes for people and the last three on improvements to the systems intended to deliver those outcomes. Each objective has a set of associated sub-objectives, and the targets and performance

indicators through which progress is to be monitored are specified. A strong national lead is to be provided through the establishment of a Learning Disability Task Force, with a membership
including people with learning disabilities and carers, and a
national Implementation Support Team. Responsibility for
ensuring implementation of the programme at local level will lie
with Learning Disability Partnership Boards.

Valuing People was generally welcomed for its person-centred
approach, which focuses on the rights of people with learning
disabilities, and for its emphasis on partnership working, but
there were also widespread concerns about the lack of long-term
funding to support the major changes required (Gates, 2001;
Revans, 2001b). Rob Grieg, who later became joint National
Director of Learning Difficulties, indicated the extent of these
changes by identifying three substantial challenges for those in
management and leadership roles (Grieg, 2001). The first is to
listen to and engage with people with learning disabilities in
order to prioritize their interests. Second, ensuring that mainstream government initiatives are inclusive of people with learning disabilities requires specialist learning disability and
mainstream services to work closely together. Finally, the
commissioning of services needs to be based on robust evidence
about the needs and wishes of people with learning disabilities
and of what works and what does not.

Evidence suggests that progress with implementing *Valuing
People* has been patchy. The problem has not been a lack of
commitment by those involved in the Learning Disability
Partnership Boards but the lack of executive power and adequate
funding to support the radical changes needed in organization
and culture, across a range of local authority and health services
(Fyson and Ward, 2004). Although there has been a significant
increase in social services expenditure on learning difficulties,
there has been no increase in spending by the NHS (Association
of Directors of Social Services, 2005). One factor has been the
delay in the closure programme of long-stay hospitals, scheduled
to be completed by April 2004 and subsequently revised to April
2006 (Department of Health, 2005e). By 2007, five long-stay
hospitals, with a total of 115 residents, were still open. The
largest of these, Orchard Hill, run by Sutton and Merton
Primary Care Trust, was the focus of media attention after a
scathing inspection report by the Healthcare Commission

revealed evidence of abuse (McCormack, 2007a). Despite such setbacks, *Valuing People* has spawned positive developments, most notably 'In Control', an innovative programme which aims to radically transform social care into a system of self-directed support. The In Control model of self-directed support, piloted in learning disability services in six local authorities, is intended to foster user control at every stage of the care process from assessment to service delivery. The programme is based on a partnership which includes the Valuing People Support Team, service users, independent organisations, for example MENCAP, and participating local authorities (In Control, 2006). Findings from the In Control pilots were to influence government plans for the future of social care for adults, and specifically the proposal for individual budgets which first emerged in the strategy for disabled people, to which we turn next.

A National Strategy for Disabled People

The Labour Government's long-term strategy for disabled people was published in January 2005 with the title *Improving the Life Chances of Disabled People* (Prime Minister's Strategy Unit, 2005). It is designed to tackle the disadvantage and social exclusion experienced by disabled people, particularly children and adults of working age. Its proposals reflect sustained campaigning by disabled activists and focus on four key areas:

- achieving independent living;
- improving support for families with young disabled children;
- facilitating a smooth transition into adulthood;
- improving support and incentives for getting and staying in employment. (Adapted from pp. 7–8)

The strategy is to be taken forward by an Office for Disability Issues, reporting to the Minister for Disabled People. The most significant proposal, with potentially radical implications for the future development of community care, is to reorganise funding for disabled people through the introduction of individual budgets. Together with other elements in the strategy, this idea re-emerged soon after in the adult care services Green Paper, *Independence, Well-being and Choice* (Department of Health,

2005a), and is described in that context below. We return to the disability strategy, to discuss the idea of independent living, in Chapter 7.

Independence, Well-being and Choice: the adult social care Green Paper

In the years following the publication of *Modernising Social Services*, the increasing separation of adult and children's services within local authorities and the growing links with health (see Chapter 5) prompted concerns about the future direction of adult services. For some time New Labour's intentions in this area remained unclear. Then in April 2004, the Government announced that it would publish a 'new vision for adult social care' to help achieve a 'person-centred, pro-active and seamless service' (Hayes *et al.*, 2004). Months of speculation followed. How might preventive services and direct payments be developed? What adjustment would be made to the performance assessment framework and to arrangements for funding? How might joint working with other agencies be promoted and what would be the future for care trusts and the relationship with health (see Chapter 5)?

Almost a year later, in March 2005 on the eve of a general election and New Labour's third successive victory at the polls, the government published its proposals as a Green Paper *Independence, Well-being and Choice* (Department of Health, 2005a) and invited consultation.

The Green Paper begins by making a case for reform that is by now familiar. Changes to the design and delivery of social care are essential because of the increased demands on services, as a result of demographic changes, and because of raised expectations within society for independent living, choice and high quality services. Current provision tends to generate dependency, whilst users and carers often lack control over the services they receive (Department of Health, 2005a, p. 6).

Also familiar are the government's aspirations for adult social care as set out in a foreword by the Secretary of State:

> Our vision is one where the social inclusion of adults with need for care or support is promoted by:

- ensuring that, wherever possible, adults are treated as adults and that the provision of social care is not based upon the idea that a person's need for that care reduces them to total dependency
- ensuring that people using services, their families and carers are put at the centre of assessing their own needs and given real choice about how those needs are met
- improving access, not only to social care services, but to the full range of universal public services
- shifting the focus of delivery to a more pro-active, preventative model of care
- recognising that carers also need support and that their well-being is central to the delivery of high quality care
- empowering the social care workforce to be more innovative and to take the risk of enabling people to make their own life choices, where it is appropriate to do so. (Department of Health, 2005a, p. 7).

Promoting independence, choice and support for carers, were central themes in *Modernising Social Services* and in the earlier White Paper *Caring for People* (Department of Health, 1989a). The emphasis on prevention and on promoting access to wider services denotes change but, as Glasby (2005) has demonstrated, it also harks back to previous attempts at reform, notably the Seebohm Report (1968) and the Barclay Report (1982). Both of these reports stressed the need for a preventative approach through the development of community resources and interagency working and through encouraging citizen participation in service planning and organisation.

If the vision for social care is, in effect, a restatement of earlier visions, this implies that earlier strategies for realising it have been unsuccessful and that a different approach is needed. So what does the Green Paper propose and what steps have been taken to implement its proposals?

The paper begins by focusing on outcomes, a key principle in the modernisation agenda and in *Modernising Social Services*. However, it goes beyond the earlier White Paper to propose seven specific outcomes for adult social care, as 'central to the values upon which services should be built, and against which they should be tested' (p. 25). These are:

- *Improved health*: enjoying good physical and mental health (including protection from abuse and exploitation). Access to appropriate treatment and support in managing long-term conditions independently. Opportunities for physical activity.
- *Improved quality of life*: access to leisure, social activities and life-long learning and to universal, public and commercial services. Security at home, access to transport and confidence in safety outside the home.
- *Making a positive contribution*: active participation in the community through employment or voluntary opportunities. Maintaining involvement in local activities and being involved in policy development and decision-making.
- *Exercise of choice and control*: through maximum independence and access to information. Being able to choose and control services. Managing risk in personal life.
- *Freedom from discrimination or harassment*: equality of access to services. Not being subject to abuse.
- *Economic well-being*: access to income and resources sufficient for a good diet, accommodation and participation in family and community life. Ability to meet costs arising from specific individual needs.
- *Personal dignity*: keeping clean and comfortable. Enjoying a clean and orderly environment. Availability of appropriate personal care. (Department of Health, 2005a, p. 26)

This selection of outcomes, covering so many dimensions of personal well-being, was the result of consultations with users and other stakeholders. However, specifying appropriate outcomes for social care is only the first step. The next is to adjust the regime for performance assessment and the inspection and regulation of adult services, so as to ensure that this promotes the outcomes envisaged. Initial proposals for how this might be achieved were published for consultation in August 2006 (Commission for Social Care Inspection, 2006c).

Prominent in the Green Paper are a series of proposals, intended to promote service user choice and control, which had already appeared in the disability strategy (Prime Minister's Strategy Unit, 2005). They include greater use of online self-assessment; the extension of direct payments and the introduction of individual budgets.

Individual budgets bring together funding streams from different agencies into a single transparent budget. This is held by the local authority on behalf of the individual who is then free to choose services, but without the responsibility for managing the budget and for employing people. Alternatively, they may receive a cash payment so they can purchase services for themselves (p. 34). Individual budgets, unlike existing direct payment schemes, may be used to purchase services provided by the local authority as well as those in the independent sector. The question of which types of funding are to be included in individual budgets is left open. Combining a range of services, such as equipment grants, Independent Living Funds and Access to Work, will require radical changes in the organisation of budgets and in service delivery, so different models for individual budgets are to be developed and piloted, with a view to full implementation by 2012 (p. 34).

These proposals, it is suggested, will also require a transformation in the social work role from gatekeeper, or rationer, of services into one of supporting individuals in making choices and taking control of their lives (p. 28). The development of different roles such as 'care navigator' and 'care broker' for providing support is envisaged. A 'care broker', for instance, might help individuals to put together a care plan, negotiate funding and arrange services, whilst more highly skilled care managers engage in assessment and care planning for people with complex needs (p. 36).

A significant element in the Green Paper is its emphasis on prevention, which is defined in two distinctive ways. It is about 'targeted, early interventions that prevent or defer the need for more costly intensive support' (p. 39). But it is also about encouraging the use of services, such as education, leisure facilities and transport, which contribute to 'the wider well-being agenda' amongst potentially vulnerable groups (p. 39). The implications of a more preventive approach for Fair Access to Care Services are noted, specifically the challenge of designing eligibility criteria that enable early interventions as well as targeting services on those with greatest need.

Delivering these changes, we are told, will require organisational adjustments. Within local authorities the role of Director of Adult Services (DASS) will need to incorporate seven key responsibilities:

- providing accountability for spending on social care and delivering quality services;
- providing professional leadership for the social care workforce and championing the rights of adults with social care needs in the wider community;
- leading the implementation of standards to drive up the quality of care;
- managing a process of cultural change to implement proactive, seamless and person-centred services;
- promoting local access and ownership and driving forward partnership working to deliver a responsive, whole-system approach to social care;
- delivering an integrated approach to supporting communities by working closely with the Director of Children's Services to support individuals with care needs through the different stages of their lives;
- promoting social inclusion and well-being to deliver a proactive approach to meeting the care needs of adults in culturally sensitive ways. (p. 44)

It is expected that the DASS and local authority will play an important role in managing the social care market, by regularly undertaking strategic assessments of the care and support needs within the local population to inform the commissioning services (p. 45). The development of local strategic commissioning frameworks with the NHS and other partners including the voluntary and community sectors is also proposed (p. 47) (see Chapters 5 and 6).

The Green Paper puts particular emphasis on the use of innovative approaches to service delivery, with examples that include extra care housing, designed as an alternative to residential care for very frail or disabled people; adult placement schemes and technology enabled services (pp. 54–6). Changes at a local level are to be supported nationally by bodies such as the Commission for Social Care Inspection, the Social Care Institute for Excellence and the Care Services Improvement Partnership (CSIP). CSIP, which was created in 2005 with a brief to develop innovative models of care, brought together seven existing bodies:

- Health and Social Care Change Agent Team;
- Integrated Care Network;

- Integrating Community Equipment Services Team;
- National Child and Adolescent Mental Health Support Services;
- National Institution for Mental Health in England;
- Valuing People Support Team; and
- Change for Children Team. (p. 53)

However, this body, like the Commission for Social Care Inspection, would seem destined to be short-lived. At the time of writing, reports that it will be broken up await confirmation in the outcome of a review scheduled for completion by April 2008. It is suggested that its social care functions are likely to transfer to the Department of Health's social care directorate, whilst its health programmes would report to regional strategic health authorities (Community Care, 2007).

Chapter 5 considers the extent to which the proposals in the Green Paper were confirmed in the health and social care White Paper *Our Health, Our Care, Our Say* (Department of Health, 2006a) which appeared 12 months later. Shortly after publication of the White Paper, the new post of Director General for Social Care was created at the Department of Health, to provide national leadership for the entire sector and to enhance the prominence of social care within the Department and across government (Byrne, 2006). The first Director General, David Behan, was appointed later in 2006.

The Green Paper claims to be 'an ambitious programme for the next 10–15 years' which will transform the lives of people who use social care (Department of Health, 2005a, p. 10). The vision of more personalised services that are focussed on outcomes that matter to users and carers has received broad backing. However, representatives of the care home sector were dismayed at the absence of a role for residential care and sceptical that alternatives such as extra-care housing would provide an appropriate care setting for people with complex needs (Leason, 2005). More generally, there are questions about how the proposals will be worked out in detail. For example, the realignment of the performance assessment framework to focus on outcomes instead of on service input, processes and volume poses substantial methodological challenges. How will these be tackled? To what extent will roles such as 'care broker' and 'care navigator' be independent of local authorities and how will they differ from that of care manager?

Some pointers to the future have emerged from the individual budget pilots, located in 13 local authorities and covering a range of user groups. Building on the experience of the earlier In Control pilots, each site has been developing and testing a Resource Allocation System (RAS) (IBSEN, 2007). The purpose of the RAS is to provide a fair and transparent process for allocating cash to particular levels of need, so that users and carers know in advance what funding they are entitled to and can select and purchase support services accordingly. This represents a significant shift away from existing arrangements, where the funding allocated for a care package or the size of direct payment reflects a professional judgement about which individual needs require a service response (Duffy, 2006). It also implies significant adjustments to the process of needs assessment. Initial findings from the evaluation suggest that the pilot projects have tackled this in rather different ways. Some had moved to a system based substantially on self-assessment questionnaires, whilst others continued to have care managers leading the assessment process, in consultation with users (IBSEN, 2007). In another key area, support planning and brokerage services, progress has been limited but the indications are that in the long term these functions are likely to be provided by the independent sector. An important question for local authority care managers is whether this implies the disappearance of their posts, or a return to a more traditional social work role where the emphasis is on helping individuals with complex problems rather than on bureaucratic client processing.

Perhaps the most widespread concerns are those relating to funding (Glendinning and Means, 2006). The expectation that the proposals will be met from existing funds and will be cost-neutral overall for local authorities (pp. 40–2) rests on particular assumptions. For instance that efficiency savings achieved through the Gershon review will release resources and that prevention will lead to a reduction in care costs. This has met with widespread scepticism. As commentators were quick to point out, the development of preventive services will require substantial initial investment particularly in the voluntary sector (Community Care, 2005).

Modernisation: a progress review

The message from the Green Paper was clear. Despite all the initiatives in the years since publication of *Modernising Social Services*, much remained to be done to ensure high quality and effective care services. So what has been achieved since New Labour came to power? Throughout this period there has been a continuing decline in the numbers of people admitted to residential care and an increase in the number of intensive home care packages (CSCI, 2005a; 2006b; Knapp *et al.*, 2005). There has also been evidence, from research, inspection reports and other performance data, as well as user accounts, of improvement in services of all kinds. However, on closer examination the evidence has yielded a complex and often confusing picture.

The Commission for Social Care Inspection has reported a 'marked improvement in overall performance against the National Minimum Standards, in residential care homes for adults and older people' since the current inspection regime was introduced in 2002 (CSCI, 2005a, p. 92; CSCI, 2006b). The figures have revealed some interesting patterns. Residential care services for younger adults have consistently out performed those for older people, with homes for younger adults with learning or physical disabilities meeting 82 per cent of the standards on average in 2005–06, whilst the figure for homes for people aged 65 and over was 79 per cent (CSCI, 2006b, pp. 41–5). As different sets of standards have been applied to homes for older and younger people direct comparison is problematic, but it appears that older people have been less likely to have access to stimulating activities and that such differences may reflect the higher fees paid to homes for younger adults (CSCI, 2005a, p. 112).

The Commission acknowledged that in all services 'the standards are at best "proxy" indicators for the things that matter most to people' (CSCI, 2006b, p. 38), so relating performance data to peoples' actual experiences of care cannot be straightforward. This can be illustrated with the findings from a CSCI report on the state of home care services for older people (CSCI, 2006d). Domiciliary care services, which became subject to inspection in April 2004, by 2005–06 were meeting on average 74 per cent of the standards against which they were assessed (p. 49), compared to 66 per cent the previous year. However, the areas in which performance was weakest – including procedures for staff recruitment, selection and supervision; staff training in relation to protection and the detection of abuse; procedures for managing medication and the recording of user needs, wishes and preferences (p. 55) – were particularly worrying given the vulnerability of many service users. It is reassuring to note that Standard 6, which relates to the flexibility, consistency and reliability of the service, was achieved by 78 per cent of organisations (p. 61). However, the report also pointed to particular shortcomings in this area, such as frequent changes of worker; missed visits and inadequate allowance for travelling time creating pressure on limited time slots, all of which were recurrent themes in consultations with users. Findings from research confirmed the difficulties of providing a consistent and reliable service without addressing these issues and pointed to the difficulties of doing so within current funding levels (Starfish Consulting, 2002; Francis and Netten, 2004).

Protection was a key area where shortcomings were recorded in all services for adults, with recruitment procedures a particular focus for concern. For example, in 2005–06, within a sample of care homes failing to meet the recruitment and vetting standard, 40 per cent of homes for older people and 53 per cent of those for younger adults had insufficient verification of the suitability of staff through recruitment checks and references (CSCI, 2006b, pp. 45–8). Such concerns were borne out by the continuing incidence of serious cases of neglect and abuse. One example, the ill treatment of people in a service for people with learning difficulties in Cornwall, prompted an audit and inspection programme of learning difficulties services nationally (Brody, 2006b). Monitoring alone has been insufficient, as indicated in an official report on elder abuse, which highlighted the absence of a research-based understanding of the varieties of abuse, effective responses to abuse and how it might be prevented (House of Commons Health Select Committee, 2004).

Another pattern noted by the Commission for Social Care Inspection was that voluntary sector providers routinely performed better against the national standards than council-run services and providers in the private sector (CSCI, 2006b, p. 40). However, whilst council-run homes for younger adults performed less well across all the standards, in homes for older people and domiciliary care services it was the private sector that performed least well (pp. 41–8). Such evidence has lent weight to the view that the contribution of public sector care services requires more careful examination and a willingness to question what is seen as a continuing ideological bias against in-house provision (Scourfield, 2006).

For social services managers and staff, the performance assessment regime with its battery of performance indicators and associated targets, and the associated strategy of 'naming and shaming' poor performers through the publication of performance league tables, became the most tangible aspect of the New Labour strategy for modernisation. Maintaining or improving its star rating has been the priority for every local authority. Dame Denise Platt, then Chief Social Services Inspector at the Department of Health, writing shortly after publication of the first star ratings for social services, strongly defended this performance regime and the methodology used. It was important, she suggested, to identify councils that needed intensive support to improve their services, as such support and monitoring enable significant changes to take place (Platt, 2002). Without doubt the star ratings awarded to authorities have recorded an overall improvement each year since their introduction in 2002, but with continuing uncertainty about what this actually means (Samuel, 2005c). It was, for example, intriguing to discover that the Commission for Social Care Inspection noted the need for greater use of evidence from inspection data to assess the quality of councils' commissioning activities, after finding for 2004–05 'no statistical correlation between a council's star rating and the performance of local services' (CSCI, 2005a, p. 167). It has to be questioned, however, whether greater use of evidence alone can improve the assessment of performance. As a detailed comparison of different methods for measuring efficiency in social care has revealed, 'an authority's position on a ranking of performance depends on the method chosen', whilst the choice of method used to examine social care performance should depend on the purpose of monitoring (Clarkson and Challis, 2006, p. 473).

Despite general agreement on the importance of information about strengths and weaknesses in service provision, the robustness of the information on which judgements have been made has been widely questioned. For example, besides the challenge of developing a common and clear set of standards for assessing local service performance there has been the problem of securing a consistent interpretation of these standards by inspection teams (Boyne, 2000). The scheduling of the review cycle has meant that the evidence sets used to assess authorities may not have been comparable (Cutler and Waine, 2003). Performance indicators, which inevitably focus on single aspects of a complex reality, may have presented a misleading picture and may have borne little relation to outcomes for services users (Plank, 2000). Whilst this underlines the need for indicators to be sensitive to outcomes, as proposed in the Green Paper, it remains important not to underestimate the difficulties involved in developing such indicators and in evaluating complex interventions such as those undertaken by social workers (Munro, 2004).

Concerns have been raised about the impact of audit and performance assessment on workforce morale. Feelings of 'being overwhelmed by bureaucracy, paperwork and targets', the most important reason for leaving employment in a survey of former public sector workers by the Audit Commission (2002, 3.1), are persistently reported by social care workers (Jones, 2001; Huxley *et al.*, 2005; Samuel, 2005d). The crisis in recruitment and retention has continued with the vacancy rates in social care in England the highest of any employment sector (CSCI, 2005a). Social care employers have become increasingly reliant on migrant labour, which has had obvious short-term benefits but cannot be seen as a sustainable strategy for meeting the sector's long-term needs (CSCI, 2005a).

Measures to improve the status and skills levels of the workforce have had an impact. The numbers enrolling on social work training courses increased after introduction of the new degree (CSCI, 2005a), although, at the time of writing, it is still too early to predict whether this trend will continue, particularly if the practice environment continues to be seen as stressful and demoralising. The values and expectations of professional practice that are central to the new social work curriculum have contrasted with students' experiences in the workplace, where bureaucracy and resource constraints have reduced the scope for skilled and meaningful interventions with service users (Preston-Shoot, 2004; Richards *et al.*, 2005). It remains to be seen whether this clash will act as a stimulus to change in practice. Amongst the wider social care workforce, where providers are required to have 50 per cent of staff qualified to at least NVQ

Level 2, progress has been slow. A survey of care facilities in Sussex by Balloch *et al*. (2004) found that only 30 per cent of staff were qualified to the level required or working towards a qualification. Similar findings emerged from other studies which found the barriers to training included its costs and availability and resistance to training in a workforce where substantial numbers have had little preparation for formal learning (Francis and Netten, 2004; Witton, 2005). Figures from the regulatory body have suggested that amongst social care providers, the qualification levels of staff have increased together with the provision of training programmes but still fall well short of meeting government targets (CSCI, 2005a).

A critical question in considering the performance of local authorities and other social care providers has been whether funding levels have been sufficient to support existing care provision, let alone the improved standards of care envisaged. Whilst funding for the personal social services undoubtedly increased under New Labour, the local authorities have consistently argued that it has been insufficient to meet growing demand and the rising costs of care. The sustainability of the arrangements for funding long-term care was also a central theme in the conclusions of the Wanless review of social care for older people (Wanless, 2006). Wanless raised issues both about the level of funding and its structure, in particular the balance between what the state should fund and what the individual should be expected to pay.

More resources for the personal social services were announced under the comprehensive spending review of July 2004. Funding was scheduled to rise from £10.6 billion in 2004–05 to £12.5 billion in 2007–08, an annual real terms increase of 2.7 per cent (HM Treasury, 2004). When the Local Government Association forecast a shortfall of £660 million in funding for adult social care services for 2006–07 (LGA, 2005), the figures were strongly contested by the government (Samuel, 2005e). Nevertheless, pressures on the system have intensified as a consequence of factors such as the Gershon efficiency savings and a deepening crisis in NHS funding (see Chapter 5). Early in 2006, a poll of 22 local authorities found that two-thirds were facing a shortfall in their adult social care budget for 2006–07. More than half were planning to cut services or to raise discretionary charges, whilst a third planned to raise their eligibility thresholds (Community Care, 2006a).

Conclusion

At the beginning of the 1990s the continuing importance of local authority social services seemed undisputed. They had become the lead agency for community care with the task of implementing a complex series of reforms in a challenging climate. By the end of the decade the process of reform was set to continue after the election of a Labour Government with a programme for modernising both national and local government and the National Health Service. As this chapter has shown, the modernising agenda has involved a yet more intricate sequence of reforms, which has been subject to continuous revision as priorities shift and government ministers come and go. It has had a considerable impact on social services, even though the exact nature of that impact is still in many respects unclear. However it is changes elsewhere that are likely to have the most radical effect on the future shape of social care. The next chapter therefore focuses on the reforms in the National Health Service and their implications for the health and social care interface, and for the future of local authority adult services.

Chapter 5

Health and Social Care: From Collaboration to Incorporation?

Introduction

Labour governments in the late 1990s announced on numerous occasions that they were determined to break down the supposed 'Berlin Wall' between health and social care agencies. This chapter focuses on both the shifting boundaries between health and social care and also on the changing approaches to encouraging effective joint working across that boundary. It explores whether or not there has been a fundamental policy shift from an emphasis on collaboration between partners to one where social services are to be largely incorporated into health. The first section, however, provides a short introduction to the problematic nature of joint working.

Working together: the theory

Over 15 years ago, Webb (1991) brutally explained that 'exhortations to organisations, professionals and other producer interests to work together more closely and effectively litter the policy landscape' yet the reality is 'all too often a jumble of services fractionalised by professional, cultural and organisational boundaries and by tiers of governance' (p. 229).

One key difficulty is that governments have often been more happy to extol the virtues of collaborative working than they have been to address the very real obstacles which exist from the point of view of the proposed collaborating partners (Sullivan and Skelcher, 2002) yet alone whether or not the outcome of partnership working is improved services for patients and service users (Dowling *et al.*, 2004). As Hudson (1987) explains:

From an agency's viewpoint, collaborative activity raises two main difficulties. First, it loses some of its freedom to act independently when it would prefer to maintain control over its domain and affairs. Second, it must invest scarce resources and energy in developing and maintaining relationships with other organisations when the potential returns on this investment are often unclear and intangible. (p. 175)

Thus in order to commit themselves to joint working, agencies need to be persuaded that it is only by this route that organisational objectives can be achieved. They have to be convinced of the possibility of what Huxham (1996) calls 'collaborative advantage'.

Hudson (1987) suggests there are three main strategies available to foster collaborative working despite these problems. These are cooperative strategies (based on mutual agreements), incentive strategies (based on 'bribes' to encourage joint working) and authoritative strategies (agencies or individuals instructed to work together). In the 1960s, the tendency of government was to request or exhort health and welfare organisations to collaborate on various initiatives. Increasingly, governments turned to the use of financial incentives (for example joint bidding for earmarked project monies) to try and persuade health and social care agencies to move in the direction that they wanted. An interesting feature since 2000 has been the willingness of government not only to use financial penalties as well as incentives (for example for delaying hospital discharges) but also to use authoritative strategies (for example the duty of partnership).

Collaboration and partnership seemed to become 'not optional but mandatory' (Clarke and Glendinning, 2002, p. 37) not just in health and social care, but as central features of policy throughout the public services (Sullivan and Skelcher, 2002). However, this is very problematic because research evidence suggests that joint working is most likely to flourish when there are high levels of trust between the partners (Cameron and Lart, 2003). It is difficult to see how trust can be enforced and outcomes may well turn out to be disappointing when based on mandated collaboration.

Hudson's framework is focused in the main on coordination and collaboration between agencies, and yet Hudson (2002) recognises there is equal concern about how to promote better cooperation on a day-to-day basis between health and welfare professionals involved in providing services for community care clients (see also Cameron and Lart, 2003; Glasby and Littlechild, 2004; Barrett *et al.*, 2005). These relationships can be equally problematic and some of the reasons for this were pulled together by Means *et al.* (1997):

- *Stereotypes* – different professional groups often hold negative stereotypes about each other. The more entrenched the stereotypes, the harder it will be to develop joint working.
- *Cultural differences* – in addition to stereotypes, there are real and very important cultural differences between professional groups in terms of how they understand and respond to need. These cultural differences include the use of jargon particular to each profession.
- *Disagreement about roles and responsibilities* – if professionals disagree over their respective roles, responsibilities and competences, then this is likely to be an obstacle to effective joint working at the local level.
- *Misunderstandings* – professionals often have only limited knowledge about other professional groups or other organisations with which they wish to liaise and work. They simply misunderstand the priorities, organisational structures, cultures and working practices of fellow professionals. There is a lack of network awareness.

The policy studies literature indicates that some professionals are adept at overcoming these obstacles and so encourage joint working. Such individuals are sometimes referred to as 'reticulists' (Friend *et al.*, 1974), whilst the Audit Commission (1986) called them 'champions of change'. They are skilled at mapping policy networks and identifying the key resource holders and fellow enthusiasts, both from their own and from other agencies. They tend to feel comfortable working above their hierarchical position, and they are willing to operate in a way not bounded by narrow organisational self-interest. However, a recent study by Hudson (2002) of working relationships between general practitioners, community nurses and social workers found that 'harmonious relationships ... [were] only patchy and partial' (p. 15).

It has long been recognised that staff equally have the capacity to undermine joint working through what is sometimes called 'street level bureaucrat' behaviour (Lipsky, 1980). Hoggett (2001) draws upon the work of Sennett (1998) to illustrate how this is likely to be magnified in times of rapid policy change:

> As the demand for change-embracing and flexible workers intensifies, those who by temperament, age or aptitude cannot maintain the pace or the adaptability required become increasingly vulnerable. (p. 54)

Public sector workers may recognise the imperative need to change but many also feel greater anger and frustration at what is expected of them. Hoggett (2001) has called for a psychosocial perspective on this phenomenon from a belief that 'our capacity to be a reflexive agent is often constrained by the difficulties we have in facing our own fears and anxieties' (p. 42). In social care, the move to quasi-markets (Le Grand and Bartlett, 1993) and the further development of a mixed economy of providers may well have served to intensify such fears.

Such perspectives underline how difficult it can be to foster collaborative working across agencies especially during periods of rapid change. The rest of this chapter illustrates just how difficult governments since the Second World War have found it to improve collaborative working.

Shifting boundaries

The issue about 'what is health?' and 'what is social care?' has been regularly disputed and redefined since the Second World War (Means and Smith, 1998b; Glendinning and Means, 2002; Glendinning *et al.*, 2005). Within the confines of this chapter, it is possible to give only a glimpse of these debates. In terms of institutional care, a key issue has always been the meaning of the term 'in need of care and attention' in the National Assistance Act 1948. Godlove and Mann (1980) argued that the authors of the 1948 Act did not envisage residential homes 'as being adequate for people suffering from incontinence, serious loss of mobility, or abnormal senile dementia'. These were health problems requiring placement in a hospital or nursing home. Yet an important aspect of the history of welfare services since 1948 has been the shift of definition of 'care and attention' to include those suffering from these illnesses and medical conditions (Means, 2001).

As early as 1953, the Minister of Health (Iain Macleod) described this whole area 'as perhaps the most baffling problem in the whole of the National Health Service' (quoted in Means, 1986, p. 94). The government decided that the best approach was to expand local authority residential care in a form which would enable such homes to cope with the needs of those labelled as 'infirm' rather than 'sick'. This approach was supported by the government, which attempted to specify the responsibilities of local authorities and hospital boards in respect of frail and sick elderly people. Ministry of Health Circular 14/57 stated that local welfare authorities were responsible not only for 'active elderly people' in need of residential care but also for those with minor illnesses requiring short periods in bed, those in need of help with dressing and toiletry and those expected to live for only a short period of time.

The group called 'the partly sick and partly well' by Huws Jones (1952, p. 22) would increasingly be directed to local authority residential accommodation even though this was meant to be a form of social rather than health care provision (Means, 2001). Although this situation was further reinforced by a subsequent circular in the mid-1960s (Ministry of Health, 1965), the reality remained one of endless disputes about how to interpret such circulars in terms of the health and social care needs of specific individuals.

The major reforms of the early 1970s in both the National Health Service and in the personal social services through the establishment of local authority social services departments did little to ease these tensions despite the assertion that they were based upon a clear separation between health and social care functions. Increasingly, disputes focused on the correct placement of adults with health and social care needs and this was often linked to the closure of long-stay hospital beds (Means *et al.*, 2002). Such arguments were often not over the correctness of the policy towards deinstitutionalisation, but the failure either to transfer adequate resources to social services or to ensure adequate health care was available for those now deemed primarily their responsibility. Cutting NHS long-stay beds was seen by many in the 1980s as a simple way to reduce costs in a health service dominated by acute care and the resource demands of teaching hospitals (Means *et al.*, 2002).

The main mechanism created by central government for overcoming these boundary disputes was joint care planning and joint finance. The NHS Reorganisation Act 1973 established joint planning machinery between health and local authorities through member-based Joint Consultative Committees. A key purpose was to help plan for the rundown of long-stay hospitals and the encouragement of community-based services for people with mental health problems, people with learning difficulties and frail elderly people (see Chapter 2). Lack of perceived progress in joint planning led to the subsequent introduction of joint finance. The arrangement was that social services could receive health authority funds for agreed projects over time-limited periods. These projects needed to be community-based and targeted at people leaving long-stay hospitals or to support people so that they would not require hospital-based care (Department of Health and Social Security, 1977; 1978b).

As already seen in Chapter 2, *Making a Reality of Community Care* (Audit Commission, 1986) castigated the failure of joint planning and joint finance to achieve effective collaboration between health and social services with the blame being placed upon organisational fragmentation and the failure to switch funds. Both Chapter 1 and Chapter 3 outlined how the NHS and Community Care Act 1990 attempted to establish a new demarcation line between health and social services. Social services were to be the lead agency for all the main community care groups with health authorities responsible for health, narrowly defined.

The emphasis of government remained on the need for social services and health to work effectively together, with the White Paper on community care devoting a short chapter to collaboration (Department of Health, 1989a, pp. 49–52). It was argued that the community care changes would clarify the respective roles of health and social care agencies so that tension and conflict would be greatly reduced. It was accepted that in some areas and over some individuals the distinction remained blurred, but health and local authorities would 'need to decide locally about how they share objectives, responsibilities and the funding of different services' (p. 50).

Such optimism proved unfounded as will now be briefly illustrated by reference to four important issues: continuing care beds in the NHS; hospital discharge; the lead role in mental health services; and joint commissioning. Each of these four issues will profile growing tensions between health and social services which helped to call into question the lead agency role of social services in community care.

Continuing care

Earlier chapters have looked at the spectacular growth of private nursing home care from the mid-1980s (Player and Pollock, 2001) and this, of course, served to speed up the decline in continuing care NHS beds (Wistow, 1995). The community care reforms gave social services the responsibility for assessing and funding people in independent sector nursing home care and this served to encourage health authorities to run down their remaining nursing home and continuing care provision (Lewis, 2001). Once again, local authorities began to complain that some people referred to them from acute hospitals had health care rather than social care needs, and hence remained the responsibility of the health service.

The Conservative Government responded to this situation by setting out *NHS Responsibilities for Meeting Continuing Health Care Needs* (Department of Health, 1995a) through Circular HSG(95)8 in a similar way to which Circular 14/57 (Ministry of Health, 1957) had attempted almost 40 years previously. The circular outlined key services which health authorities and GP fundholders had to continue to arrange and fund. Continuity in patient care arranged and funded by the NHS was reserved for those needing ongoing specialist clinical supervision. This was distinguished from the small number needing a rehabilitation and recovery plan arranged and funded by the NHS and the large number able to be discharged from the NHS either into the community with a health and social care package or into a care home. Conservative governments had encouraged a massively reduced role for the NHS but had become concerned that this trend had gone too far. This guidance was designed to ensure agreed local policies would establish 'a line in the sand' beyond which this withdrawal would not go. However, subsequent research was to show that there was considerable local variation in how this guidance was interpreted by the health service (Samuel, 2006).

Hospital discharge

The second issue concerns hospital discharge arrangements for those entering care and for those returning home. This was seen from the outset as a major issue in the implementation of the community care reforms. The Deputy Chief Executive of the National Health Service Management Executive and the Chief Inspector of the Social Services Inspectorate set local authority and health care agencies eight key tasks for 1992–93 in terms of the initial implementation of the community care changes. These included ensuring the robustness and mutual acceptability of discharge arrangements. Subsequently, the handover of social security transfer monies to individual social services authorities became dependent on signing hospital discharge agreements with their health authorities.

Considerable efforts were made to improve the way health and social care professionals worked together over hospital discharge issues, including the production of a hospital discharge workbook (Henwood, 1994). However, research continued to identify major deficiencies in the coordination of health and social care agencies over hospital discharge (Audit Commission, 1997; Department of Health, 2000c) and this was soon to become a major concern to post-May 1997 Labour governments. For example, the major review of the National Health Service produced in 2000 stressed how:

> on one day in September last year, 5,500 patients aged 75 and over were ready to be discharged but were still in an acute hospital bed: 23% awaiting assessment; 17% waiting for social services funding to go to a care home; 25% trying to find the right care home; and 6% waiting for the right care home package to be organised ... The 1948 fault line between health and social care has inhibited the development of services shaped around the needs of patients. (Department of Health, 2000d, p. 29)

The clear suggestion of the above quotation is that the fault in such delayed discharges often lay with social services, a point confirmed when the government announced financial penalties for local authorities deemed responsible for such delays (Glendinning, 2002a; Henwood, 2006).

Mental health issues

The third issue relates to mental health services and from the outset there was no shortage of people sceptical of the competence of social services to play a lead role in the way proposed by the White Paper on community care. Thus, the British Medical Association (1992) indicated that 'there is concern ... that most local authorities lack the skills and expertise to take on the responsibility for supporting mentally ill people in the community' (p. 30).

In addition the capacity of social services to take on this lead role was made problematic because of the development of the care programme approach (CPA) (Department of Health, 1995b) as a parallel system to care management for developing user-centred care plans. CPA was introduced in order to provide a clear framework for the care of people with mental health problems outside hospital. However, since the vast bulk of care programme staff were employees of health care agencies, the relation of CPA to the new system of care management began to be identified as a major source of confusion and tension between health and social services (Mental Health Foundation, 1994; Department of Health/Social Services Inspectorate, 1995). In addition, the Audit Commission (1994) pointed out that too many resources remained locked into hospital provision, the development of community services was patchy and service management and coordination had to be improved.

These concerns were dramatically heightened by a number of mass media portrayals of people with severe mental problems who had killed either care workers or members of the public. For example, on 9 October 1993 John Rous, diagnosed as suffering severe schizophrenia, killed Jonathan Newby, a 22-year-old graduate, working as a volunteer for the Oxford Cyrenians. Ten months previously, Jonathan Zito had been stabbed on the London Underground by Christopher Clunis, also diagnosed as schizophrenic. Reports into both these incidents pointed to a lack of specialist expertise, poor coordination of services, a failure to respond to warning signs and a lack of long-term accommodation specifically targeted at those with the most severe mental health problems (Ritchie *et al.*, 1994; Davies Report, 1995).

The initial response of government was to provide good practice guidance on joint working in this area (Department of Health, 1995b) and further changes to the law. In terms of the latter, the Mental Health (Patients in the Community) Act 1995 established a new system of supervised discharge for many of those leaving hospital with the most severe mental health problems. In February 1996 this was followed up with the announcement of a 'new "asylum" plan for the severely mentally ill' which would provide 24-hour nursing care for at least 5,000 of the most disturbed mentally ill patients in some 400 new residential homes (*The Independent*, 21 February 1996, p. 1). Since then, as explained in Chapter 2, there has been a bitter argument over the desire of the government to introduce compulsory detention and treatment for those considered to have a severe and dangerous personality disorder (Pilgrim, 2007).

In terms of good practice, the Department of Health (1995b) issued *Building Bridges: A Guide to Arrangements for Inter-Agency Working for the Care and Protection of Severely Mentally Ill People*. The guide stressed that the care programme approach and care management were based on the same principles and so 'the two systems should be capable of being fully integrated' (p. 56) as long as each client had an agreed single care plan and single key worker.

The 'culprit' was defined as a failure in joint working caused by lack of agreement on roles and responsibilities and poor awareness of each other's networks. Until these deficiencies were resolved, the message of *Building Bridges* was that some people with severe mental health problems would continue to slip through the 'net' of available support into homelessness and possibly worse. However, reviews of CPA continued to identify a failure of coordination or integration with care management (Department of Health/Social Services Inspectorate, 1999).

Joint commissioning

One of the themes running through the mental health debate was the lack of adequate community services to support the objective of providing care in the community rather than in long-stay hospitals. This led to a major emphasis on the need for health and social services to work together on joint purchasing strategies, the final issue to be considered in this section.

By the mid-1990s the Conservative Government had become convinced of the great value of joint commissioning and was keen to offer advice on how obstacles could be overcome. Guidance distinguished between joint commissioning (two or more commissioning agencies act together to coordinate commissioning), joint purchasing (two or more agencies coordinate the actual buying of services) and joint provision (agencies jointly provide a service) with a clear view that effective joint commissioning was likely to lead on to the second two activities (Department of Health, 1995c; 1995d). The overall message was that the Department of Health (1995c) remained committed 'to helping authorities achieve the potential benefits for service users and their carers that effective joint commissioning can bring' (p. 9).

Initially, many of the most high profile joint developments were in the areas of learning difficulties and mental health. Peck *et al.* (2002) explain the origins of one of these in the following way:

> In 1996, Somerset Health Authority and Somerset County Council undertook a review of mental health services in Somerset. The ensuing report catalogued a series of problems that would have been familiar to most localities around England. Amongst the recommendations for dealing with these problems were the proposals to introduce joint commissioning and the creation of the first combined mental health and social care provider in the UK, Somerset Partnership NHS and Social Care Trust, which was formally established in April 1999. (p. 4)

The incoming Labour Government in 1997 was soon to make its enthusiasm for such arrangements clear (see below). However, it almost certainly failed to grasp the message of the first section of this chapter, namely just how difficult it is to achieve this kind of outcome.

Modernising health care (1): partnerships, frameworks and milestones

Reforming the National Health Service has been a central concern of Labour governments from 1997 onwards, and its ideas have been set out in a plethora of publications that have included a White Paper on the NHS in general (Department of Health, 1997), the NHS Plan (Department of Health, 2000d) and follow up publications (Department of Health, 2001h; 2004) as well as a White Paper specifically on public health (Department of Health, 1999a) and another one on community services (Department of Health, 2006a). The last three sections of this chapter draw out the implications of all this for community care. The first of these explores the initial enthusiasm for partnership working, national service frameworks and service development milestones and targets. The second section shows how this became increasingly tempered by a renewed enthusiasm for markets – competition was required after all in order to generate efficiency and user responsiveness. The final section returns to the four problematic issues we have just examined and explores the extent to which they have been moved forward by policy initiatives since 1997.

The proposed public health changes stressed the need to balance a recognition of the wider determinants of health with the fact that decisions by individuals (for example, to smoke or not) were equally crucial to health outcomes. A key development was related to a requirement for each health authority to publish a health improvement programme (HiMP) in consultation with a range of other agencies including social services. HiMPs were expected to reflect both local needs and concerns but also national health targets in priority areas such as accidents, cancer, coronary heart disease and mental health (Department of Health, 1999a). HiMPs were to be driven by health and seemed to largely supersede the lead role of social services in producing community care plans (see Chapters 3 and 4).

The NHS White Paper was entitled *The New NHS: Modern, Dependable* (Department of Health, 1997) and emphasised the need for a major switch of focus and resources away from hospitals and towards primary care. However, this was not to be achieved through an extension of the GP budget-holding approach preferred by the previous Conservative administration (Department of Health, 1989b). Budget-holding was to be replaced by a completely new system of primary care groups/primary care trusts (PCGs/PCTs) each to serve populations of around 100,000. A four-stage development process was outlined in which the 'loose' administrative structure of the PCG emerges into a PCT with its own budget and eventually with added responsibility for providing community services through pooled budgets with social services.

It was immediately obvious that this primary care revolution in the NHS would have massive implications for social services and that one of the key agendas of the government was to improve joint working between health and social care (Poxton, 1999; Bradley and Manthorpe, 2000; Rummery and Glendinning, 2000). The Health Act 1999 not only created a duty of partnership but also introduced new financial flexibilities. These were designed to support the ability of local authorities and the NHS to pool budgets for specific groups of services, to delegate commissioning to a 'local' organisation and to create single provider organisations (Clarke and Glendinning, 2002). The government was determined to 'smash' the so-called Berlin Wall and to achieve effective joint working between health and social care.

The determination of the government to achieve radical change in the health service was emphasised by its decision to pull together all the strands of policy change and all the proposals for reinvestment into *The NHS Plan: A Plan for Investment, A Plan for Reform* (Department of Health, 2000d). The main publicity for the plan focused on the major expansion in training numbers for doctors, nurses and the professions allied to medicine, but the plan also emphasised the need for a much stronger role for independent sector health care providers in the treatment of NHS patients. The overall vision was of an NHS which ensured 'services would be available when people require them, tailored to their individual needs' (p. 17).

The plan also announced a significant further expansion in the development programme for primary care trusts:

> We now propose to establish a new level of primary care trusts, which will provide for even closer integration. Health and social services are already working together extremely closely and wish to establish new single multi-purpose legal bodies to commission and be responsible for all local health and social care. The new body will be known as a 'care trust' to reflect its new broader role. (p. 73)

Localities were being encouraged to bid for care trust status although these were never to take off in large numbers despite the new flexibilities under the Health Act 1999 (see above).

Such developments only served to confirm the relevance of the question of whether or not social services were losing their lead agency role in community care by stealth (Glendinning and Means, 2002). Such suspicions were further aroused by the publication of *Shifting the Balance of Power within the NHS* (Department of Health, 2001h). This set out an implementation strategy for the NHS Plan but in a way which stressed the dominant role of health rather than local authorities in long-term care and through a discourse which referred to social care rather than community care.

One year prior to the publication of the NHS Plan, the government had published the first of its national service frameworks (NSFs). The NHS Plan made clear the high priority placed by the government on the targets and milestones contained in such NSFs as a way of driving forward health and social care modernisation. These frameworks can been seen as brave attempts to think across health and social services and hence to encourage improved joint working underpinned by clear service benchmarks. However, they can equally be criticised for the failure to ensure a clear connection between such targets and available resources. Three of these NSFs will now be looked at in some detail because of their implications for community care policy and practice. These are the ones on mental health (Department of Health, 1999b), older people (Department of Health, 2001g) and long-term conditions (Department of Health, 2005b).

The National Service Framework (NSF) for mental health built upon the earlier report *Modernising Mental Health Services* (Department of Health, 1998b) and focused on the needs of working age adults up to 65, and hence excluded the mental health problems of both children and older people. The framework set out seven standards across the five areas of mental health promotion, primary care and access to services, effective services for people with severe mental illness, caring about carers and preventing suicide. For example, the two standards in the area of primary care and access to services were:

- Any service user who contacts their primary care team with a common mental health problem should:
    - have their mental health needs identified and assessed;
    - be offered effective treatments, including referral to specialist services for further assessment, treatment and care if they require it.

- Any individual with a common mental health problem should:
  - be able to make contact round the clock with the local services necessary to meet their needs and receive adequate care;
  - be able to use NHS Direct, as it develops, for first-level advice and referral on to specialist helplines or to local services. (Department of Health, 1999b, p. 28)

The two standards with regard to effective services for people with severe mental illness included the following on the care programme approach (CPA). All mental health service users on CPA should:

- Receive care which optimises engagement, anticipates or prevents a crisis, and reduces risk.
- Have a copy of a written care plan which:
  - includes the action to be taken in a crisis by the service user, their carer and their care coordinator;
  - advises their GP how they should respond if the service user needs additional help;
  - is regularly reviewed by their care coordinator.
- Be able to access services 24 hours a day, 365 days a year. (p. 41)

All seven standards were backed up by detailed milestones which were intended to ensure the gradual full achievement of all the standards in all localities.

So what specifically did this NSF have to say about the lead agency role of social services and joint working across the health and social care divide? The NSF starts by stressing that implementation 'will require new patterns of local partnership, with mental health a cross-cutting priority for all NHS and social care organisations and their partners' (p. 6). It also stressed that the range of mental health services could never be unified into a single provider so that 'interfaces and boundaries must be managed effectively to provide and commission integrated services' (p. 9). However, the clear flavour of the NSF is that the central interface is between NHS trusts (increasingly specialist mental health trusts) and emerging primary care arrangements. In reading the NSF for mental health, it is hard to avoid the conclusion that the concept of social services as the lead agency for people with mental health problems had been quietly shelved some time before.

The NSF for mental health claimed the forthcoming NSF for older people would be available in spring 2000 and yet it was not published until March 2001. Major delays were caused by the production of the NHS Plan and probably the sheer complexity of an NSF for this client group. The NHS Plan devoted a whole chapter on 'dignity, security and independence in old age' (Department of Health, 2000d, pp. 123–9). This outlined the establishment of 'a single assessment process for health and social care' backed up by 'a personal care plan' (p. 125) to be held by the service user. The significance of the single assessment process is that it represented a commitment that key agencies at the local level would share assessment tools and approaches rather than each being allowed 'to do their own thing'.

However, the chapter on 'changes between health and social services' (pp. 70–3) had equally far-reaching implications for services for older people. In addition to the description of care trusts, the NHS Plan announced a £900 million investment by 2003–04 on new intermediate care and related services to promote independence. Such schemes were seen as including rapid response teams, intensive rehabilitation services, integrated home care teams, and social work attachments to primary care. Their main focus was seen as (i) reducing the need for older people to enter hospital and (ii) speeding up their ability to leave hospital after their acute care needs were met. This new investment did stimulate the development of a wide range of new joint rehabilitation and intermediate care services although this was perhaps at the cost of a further fragmentation of services funded by different 'pots of money' and targeted at slightly different groups of people with combined health and social care needs. The ambitious claim was made that such investment in intermediate care would mean that 'by 2004 we will end widespread bed blocking' (p. 102).

The NSF itself set out eight standards (and related milestones) relating to age discrimination, person-centred care, intermediate care, general hospital care, stroke, falls, mental health in old age and health promotion. As with the NSF for mental health, the question needs to be asked about the implications of the NSF for the future lead agency role of social services in community care for older people. The most striking gesture of the NSF in this regard is the complete absence of comment on this issue. Instead, the new flexibilities under the Health Act 1999 and the new possibilities through primary care trusts/care trusts are stressed with the emphasis on partnership, joint commissioning, integrated service and a single assessment process.

Earlier in the chapter, the NHS Plan (Department of Health, 2000d) was quoted in terms of the 5,500 patients over 75 who were blocking acute beds in September 1999 and how this was linked to the major investment in intermediate care. The NSF for older people set formidable milestones in this regard so that by March 2004, the government expected there to be:

- at least 5,000 additional intermediate care beds and 1,700 non-residential intermediate care places compared with the 1999/2000 baseline;
- at least 150,000 additional people receiving intermediate care services which promote rehabilitation and supported discharge compared with the 1999/2000 baseline;
- at least 70,000 additional people receiving intermediate care which prevents unnecessary hospital admission compared with the 1999/2000 baseline. (Department of Health, 2001g, p. 50)

Such milestones raised numerous questions. What is the evidence that intermediate care is cost-effective? What types of intermediate care work best with what types of client? Are the milestones realistic? Above all, will this new investment in intermediate care produce the dramatic effects so strongly desired or, as Martin (2001) put it, 'can it do what its backers promised when it becomes mainstream, the gloss has faded and the charismatic leaders have been promoted away' (p. 18). Audit work by the government has provided an unequivocal answer to this last question, and that is 'no'. A joint review by the Commission for Social Care Inspection, the Audit Commission and Healthcare Commission found a lack of progress against standards and milestones as well as weaknesses in partnership working between agencies (Healthcare Commission, 2006).

The final NSF is for long-term conditions, although this in fact only covers those suffering from neurological diseases

(Department of Health, 2005b). However, this is only one of a number of policy documents addressing the issues of long-term health care conditions which also featured as a priority area in the White Paper on community services (Department of Health, 2006a).

Chapter 2 demonstrated the long history of neglect of all the main community care groups in terms of access to good quality health care services, a weakness that continues through to today (Challis *et al.*, 2004). Hence, much of the government's effort to improve health care for all those with long-term conditions is to be praised, even if a key motivation is to reduce health care costs by reducing the role of the hospital (Hudson, 2005). Our main criticism is that this focus on long-term conditions is being pursued within a narrow medical paradigm which marginalises quality of life issues (Hunter, 2005).

In 2005, the Department of Health (2005c) published *Supporting People with Long Term Conditions: An NHS and Social Care Model to Support Local Innovation and Interpretation*. This report defined the problem as the discomfort and stress experienced by the 17.5 million people with a long-term health condition but went on to emphasise that just 5 per cent of inpatients, many with a long-term condition, account for 42 per cent of all acute bed days. The new model was seeking to embed an effective, systematic approach to the care and management of patients with a long-term condition into local health and social care communities with an overall target to reduce inpatient emergency bed days by 5 per cent by March 2008 using 2003–04 bed days as the baseline.

Some of the pitfalls of this new approach can immediately be seen from a social model perspective. The document refers to patients, not service users. It stressed the discomfort and stress of patients but the main target is not the reduction of this but rather a reduction in emergency bed days. In fairness, the report does stress that one of the aims is to prolong and extend the quality of life (p. 7) but this is not followed through. An improvement in quality of life is seen as coming almost solely through targeted health care intervention organised through a new system of case management for those with multiple needs controlled by a new group of highly experienced nurses to be called community matrons. The report defines the role of the community matron in the following way:

Community matrons are likely to have caseloads of around 50–80 patients with the most complex needs and who require clinical intervention as well as care coordination. They will work across health and social care services and the voluntary sector, so that this group of patients receives services that are integrated and complementary. Whether they work from the PCT, general practice or a hospital, community matrons need to have close working relationships with general practices, hospital wards and local social service teams. (p. 16)

It is hard not to see this stress on a matron, as the coordinator for those with the most complex needs, as a return to the medical model. It is even harder to see how this fits with the rhetoric of user empowerment or draws upon all that local authorities have learned about care management and coordination (see Chapters 3, 4 and 6). In fairness, it can be argued that the 2006 White Paper has shown some recognition of the need to draw in a social care perspective more centrally into its long-term conditions thinking and it does acknowledge the social care leadership role of the new Directors of Adult Social Care Services (Department of Health, 2006a).

Modernising health care (2): a return to markets

The origins of the NHS Plan seems to have been a frustration with the slow pace of reform in the early years of the 1997 Labour Government. One feature of that government had been a distancing from the market and quasi-market reforms of previous Conservative administrations. Markets seemed to be 'out' and a stress on partnership planning and milestones seemed to be 'in'. At first glance, the NHS Plan seemed to follow this logic with its stress on public service agreements, modernisation action teams and ambitious targets and performance indicators. However, the enthusiasm of the government for this as the main modernisation driver has cooled somewhat and instead the emphasis began to shift to the use of markets and competition.

From the outset, it needs to be remembered that the NHS Plan talked of a new partnership with independent sector health care providers. It was soon becoming clear that the government was willing after all to encourage a market of multiple health service providers. A key feature of this was to be the ability of NHS Trusts to apply for Foundation Hospital status which would effectively enable them to operate as independent 'not-for-profit' health care providers, a development justified in terms of the need for successful trusts to be free to innovate by no longer being restricted by NHS bureaucracy.

A key review of implementation progress on the NHS Plan in 2004 made clear how Foundation Hospitals fitted into a wider strategy to generate diversity. *The NHS Improvement Plan: Putting People at the Heart of Public Services* (Department of Health, 2004) made three key commitments in this area:

- all hospital trusts to be in a position by 2008 to apply for NHS Foundation Trust status;
- a wider range of primary care services;
- independent sector providers to increase their contribution to provide up to 15 per cent of operations and an increasing number of diagnostic procedures to NHS patients by 2008.

The overall rationalisation for these developments was that 'NHS Foundation Trusts, treatment centres and independent sector providers of NHS services will enable patients to have a greater degree of choice' (p. 51). However, this was a choice to be exercised in the growing market of health care providers in which cost would follow patients so that patient choice would define how much income was generated by each provider. Health care providers which were popular with patients would flourish while unpopular ones would either have to change, reduce services or even close down. Table 5.1 pulls together the sheer scale of the implementation challenge faced by the NHS in order to deliver this 'marketisation' of the NHS (Department of Health, 2006b).

As already indicated, the justification for these reforms is that this emphasis on a diversity of providers is the only way to generate a modern, responsive NHS appropriate to the 21st century. The Government continually stresses that the NHS remains underpinned by public expenditure and is based on a response to need rather than the ability to pay. As such this 'resuscitation of the internal market' (Crinson, 2005, p. 510) represents a clear return to the reform logic of the Conservative Government of the late 1980s. Le Grand and Bartlett (1993) argued that the NHS

TABLE 5.1 *Implementing reform: expectation of change by March 2007*

	By March 2006	By March 2007
Practice-based commissioning	20% of practices	Universal coverage
Number of PCTs	303	120 to 160+ depending on consultation
Choice of hospital	4+	Extended
Choose and book	25%	90%
NHS Foundation Trusts	32 (acute)	65 to 80 including 5 to 10 mental health
Independent Sector Treatment Centre (ISTC) capacity	18	24
Payment by results	£9 billion of services covered	£22 billion of services covered
More service delivered in the community		The forthcoming White Paper will create new levers and incentives for shifting care

Source: Department of Health (2006b) p. 7.

education and community care reforms of that period had a common strand which was the introduction of what they termed 'quasi markets' into the delivery of welfare services. They argued that the intention was for the state to be primarily the funder, with services being delivered by a wide range of private, voluntary and public providers who operate in competition with each other. Le Grand (2003) has continued to argue that 'services delivered by appropriately designed quasi market mechanisms can be empowering, efficient and equitable' (p. 163) and are much more likely to deliver high quality services than an approach which emphasises the 'public service ethos'.

Other commentators disagree totally with this perspective. The title of Pollock's (2004) book *NHS plc: The Privatisation of our Health Care* makes clear her belief that the emphasis is really on the market rather than 'the quasi' and that this might endanger the whole NHS (see also Mandelstam, 2007). Pollock believes that 'the destiny of the NHS' is 'to become progressively residualised within an increasingly private health care system' (p. 261). She also argues that the new modernised NHS is inherently unstable so that 'private providers will be subject to failures and takeovers. There will be workforce shortages and gluts. Trusts will seek safety in mergers, including mergers with PCTs' (p. 261). She fears that all this will undermine confidence in a health care system free at the point of delivery and open up the way for the introduction of an American-style health care insurance system.

What does all this (quasi) marketisation mean for community care? It does seem to create an even more complex environment within which to achieve any effective coordination of services across health and social care. Foundation Hospitals, in particular, represent a major challenge given their autonomy from the health service and their need to perform in their market if they are to survive financially. Above all, the health service seems to be trapped in a state of almost permanent organisational flux which represents a major problem for any social care stakeholder wishing to engage with it.

However it can be argued that this is an unnecessarily negative view given the reassuring tone of the White Paper on community services (Department of Health, 2006a). Indeed, given the enormous reform agenda outlined in Table 5.1, this document is a strangely tepid affair. Four main goals are outlined, namely better prevention and earlier intervention; 'more voice and a louder choice' (p. 7) for patients and service users; the tackling of health inequalities and access to community services; and more support for those with long-term health care needs. No dramatic statements are made about the new market in health care providers although this commitment is supported (often implicitly) throughout. Joint commissioning and coordination between health and social care is stressed – but this is to be supported by a new procurement model and best-practice guidance rather than the national system of Care Trusts which many commentators had predicted (Glendinning and Means, 2002). The implications of the White Paper for future approaches to joint commissioning is picked up in the last section of this chapter.

Interestingly, it should be noted that the modernisation of health and social care in Wales has continued to concentrate upon partnerships, frameworks and milestones rather than upon markets. For example, the NSF for older people in Wales was not published until 2006 – it covered the same eight standards as in England but added 'challenging dependency' and 'medicines and older people' (Welsh Assembly Government, 2006b). Each standard is accompanied by detailed action points which also specify 'by when' and 'by whom'. *Design for Life: Creating World Class Health and Social Care for Wales in the 21st Century* (Welsh Assembly Government, 2005) lists three sequential strategic frameworks (Welsh Assembly Government, 2006b) which are redesigning care (2005–08); delivering higher standards (2008–11); and ensuring full engagement (2011–14). The first strategic framework on redesigning care is accompanied by detailed action points and a commitment to generate these for the later frameworks is also made. This is a rhetoric largely abandoned in England and it does not seem to be accompanied by a growing stress on the use of markets to deliver user responsiveness. The importance of this is returned to in the last chapter.

Continuing tensions

The second section of this chapter looked at four sources of tension after the introduction of the 1993 community care reforms through to the election of the 1997 Labour Government. The issues focussed upon were continuing care, hospital discharge, mental health policy and joint commissioning. These are now returned to in terms of what progress if any has been made between 1997 and the publication of the 2006 White Paper on community services (Department of Health, 2006a).

Continuing care and long-term care

Continuing care and the respective roles of health and social services has continued to be a source of conflict. This is despite the early decision of the incoming Labour Government to set up a Royal Commission on Long Term Care. Sir Stewart Sutherland was asked to chair the commission with a remit:

To examine the short and long term options for a sustainable system of funding of long term care for elderly people, both in their own homes and in other settings, and within 12 months, to recommend how and in what circumstances the cost of such care should be apportioned between public funds and individuals. (Sutherland Report, 1999a, p. 9)

There was growing criticism of how the capital resources (and especially the home equity) of older people were being used to fund their nursing home care in later life, because it was felt such care should be free under the National Health Service (Rummery and Glendinning, 1999). However, Commission members were unable to agree on the best way forward for funding and so they were forced to publish both a main report (Sutherland Report, 1999a, pp. 1–111) and a note of dissent (Joffe and Lipsey, 1999, pp. 113–43).

The main report argued for free personal care on the grounds that no logical distinction could be made either between health care and social care or between those services which should be free and those which should be means-tested:

Older people need long term care not simply just because they are old, but because their health has been undermined by a disabling disease such as Alzheimer's disease, other forms of dementia or a stroke. As yet these diseases cannot effectively be cured by medical care but people suffering from them will require ongoing therapeutic or personal care of different kinds in order to enable them to live with the disease. In this regard, the only difference between cancer and Alzheimer's disease is the limitation of medical science. (Sutherland Report, 1999a, p. 67)

The main report, therefore, felt justified in calling for a common system of funding for what it defined as personal care (see Box 5.1). This common system was to be based on general taxation so that all personal care would be free at the point of consumption rather than being means-tested or based upon some system of insurance. It was argued that although the resultant public expenditure costs would be considerable (see Table 5.2), they were perfectly affordable.

The authors of the note of dissent were unconvinced by the

BOX 5.1   Definition of personal care

Personal care would cover all direct care related to:

- personal toilet (washing, bathing, skin care, personal presentation, dressing and undressing and skin care)
- eating and drinking (as opposed to obtaining and preparing food and drink)
- managing urinary and bowel functions (including maintaining continence and managing incontinence)
- managing problems associated with immobility
- management of prescribed treatment (e.g. administration and monitoring medication)
- behaviour management and ensuring personal safety (e.g. for those with cognitive impairment – minimizing stress and risk).

Personal care also includes the associated teaching, enabling, psychological support from a knowledgeable and skilled professional and assistance with cognitive functions (e.g. reminding, for those with dementia) that are needed either to enable a person to do these things for himself/herself or to enable a relative to do them for him/her.

Source: Sutherland Report (1999a) p. 68.

affordability argument. They were concerned that 'this huge addition to the burden on public expenditure would not, however, increase spending on services for elderly people by a single penny' (p. 113). The Labour Government proved to be much more supportive of the note of dissent than the main report. It decided that the nursing care component of personal care in nursing homes should be free, but that social care in nursing homes, residential care and the community would continue to be means-tested and chargeable. This rejection of the central recommendation of the main report was justified on the grounds that actioning the proposal would have absorbed large sums of money without increasing the range and quality of care available to older people (Department of Health, 2000d). The Government had decided to reassert that a real distinction continued to exist between health and social care even if this was

TABLE 5.2   *Estimates of health and social care services expenditure where personal care is provided without charge in residential and domiciliary settings (normal living costs in residential care of £120 per week, personal care costs of £122 in residential care and £217 in nursing home care) for UK, at 1995 prices*

	1995 prices	2010	2021	2031	2051
Cost £billion	8.2	10.9	14.7	20.8	33.4
Tax base on earnings + pensions + investments (%)	2.5	2.1	2.1	2.4	2.6
% GDP	1.2	1.1	1.2	1.3	1.4

Source: Taken from Sutherland Report (1999a) p. 70.

done because of pragmatic concerns about public expenditure rather than through ideological beliefs. The extent of this practical concern was confirmed subsequently by the way in which free nursing care was defined in government guidance – as care provided by registered nurses only and not by nursing assistants (Pearce, 2001).

The debate about free personal care continued apace rather than abated. This was driven by the decision of the Scottish Assembly to support the majority report of the Royal Commission and fund free personal care for older people (Jerrom, 2002). Interestingly, recent research has shown that the difference between Scotland and the rest of the UK in public expenditure on personal and nursing care is smaller than often assumed. This is for a number of reasons, the most important of which is that people in care homes in Scotland do not receive attendance allowance (Bell and Bowes, 2006). In addition, the Welsh Assembly decided not to pursue its original intention to introduce free personal care because of concerns about affordability (*Community Care*, 2–8 March, 2006).

England and Wales saw considerable acrimony develop over the complex procedures for defining the now 'free' nursing component of nursing home care. The following years have suggested that governments are no nearer a genuine settlement of how best to deliver and fund long-term care than they were before the Royal Commission. Debates continue over both how best to fund long-term care (Glendinning *et al.*, 2004; Clarkson *et al.*, 2005; Hirsch, 2005) and also over exactly where the boundary between health and social care should fall. The Wanless Review (2006) on the funding options for securing good quality social care in later life is perhaps the most detailed and high profile of these and its main recommendations on a partnership model are discussed further in Chapter 9. The Wanless Review does not tackle the health and social care divide in such 'a root and branch' way as the majority report of the Royal Commission (Sutherland Report, 1999a) but it does acknowledge that 'it is sometimes very difficult to distinguish between the need of someone with cancer receiving free continuing NHS care (including free accommodation) and someone with very high personal care needs due to, for instance, severe dementia' (p. 104).

There is still no clear consensus on the legal obligations of the NHS to fund long-term care and continuing care and hence there is no consensus over the eligibility of people to claim such support. Box 5.2 list eight key decisions relating to this issue between 1996 and March 2005. More recently, the Grogan judgment has confirmed that the original Coughlan judgment that the NHS is responsible for paying for the care of patients whose needs are primarily health based is still being flouted (Samuel, 2006). This confused situation led the then Community Care Minister to call for a national approach to continuing care to improve consistency and ease of understanding, (see also Heywood, 2005; Stephenson, 2005). Despite this the White Paper on community services could only promise that during 2006 'we will support NHS and social care professionals' decision-making on responsibility (and funding) through a national framework for NHS-funded continuing care and nursing care. At the start of the chapter we quoted the Minister of Health in 1953 as saying the health and social divide in long-term care 'as perhaps the most baffling problem in the whole of the National Health Service'. Over 50 years later, little seems to have changed despite the almost endless stream of policy initiatives during the intervening years.

BOX 5.2   The history of funding eligibility for continuing care

- 1996: Written criteria are first used in assessing funding for continuing care.
- 1999: The Coughlan judgment rules that the NHS is responsible for paying for the care of patients whose needs were primarily health-based.
- 2001: Department of Health issues guidance on continuing care eligibility.
- August 2002: Department of Health asks strategic health authorities to bring all former health authority criteria for eligibility into a single set.
- February 2003: Health Ombudsman Ann Abraham publishes a report highlighting problems across England for people trying to secure funding for continuing care and calls for reassessment of claims.
- April 2003: Department of Health issues a suggested procedure for carrying out the retrospective reviews by December 2003; this is later revised to March 2004.
- December 2004: Ombudsman publishes a follow-up report on NHS funding for long-term care. It says not all claims have yet been reviewed and calls for national eligibility criteria. Days prior to publication, Health Minister Stephen Ladyman says a national approach will be commissioned.
- March 2005: Ombudsman says huge number of cases still waiting to be finished.

Source: Stephenson (2005) p. 17.

Hospital discharge

The White Paper took a very positive view of progress on speeding up hospital discharge, claiming a 64 per cent reduction in delayed discharge from acute hospitals between 2001 and September 2005, which was seen as releasing about 1.5 million bed days per year (Department of Health, 2006a, p. 143). The White Paper claimed that this was a direct result of the investment in intermediate care which was now helping 360,000 people per annum. This would suggest that pessimism about the robustness of the plans for intermediate care (Martin, 2001) as outlined in the NHS

Plan (Department of Health, 2000d) was unfounded. However, detailed research on intermediate care and on leaving hospital since the NHS Plan was published has painted a more complex picture than the one offered in the White Paper. Intermediate care services proved highly challenging to establish and developed in a very uneven way across the country (Godfrey *et al.*, 2005; Barton *et al.*, 2006). A follow-up study by the Commission for Social Care Inspection (2005b) of 70 older people discharged from hospital in March 2004 found that a permanent move from hospital to a care home was often a hurried decision designed to minimize risk. This attitude of mind from professionals led to a failure to explore alternatives such as referral to an intermediate care service prior to a return to the patient's own home.

There does seem little doubt that delayed discharge has been reduced but it is not clear how important intermediate care services have been in this. First, some of this improvement may have reflected a sustained attempt to develop joint working skills at the local level through the impact of the Change Agent Team (subsequently renamed Care Services Improvement Partnership) as argued by Henwood (2006). Second, this improvement could have been partly the result of the reimbursement penalties for local authorities brought in by the Community Care (Delayed Discharges etc.) Act 2003 or at least the threat of these fines (Glasby, 2004). However, even if such penalties and threats can be shown to be effective, there are still important questions about how the pressure for a quick decision impacts upon individual patients (Henwood, 2006). The research just reviewed by the Commission for Social Care Inspection suggests that this might often mean pressure to enter a care home as the most straightforward (and hence the quickest) solution.

Mental health issues

The National Service Framework for Mental Health (Department of Health, 1999b) has already been outlined in this chapter as the main policy statement by central government about how it intended to overcome the problems of the past. In the following years, three main issues continued to dominate debates about mental health services. As already indicated, the first of these related to the desire of government to strengthen legislation with regard to those with severe and dangerous personality disorders in order to protect the public (Department of Health, 2000e). Pilgrim (2007) has plotted in detail the opposition from the Mental Health Alliance of user groups, professional groups and the voluntary sector to these plans to greatly increase compulsion without the balance of the state having a duty to ensure good quality mental health services in every locality. He points out how the extent of the unease with the proposals has meant that 'despite being in a third term of office and still enjoying a comfortable majority in the House of Commons, the New Labour administration had still failed to complete its intended legislation reforms' (p. 79) in terms of either amendment or replacement of the Mental Health Act 1983.

Second, concerns have continued about the need to improve the integration of services. This has included the desire to improve integration within the NHS with a view that mental health services need to work much more closely with other NHS services so that people with both physical and mental health needs receive a seamless package of care which covers all their needs. It has also included continuing concern over the lack of integration across health and social care especially for older people with mental health needs (Care Services Improvement Partnership, 2005). However, despite such worthy sentiments, little has changed in terms of the 'Cinderella' tag described in Chapter 2. It has been mental health and older people's services which have felt the brunt of the NHS cash cuts brought in as a result of the financial crisis which beset many NHS trusts in 2006–07 (*Community Care*, 27 April–3 May 2006).

The third issue concerns a debate about the inadequacies of many traditional mental health services such as day care and the relationship of this to the social exclusion of many people with mental health problems. The Mental Health Foundation (2005) called for ineffective traditional services to be scrapped and diverted to alternatives such as cognitive behavioural therapy, supported employment and therapeutic communities. The emphasis on supported employment chimed well with the government emphasis upon getting disabled people back to work and off incapacity benefit (Department for Work and Pensions, 2006a). Indeed, one in five such claimants cite mental health as the main cause of incapacity leading to concerns from some mental health charities that people could be manipulated back to work before they are ready (Leason, 2006) (see also Chapter 9).

Joint commissioning

This chapter has illustrated that how best to commission services across health and social services has continued to confound politicians and civil servants. It has been shown how the early emphasis on a duty of partnership moved towards to what at the time appeared to be the inevitable creation of a national system of care trusts which would span health and social care. However, this chapter has also outlined the re-emergence of the belief that (quasi) markets, choice and competition for patients is the only way to bring increased efficiency to the NHS. What has this meant for joint commissioning?

The government's thinking in the mid-2000s is most clearly outlined in the White Paper on community services (Department of Health, 2006a). As already indicated, the starting point was that the GP practices and primary care trusts would have a major focus on commissioning with money increasingly following the patient, a process called practice-based commissioning. Such commissioning is seen as requiring close working with local authorities especially if well-being and public health objectives are to be met. More specifically, Directors of Adult Social Care and Directors of Public Health:

> will play key roles with directors of children's services, in advising on how local authorities and PCTs will jointly promote the health and well-being of their local communities. They will need to undertake regular joint reviews of the health and well-being status and needs of their populations. They will be responsible for a regular strategic needs assessment to enable local services to plan ahead for the next 10 to 15 years and to support the development of the wider health and social care market, including services for those who have the ability to pay for social care services themselves. (Department of Health, 2006a, p. 42)

A sceptic might say that what is being described is something very much like the old community care plan but with health rather than social care in the driving seat. A sceptic might further say that it is an approach that is getting far too complicated for field-level staff and service users to follow. And such a person might also point to how NHS debts can lead health authorities to withdraw funding from new jointly commissioned services at the last minute. The White Paper tried to reassure with the news that the government is to develop general guidance on joint commissioning for health and well-being combined with specific guidance on those with ongoing problems since 'commissioning for people with long-term needs has too often been episodic and organisational rather than focussed on individuals' (p. 167). Time will tell whether or not the White Paper has helped to move joint commissioning forward. The *Commissioning Framework for Health and Well-being* has since been published (Department of Health, 2007) and it covers both commissioning for individuals and for populations. Although the report argues that the core theme is partnerships between health and local authorities, it is very clear that primary care trusts are in the driving seat.

Concluding comments

The government has often seemed to lose patience with the Berlin Wall between health and social services and in consequence has considered a range of options from financial sanctions on social services for delayed hospital discharge through to the establishment of joint health and social care trusts. The move towards care trusts has been much slower than we predicted in the third edition of this book. The incorporation and subservience of social care to health still seems to be occurring but mainly through a gradual and slow process which almost represents 'a death by a thousand cuts' in terms of the original Griffiths Report (1988) vision of social services as 'the leaders in community care' (see Chapter 3). Indeed, it can be argued that the very concept of a lead agency role in community care has lost all salience. The stress is now all about what the Wanless Review (2006) called 'the language of integration' (p. 26) although it is open to doubt about whether or not it is about the substance of integration.

The full extent of this integration challenge has been underlined by the review of social care services for older people in Northumberland County Council by the Commission for Social Care Inspection (CSCI, 2006e). Northumberland operates the first care trust designed to commission both health and adult social care services but the inspection found that health priorities were winning out in a tight financial climate over social care priorities. We have seen in this chapter how the most recent enthusiasm of government seems to be for a harmonisation of commissioning by health and social care rather than the formation of care trusts but it is still unclear how this change of emphasis will protect social care.

Many of these issues are returned to in the final chapter which is framed by the difficult context of the major financial crisis that overtook the NHS in 2006–07. This chapter has profiled the high hopes of the NHS Plan with its major reinvestment in health and social care but, at the time of writing, community hospitals are being closed and many newly qualified health care professionals are unable to find employment. Chapter 9 will consider whether this NHS crisis represents one last chance for social care to take 'centre stage'.

Chapter 6

Housing and Community Care

It has long been accepted that the 1989 White Paper on community care was right to stress that 'suitable good quality housing' was essential to social care packages (Department of Health, 1989a, p. 9) and that as a result 'social services authorities ... need to work closely with housing authorities, housing associations and other providers of housing of all types in developing plans for a full and flexible range of housing' (p. 25). This message has been subsequently reinforced through the Audit Commission (1998), independent research (Cameron *et al.*, 2001; Foord and Simic, 2001; Appleton, 2002; Means, 2006) and a range of government reports and policy documents (Sutherland Report, 1999a; Department of the Environment, Transport and the Regions, 2001; Department of Health, 2005a).

This chapter focuses on housing issues from the perspective that housing is an essential element of community care. However, the emphasis of the chapter is not solely on the politics of what is usually called 'special needs' or supported housing, but will also include a consideration of much broader issues such as the meaning of home and the impact of general housing policies on frail elderly and disabled people. It will conclude with reflections on whether the housing dimension of community care is likely to be reinforced or undermined by the key 'modernisation' changes in health and welfare which were outlined in the two previous chapters.

The meaning of home

Clough *et al.* (2004) argue that three core assumptions underpin community care policy, namely people want to live at home; people do not want to live in care homes; and people want independence. Higgins (1989) argued that the key 'distinction is actually between the institution and home which differ markedly in terms of their core characteristics' (p. 15). Ordinary houses (homes) are preferable to institutions because it is claimed that they offer more privacy, informality, freedom and familiarity. The rest of this section explores the theory about the home and goes on to consider the implications of this for the users of community care services.

In attempting this, one is immediately struck by the complexity of the term 'home' and the extent to which it does or does not relate to living in specific buildings. Even 'what does home mean to you?' can generate a wide set of responses, including:

- a set of relationships with others;
- a relationship with the wider social group and community;
- a statement about self-image and identity;
- a place of privacy and refuge;
- a continuous and stable relationship with other sources of meaning about the home;
- a personalised place;
- a base of activity;
- a relationship with one's parents and place of upbringing;
- a relationship with a physical structure, setting or shelter. (Rapaport, 1995)

The extensive literature on the home emphasises how responses will vary according to gender, class, ethnicity, country and age of the respondent, and that ideas about 'home' are constantly changing and evolving within any given society and throughout any individual lifecourse (Heywood *et al.*, 2002; Andrews and Phillips, 2005; Clapham, 2005; Peace *et al.*, 2006).

The meaning of home became a source for fierce debate in urban sociology during the late 1980s and early 1990s, although such arguments paid little attention to elderly and disabled people. The background to the debate was a belief in the emergence of a new 'middle mass' in British society with shared goals and aspirations, one of which was the desire to be owner-occupiers. Britain had become, as Saunders (1990) put it, *A Nation of Home Owners*. In terms of concepts of home in the UK, Saunders argued that owner-occupiers identified their house as a home and 'a place where they feel relaxed and where they can surround themselves with familiar and personal possessions'

(p. 272). Council tenants, on the other hand, associated 'home' much more with their relationships with family and neighbours. He concluded from this that the great advantage of owner-occupation over other tenures was its capacity to enable people to express themselves and their identity in a private realm which was free from surveillance. However, his work was highly contentious because of its apparent celebration of owner-occupation over renting, a point made by his critics, especially after the collapse of the housing market in Britain in the early 1990s (Forrest *et al.*, 1994). Owner occupation could be the cause of misery through negative equity and mortgage foreclosure, rather than always being a place of security. The subsequent resurgence of house prices has led to a critique of owner-occupation because of how high prices exclude many young people from the housing ladder unless they are able to inherit wealth from parents or grandparents (Rowlingson, 2006).

In terms of elderly and disabled people, a number of authors have criticised the heavy emphasis placed by Saunders on tenure difference as the core of the meaning of home and have called for a greater stress on 'the emotions of home' (see also Heywood *et al.*, 2002; Clough *et al.*, 2004). These emotions can be both negative and positive. For the majority, home is a positive experience since it is where supportive and loving relationships most often take place. This is certainly true for many older people as the research by Phillipson *et al.* (2001) on social networks and social support in late 20th century Britain clearly demonstrated. Their updating of the three seminal studies by Young and Willmott (1957) in East London, Sheldon (1948) in Wolverhampton and Willmott and Young (1960) in a London suburb supported a growing role for friends but also 'that kinship ties have stood up well to the developments affecting urban societies over the past fifty years' (p. 251). Marriage remained a crucial support for many, while close kin tended to act 'as the first port of call if help is needed in the home' (ibid.).

It has long been noted that older people develop a strong emotional attachment to their home:

> home was the old armchair by the hearth, the creaky bedstead, the polished lino with its faded pattern, the sideboard with its picture gallery and the lavatory with its broken latch reached through the rain. It embodied a thousand memories and held

promise of a thousand contentments. It was an extension of personality. (Townsend, 1957, p. 27)

Such views may appear dated and hence irrelevant to present-day debates. However, much more recent research by Askham *et al.* (1999), Clough *et al.* (2004) and Godfrey *et al.* (2004) suggests that many older people continue to retain a strong bond with their homes. As one respondent explains in Clough *et al.* (2004):

> Our home is, an old phrase, is our castle. Our home is our place of refuge, a place of comfort, a place of love. Well a place of comfort. We want our things around us. They all mean something. Our home is very special to us, it's not just bricks and mortar, it's the love that goes into a house to build a home. (p. 91)

This emphasis on the positive aspects of home must not be allowed to obscure the fact that it can also be a negative experience for some. For many elderly owner-occupiers house repair can become a major worry, while this can also be true of more general maintenance, including gardens (Heywood *et al.*, 1999; 2002). Means (2006) has drawn upon three different studies of vulnerable older people in order to illustrate the problematic nature of 'ageing in place' for a minority. The three studies looked at older homelessness (Pannell *et al.*, 2002), older people in the private rented sector (Carlton *et al.*, 2003) and home improvement and adaptions for people with dementia (McClatchey *et al.*, 2001). The Carlton *et al.* (2003) study, for example, illustrated the vulnerability of older tenants to harassment from landlords, especially when the landlord wishes them to leave prior to selling off into owner-occupation. One such tenant remembered how:

> He harassed me. He wants me out. He rang the hospital to say I'm insane ... My landlord, he came to me and offered me £1,000 to get out, then he said to me, 'Oh, Mrs, you haven't got long to live.' (p. 24)

The overall argument in Means (2006) is that a stress on 'staying put' needs to be much more than a slogan and hence needs to be backed up by (i) investment in mainstream housing targeted at older people on low incomes; (ii) a much wider range of specialist support and advice services to help those in vulnerable housing situations; and (iii) developing a positive view of a wide range of housing with care options in later life. A common feature in all three studies drawn on by Means (2006) was the financial and staffing insecurity of the small voluntary organisations seeking to support older people in problematic housing circumstances.

Despite the earlier emphasis on the strong link between 'feeling at home' and attachment to specific houses for many older people, great care must be taken not to overgeneralise. There is evidence that owner-occupiers who move to a different part of the country on retirement establish a sense of home in their new accommodation and environment. Langan *et al.* (1996) looked at a small number of households which had moved from the Midlands to Lake District villages. One stressed that 'I love my little cottage, you know', while a second stressed the friendliness of her village which also had excellent facilities, including a shop and easy access to a GP. It seems likely that many middle-class older people are used to moving periodically for career and other reasons, and perhaps have always seen their house as an asset through which wealth can be released as a result of trading down in later life (Rowlingson and McKay, 2005). Such individuals are likely to have learned the skill of how to transport a sense of emotional security from one building (home) to another, especially if they feel that they have retained a strong sense of control over their housing move (Clough *et al.*, 2004; Clapham, 2005).

There is also extensive evidence that many older people do manage to re-establish a sense of home when they move into good quality sheltered housing (Heywood *et al.*, 2002, ch. 7) and that this includes very sheltered or extra-care housing schemes which aim to promote a high level of care (Oldman, 2000; Vallelly *et al.*, 2006). Such findings have led Oldman to argue that 'it cannot be always assumed that older people do not want to move' to specialist housing environments (p. 18). Some care must be taken in making this argument. A literature review by Croucher *et al.* (2006) on sheltered housing does not refute such findings but does point out that the very frail are often at the margins of social groups and networks within their sheltered schemes and that there is still a significant movement of such people from sheltered housing into care homes.

There has certainly been a growth in sheltered housing options which is much wider than the distinction between those who do and those who do not provide care. These options include retirement villages, both in terms of those exclusively for older people needing to rent (Bernard *et al.*, 2004) and those which are mixed tenure developments (Evans and Means, 2007). Brenton (2001) has shown that it is possible to be even more imaginative than this. She has studied the popularity of co-housing schemes in the Netherlands and their relevance for the UK. Although the details of such schemes vary, their essence tends to be self-contained units with some communal support facilities in which each scheme member knew others prior to moving in. Thus, such schemes build on existing friendships and networks rather than artificially creating a community of strangers.

Despite this largely positive picture of sheltered housing, the research by Clough *et al.* (2004) suggested the popularity of such housing would be massively extended if space standards were not so restrictive. One of their respondents rejected such 'rabbit hutches' since 'you don't necessarily lose your desire for space and taste just because you've got a bit older and infirm' (p. 163).

The conventional wisdom is that a willingness to move does not extend to the more institutional environments of residential care and nursing homes. Willcocks *et al.* (1987) suggested that strong emotions and attachments to houses are expressed by many elderly people when they feel threatened by a possible move into residential care, since 'to leave homes which may be inconvenient and difficult ... would be to relinquish a hold on a base from which personal power can be generated and reinforced' (p. 8). Or, as Steinfield (1981) explains, housing moves in later life are often linked to negative rather than positive status passages and hence the desire of many to 'stay put'. However, the research by Willcocks *et al.* (1987) also indicated that once in such a home, older people often appreciate the care support from staff, but continue to dislike the lack of privacy and private space. These authors used their findings to argue the need to develop flatlets in which residents would have a key to their own rooms (see also Peace *et al.*, 1997; Brenton *et al.*, 2002, p. 28). This is close to what very sheltered housing actually provides (Means, 1999) and suggests that such types of specialist and age-segregated accommodation can become a home if the privacy issue is properly tackled. This underlines just how stressful it is likely to be when older residents have to leave their residential or nursing *home* because of refurbishment or closure (Wild *et al.*, 2002). Against this, it also needs to be remembered that staying put in one's own home when one has very high dependency needs may be the best option for many, but the reality of near 24-hour health and welfare support can be a loss of control and privacy as one's own home almost begins to take on the features of an institution (Wiles, 2005). The growth of assistive technology will open up the 'staying put' option for many more elderly and disabled people, but this could involve high degrees of surveillance which are in stark contrast to Saunders's view of the private domain of the owner-occupied home (Holland and Peace, 2001; Audit Commission, 2004b).

Finally, there is the need to address the tenure difference question since relatively little is known about the meaning of home to older people in rented accommodation (Heywood *et al.*, 2002). Is it easier to settle in a residential home if one had previously rented rather than owned? Are attachments to particular rented houses less strong? Certainly, older tenants of both local authorities and housing associations are often under pressure to move from the house where they brought up their children in order to release family housing to those on the waiting list. Many such tenants have been willing to consider a move to modern prestigious sheltered housing schemes (Means *et al.*, 1997) yet seem increasingly willing to reject offers from older schemes, many of which are becoming hard to let (Tinker *et al.*, 1995). However, there is a shortage of research about the emotional feelings experienced by older people on leaving rented accommodation. One key factor is almost certainly the quality of rented accommodation lived in in the past and the extent to which there has been a single 'family' home rather than a series of moves into different rented accommodation during the life course. For some elderly people their present rented accommodation may hold little emotional attachment and for some the memories may be largely negative. A move in later life may represent an opportunity to establish a sense of home (Carlton *et al.*, 2003).

Towards independent living?

So far the focus of this chapter has been on the meaning of home for older people and how this has been used to justify the emphasis of community care policy on remaining in one's own home rather than moving into residential or nursing home care. However, the same assumptions have also been applied to other community care groups, namely people with learning difficulties, people with mental health problems and physically disabled people. Independent living is usually seen as requiring one to live in as ordinary a home as possible. Morris (2002) has stressed how moving into your own home can be a key element to moving into adulthood for many young disabled people.

In terms of people with learning difficulties, the key policy thrust of the 1990s was resettlement from institutions where they had lived for many years to new homes and hostels in the community. The justification for this was the nature of the institutions, as stressed earlier by Higgins (1989) and as described in Chapter 2. This policy change was often supported by individuals with learning difficulties: 'It's a lot better to live on your own. It's important that people with learning disabilities have the right to their own home and their own key and live by themselves' (quoted in Mental Health Foundation, 1996, p. 50). However, Saunders (1990) did underline that home for some can be as much a matter of networks and relationships (for council tenants) as of privacy (for owner-occupiers). One danger of the resettlement process was that the hospital-based networks and relationships would be shattered but not replaced by equivalent networks in new surroundings. The privacy of the new home or hostel might end up being experienced by some as a prison of loneliness and despair (Crane, 1999).

Research evidence was to dispel such pessimism. Cambridge *et al.* (1994) tracked 200 people with learning difficulties from 12 localities over a five-year period from when they left long-stay hospital care. Their overall conclusion was unambiguous:

From our involvement with the twelve services included in the evaluation, we know of no reasonable basis on which to challenge the policy of care in the community for people with learning disabilities who would otherwise be long-term hospital residents. In fact, most people are demonstrably better off living in the community than in hospital, over both the short and long term. (p. 105)

Positive outcomes included more choice for most over living environments and improved support networks. Emerson and Hatton (1996) reviewed 71 resettlement studies of people with learning difficulties going right back to 1970. The overall message was of improvements in standards of living and quality of life with a wide degree of acceptance by neighbours and local businesses.

Recent Labour governments have remained committed to the link between independent living and access to mainstream housing options. *Valuing People: A New Strategy for Learning Disability for the 21st Century* (Department of Health, 2001a) listed one of its key objectives as enabling 'people with learning disabilities and their families to have greater choice and control over where and how they live' (p. 70). The White Paper argued that people with learning disabilities can live successfully in a variety of settings from self-contained properties to village communities but stressed the advantages of ordinary housing:

> David inherited the tenancy of a housing association bungalow following his mother's death. He has a support package from a care provider and had some intensive support from the Community Team for Learning Disabilities to improve his cooking and domestic skills. His brother and sister-in-law live nearby and provide emotional and practical support. He is now coping well. (quoted in Department of Health, 2001a, p. 270)

The range of schemes and initiatives designed to foster independent living continues to increase (Prime Minister's Strategy Unit, 2005). Race (2005), however, takes a very critical view of what has so far been achieved, arguing that policy-makers and service providers continue to think in terms of 'special people with special needs' rather than the need for what Wolfensberger and Thomas (1983) called 'normalisation'. More specifically, Race feels too many supported housing schemes remain institutional and he is particularly critical of the 2001 White Paper on learning disabilities for retaining 'village and intentional communities' (Department of Health, 2001a, p. 73) as acceptable options.

Race is also critical of how people with learning disabilities are increasingly expected to live with their parents because of the shortage of independent housing options. In fairness, this issue was flagged up in the White Paper and it has also been underlined by research by Mencap (2002) which exposed the lack of planning by local authorities for the estimated 29,000 people with learning disabilities who live with parents aged 70 or over. The tendency was 'to act in a crisis situation, only arranging alternative accommodation when parents die' (p. 2). This does raise a major issue about housing and community care policies. Although it is argued that institutions undermine independence, is there not a danger that this is just as likely to happen to young adults in the family home if they are not supported to 'move on'? Under these circumstances, greater independence may be achieved through some kind of housing with support accommodation rather than through over reliance on parents.

This is also an important issue for those physically disabled people who have been brought up in the family home but now wish to branch out as adults who are largely independent from their parents (Hendey and Pascall, 2002). However, Morris (2002) cautions that housing with support options are accepted rather than chosen by young disabled people because of the lack of mainstream housing opportunities. The government has itself admitted that a major reason for this has been deficiencies in the disabled facilities grant (DFG) as the main mechanism for adapting ordinary housing (Prime Minister's Strategy Unit, 2005) (see discussion below).

The issue for large numbers of people with mental health problems may also be the limits of a family home, although for many others it is the lack of any home at all. The National Service Framework for mental health estimated that 'between a quarter and a half of people using night shelters or sleeping rough may have a serious mental disorder, and up to a half may be alcohol dependent' (Department of Health, 1999b, p.14). Despite such figures, the seven standards of the NSF (see Chapter 5) make only minimal reference to the potential role of housing and housing organisations in achieving these standards, apart from the passing recognition of the need for an expansion of specialist housing with support schemes. This is despite the growing research evidence of the scope for supporting people

TABLE 6.1   *Local authority supported residents in staffed residential and nursing care at 31 March (1997–2002)*

People aged under 65	1997	1998	1999	2000	2001	2002
Physically/sensorily disabled adults	10,356	8,734	9,094	9,960	9,498	9,755
People with mental health problems	7,965	9,277	10,208	10,560	10,995	11,275
People with learning disabilities	25,446	26,029	27,799	29,495	29,705	30,345

Source: Prime Minister's Strategy Unit (2005) p. 79.

with mental health problems in both mainstream housing and in specialist housing with support schemes (Audit Commission, 1998; Simic, 2005). One explanation for this slow progress is that responses to people with mental health problems is played out within what Simic (2005) calls 'thinking in headlines' and 'dramatic narratives' (p. 126), namely the association of mental illness with violence by the media.

The policy of long-stay hospital closure has now been embedded as a priority for over 20 years. Labour governments since 1997 have not only reinforced this policy but also stressed the need to socially include disabled people within broader society. However, the government's own statistics (see Table 6.1) show that the very opposite to these intentions has in fact happened:

> The numbers of those with learning disabilities or mental health support needs who are placed in residential care increased by 20 per cent and 40 per cent respectively between 1997 and 2002. The numbers of people with physical and/or sensory impairments in residential care, having initially fallen, are now increasing. (Prime Minister's Strategy Unit, 2005, p. 79)

The next section looks at the policy initiative which was expected to play a key role in avoiding this situation from happening, namely *Supporting People*.

Supported housing or supporting people

The Higgins typology of home and institution which was outlined at the start of this chapter left open the question of exactly what an institution is and how neatly it can be distinguished from a home and ordinary housing. This has become an important issue given the increasing range of specialist housing and housing with support options available to all the main community care groups.

'Supported housing' is increasingly the term used to describe this varied provision. It is seen as encompassing all forms of sheltered housing as well as a wide variety of staffed and unstaffed shared housing and self-contained accommodation with support attached. The main distinguishing feature is that services are provided that would not be provided to occupiers of general needs housing. In 1998, the Audit Commission (1998) estimated in *Home Alone: The Role of Housing in Community Care* that in England and Wales there were 450,000 units of sheltered housing with on-site wardens and a further 82,000 units of supported housing for people with mental health problems, physical disabilities, learning difficulties and other needs. The report noted that 'the development of specialised housing was not the result of a planned, multi-agency approach but the ragged inheritance of uncoordinated historic decisions' (p. 23).

Supported housing came under increasing criticism, partly because of the complex funding and lack of rational planning identified by the Audit Commission (1998). Schemes were seen as developing in response to the availability of subsidy and local political popularity rather than through the targeting of resources to meet identified need. In addition, the financial viability of many supported housing schemes required the increasing use of housing benefit (HB) to allow people on low incomes to pay for the support element of their housing with support. Even if this was a justified use of 'housing' benefit, the Audit Commission (1998) pointed out that the service charge element of HB could be paid only to tenants of specific housing schemes and was not generally available to those in mainstream housing, even though their need for help might be similar. Finally, this 'bricks and mortar' approach to funding had encouraged the building of specialist accommodation long after it was still required with the growing problem of 'hard to let' sheltered housing schemes being the most obvious example (Tinker *et al.*, 1995).

The main response of government was the development of the *Supporting People* initiative (Interdepartmental Review of Funding for Supported Accommodation, 1998; Department of Transport, Local Government and the Regions (DTLR), 2001b). *Supporting People* was a complex programme which combined housing benefit and supported housing management grant into an integrated programme. Local authorities were expected to run the new system in collaboration with health and to do this on the basis of a detailed analysis of the need for supported housing within their locality (Foord and Simic, 2001; Foord, 2005). Resultant 'subsidies' could be used to underpin specialist supported housing schemes but equally to bring support services to people who live in mainstream housing. The new system did not become fully operational until April 2003.

Supporting People raised massive implementation issues (DTLR, 2001b), including over issues such as which groups would be prioritised for funding support and how the distinction between housing support and community care needs would be worked through in practice. Initially, difficult decisions were largely avoided through the 'generosity' of funding for the *Supporting People* programme. Estimated costs of between £300 to £500 million per annum turned into actual expenditure of £1.8 billion in 2003 when the scheme was launched leading to the government announcing major cutbacks for the following three years (Brody, 2005a). The resultant financial pressures resulted in 978 *Supporting People* services being decommissioned by local authorities between 2003 and 2005, with 414 of these targeted at people with learning disabilities, followed by 136 schemes for people with mental health problems and 103 for older people (*Community Care*, 5–11 May 2005, p. 6). As Foord (2005) put it, ' "crisis" and "retrenchment" is in the air ... as the supporting people's budget cuts begin to bite' (p. 3).

However, equally problematic for the *Supporting People* programme was continued debate and disagreement over the boundaries between housing costs (the province of housing benefit, housing support to be funded by *Supporting People*) and health/community care needs. *Supporting People* became yet another policy to be reviewed by the government almost as soon as it had been created (Office of the Deputy Prime Minister

(ODPM), 2004a; 2004b; 2005). The outcome of these reviews was confirmation of reduced expenditure but also a stress upon how *Supporting People* was designed to help three groups:

- people in receipt of care with support for whom housing related support underpins health and social care services;
- people living with support only, for whom a small amount of support (such as a warden or a community alarm) makes a critical difference in being able to remain independent;
- people experiencing or at risk of social exclusion, for whom housing-related support plays an essential part in preventing or dealing with a crisis situation and restoring independence in a sustainable way.

The November 2005 discussion paper from ODPM (2005) acknowledges the artificiality of the housing support and care division especially for the first of these three groups and for this reason queried whether the ring fencing of *Supporting People*'s money should continue. Three options were offered, namely, a separate grant not ring-fenced; full integration into the council block-revenue support grant system; or delivery through local area agreements. Optimists have seen this as the sweeping away of bureaucracy and artificial divisions (Johnson, 2006) while pessimists fear that the money will be diverted to meet community care needs with those requiring low-level services losing out (Brody, 2005b). It could also be argued that the government was moving to place emphasis on individual budgets for people with support needs (see later in this chapter and Chapter 7) as the best way to achieve empowerment and individualised services.

Mainstream housing and community care

It can be argued that an emphasis on 'special needs' housing and supported housing deflects attention away from inadequacies within mainstream housing provision which, in turn, can lead people to drift into residential care or end up homeless. This section therefore looks at mainstream housing provision in terms of availability, affordability, repair and access, drawing out the implications of the findings for the users of community care services. These housing policies have been the responsibility of a

TABLE 6.2   *Responsibility for housing policy*

Name of Department	Period
Department of the Environment	Up to 30 April 1997
Department for the Environment, Transport and the Regions	1 May 1997–30 April 2001
Department for Transport, Local Government and its Regions	1 May 2001–31 May 2002
Office of the Deputy Prime Minister	1 June 2002–4 May 2006
Department for Communities and Local Government	5 May 2006–present

bewildering range of different and sometimes simply renamed government departments (see Table 6.2).

Any review of mainstream housing needs to be understood in the context of the emphasis by recent Conservative and Labour governments on the superiority of owner-occupation over renting. A key element of this growth was the sale of around 2.2 million council houses into owner-occupation from 1980 to 1996 as a result of the 'right to buy' (Office for National Statistics, 1997). The majority of elderly people are now owner-occupiers (Heywood *et al.*, 2002) while significant numbers of physically disabled people and people with mental health problems are also owners. The present number of owner-occupiers with learning difficulties may be very small but more and more are likely to inherit the family home and the 2001 White Paper on learning disabilities stressed that 'they can cope with the full range of tenures, including home ownership' (Department of Health, 2001a, p. 70). Such trends have resulted in a growing debate about the role of social housing (council housing, housing provided by housing associations, etc.) in supporting those unable to own (or not willing to do so) (Hills, 2007).

Availability and affordability

Whether or not there is a shortage of housing in England and Wales is a more difficult question than it first appears since it requires much more than just checking the overall number of units against the overall number of households. To be used by existing or potential households, houses must be affordable, in the right part of the country and of an appropriate design and size, as well as being in good condition. Studies which try to take all these factors into account suggest major housing shortages exist in London and the wider south east (Joseph Rowntree Foundation, 2002; ODPM, 2004c). Conversely there has been a growing acceptance from central government that there is nevertheless a problem of very low demand for certain types of housing in certain areas. This has resulted in concentrations of vacant properties in some estates and neighbourhoods especially in the north of England (Audit Commission, 2005b; Lund, 2006).

In terms of the focus of this book, it is interesting to speculate how many people with support needs could manage in mainstream housing if it was available, affordable and in reasonable repair, and if the necessary support services could be brought to such housing. It is certainly the intention of the *Supporting People* programme (ODPM, 2005) to help more vulnerable people to remain in mainstream housing by enabling them to access support services. However, it is also the case that supported housing is often used to 'rescue' homeless people who have suffered from the shortage of affordable mainstream housing (Pannell *et al.*, 2002) and the above discussion on house shortages suggests that this will continue to be the case in the south east. There is an equally strong possibility that homeless people and others in the most vulnerable housing situations will end up concentrated in low demand areas in the north despite the desire of government to generate 'balanced communities' (Lund, 2006, pp. 182–5).

In terms of affordability, our main focus is on rented housing. This is not to deny that issues of affordability in owner-occupation do not arise, as the growth of repossessions in the 1990s served to illustrate. However, older owner-occupiers tend to have paid off their mortgages by the time of retirement (Peace and Holland, 2001) and hence the major issue for them is often house disrepair (see below). In contrast, younger owners of properties do experience mental health problems; younger physically disabled adults who are owner-occupiers get made redundant; and the house-owning parents of people with learning difficulties die. All three of these situations can raise affordability issues.

However, issues of affordability are most visible in terms of rented property. A raft of housing legislation has had the effect of driving up rents in the council house, housing association and private sectors (Heywood *et al.*, 2002). At the same time the growth of owner-occupation has inevitably meant that renting, apart from the 'de luxe' end of the private sector, has seen an ever more intense concentration of vulnerable households comprising the unemployed, disabled people, low income elderly people and people with multiple problems (Carlton *et al.*, 2003). In terms of social renting, this trend has been reinforced by the fact that homelessness has become the main route into new tenancies.

The vast majority of 'vulnerable' tenants in the public and private sectors have been able to afford their accommodation only because of the housing benefit system. This can be seen in a very positive light:

> Housing benefit is uniquely adaptable to the accommodation-related needs of people who require support to live in the community. It is cost-effective – payments can be tailored to the type of supported accommodation required as the individual's capacity for community living increases or diminishes over time. (Griffiths, 1997b, p. 23)

However, the response of government was one of horror at the rapidly increasing level of housing benefit, the annual costs of which rose from £4.5 billion in 1986 to £14.7 billion in 1996 (Wilcox, 1997). One of the key reasons for this growth was the increased use of housing benefit to pay for support needs, especially for those older tenants in sheltered housing. Another reason has been rising rents because of lower capital grants and the decline in secure tenancies in the private rented sector (Carlton *et al.*, 2003).

The government strategy for reducing costs has included the development of the *Supporting People* programme (see previous section) as a ring-fenced alternative to the continued use of housing benefit to meet support costs. The second approach has seen the introduction of a series of restrictions on housing benefit through the Housing Act 1996 over such issues as the amount of space for which benefit will be paid on new tenancies and the 'setting [of] "local reference" rents for an area, leaving tenants to find the difference out of money intended for their minimal sustenance needs' (Heywood *et al.*, 2002, p. 46). More recently the government has piloted a new means-tested housing benefit approach in which the benefit is normally paid direct to the tenant which revolves around a new system of standard rents based on property size and location. The main justification for this change is that tenants could 'keep the difference' if they rent property below the standard allowance or if they move to a cheaper property in the same area (Department for Work and Pensions, 2002). Research evidence suggests, however, that the real impact has been to increase rent arrears (Kemp, 2006).

Overall the concern for the public purse has far outweighed concern for low income vulnerable people who rent. This leads Heywood *et al.* (2002) to conclude that:

> All these attempts to reduce the cost of housing subsidies fail to accept the economic realities of housing poorer people in a society with such an uneven distribution of incomes. The lesson the Victorians took so long to learn, that the market unassisted by redistributive taxation could not meet the housing needs of those who had never been paid enough, is in danger of being forgotten again. (p. 47)

Finally, the link between tenure options and affordability needs to be recognised. Morris (2002) points out how high social housing rents deny young disabled people the opportunity to save up the resources to become owner-occupiers in a situation where 'their family is less likely than the families of non-disabled young people to be able to assist them with buying their first home' (p. 9) since they tend to have lower incomes than families with children who are not disabled.

Housing conditions

In all tenures, some appalling housing conditions can be found and the implications of such conditions for people with support needs are immense. In terms of housing estates with a large amount of socially rented housing, a concentration of people with social and health difficulties in poor housing has helped to generate almost total environmental and social collapse requiring broad strategies of regeneration to tackle the resultant problems rather than just the repair of the housing stock (ODPM, 2004c). More specifically, there is growing research evidence about the impact of poor housing on health in areas such as excess winter deaths related to inadequate home heating (Marsh *et al.*, 2000; Easterbrook, 2002).

The response of government has been to make a commitment to provide 'a decent home' for everyone in the socially rented sector by 2010 and also to make significant improvements in the proportion of private housing in decent conditions occupied by vulnerable groups (ODPM, 2004d). A decent home is defined by reference to four criteria, namely meeting the current statutory minimum standard for housing, being in a reasonable state of repair, having reasonably modern facilities and services, and providing a reasonable degree of comfort (see Box 6.1). The national baseline was set at 1 April 2001 using data from the 2001 English House Condition Survey and identified '1.6 million non-decent homes in the social sector at that time' (ODPM, 2004d, p. 21). A further 1.2 million private sector homes were defined as offering 'non decent' accommodation for vulnerable households. A vulnerable household is in turn defined as one 'in receipt of at least one of the principle means-tested or disability related benefits' (p. 19).

For those in owner-occupation, and especially for low-income elderly people, there is constant pressure about how best to maintain property to a reasonable standard. Recent years have seen a dramatic reduction in the availability of local authority home improvement and repair grants. July 2003 did see the introduction of new broad discretionary powers in these areas but the reality was that this included neither any mandatory home improvement grants nor any ring-fenced monies to support home repair by owners on low incomes. The assumption is that the responsibility for maintaining privately owned homes should rest first and foremost with the owner (DETR, 2001). Local authorities are expected to intervene only where a specific property is deemed a high category hazard risk under the new Housing, Health and Safety Rating System introduced by the Housing Act 2004 (Lund, 2006, Chapter 7).

One option used by elderly and disabled people with repair

BOX 6.1　What is a decent home? A summary of the definition

2.1　A decent home is one which is wind and weather tight, warm and has modern facilities. It reflects what social landlords spend their money on. To set a national target a common definition of decent is needed so all social landlords can work towards the same goal.

2.2　A decent home meets the following four criteria:

a – It meets the current statutory minimum standard for housing
Dwellings below this standard are those defined as unfit under section 604 of the Housing Act 1985 (as amended by the 1989 Local Government and Housing Act).

b – It is in a reasonable state of repair
Dwellings which fail to meet this criterion are those where either:

- One or more of the key building components are old and, because of their condition, need replacing or major repair; or
- Two or more of the other building components are old and, because of their condition, need replacing or major repair.

c – It has reasonably modern facilities and services
Dwellings which fail to meet this criterion are those which lack three or more of the following:

- A reasonably modern kitchen (20 years old or less);
- A kitchen with adequate space and layout;
- A reasonably modern bathroom (30 years old or less);
- An appropriately located bathroom and WC;
- Adequate insulation against external noise (where external noise is a problem);
- Adequate size and layout of common areas for blocks of flats.

A home lacking two or less of the above is still classed as decent therefore it is not necessary to modernise kitchens and bathrooms if a home passes the remaining criteria.

d – It provides a reasonable degree of thermal comfort
This criterion requires dwellings to have both effective insulation and efficient heating.

Source:　Office of the Deputy Prime Minister (2004d) p. 7.

problems is to turn to a specialist home improvement agency (HIA) for advice. These are non-profit-making bodies which offer independent advice and support on how to repair, improve and adapt homes (Heywood *et al.*, 2002, Chapter 6). Such agencies are often called Care and Repair or Staying Put projects, although some agencies use other names. The Office of the Deputy Prime Minister has agreed to invest a further £2 million to help expand the availability of HIA services in England to areas where there was no or very little coverage (ODPM, 2004d, p. 18). HIAs used to have a pivotal role in helping vulnerable clients to obtain local authority grants to improve their home. Although this work has declined because of the lack of availability of grants, they continue to play an important role in home adaptations (see next section) as well as in the development of a range of services such as handyperson, home energy, home security and home safety schemes (Adams, 2006).

Owner-occupation in later life will be a boon to many. With the mortgage paid off, housing costs will drop at a time when weekly income is reduced, thus avoiding a major decline in living standards. For many, there is the prospect of a move from a family home to a smaller property, thus releasing equity to be used in a variety of ways, including meeting future care needs. But others will be trapped in poorly repaired property of limited value with few assets with which to develop a maintenance and repair strategy. The housing dimension of community care needs to include a strategy for offering support to elderly and disabled people facing these kinds of repair problems.

Access (new build and adaptation)

Recent years have seen the emergence of government concern about the importance of access standards (Prime Minister's Strategy Unit, 2005). In looking at the issue of access, it is crucial to distinguish between the concept of visitability and that of life-time homes. The concept of visitability derived from the idea of mobility housing and reflected an awareness that most ordinary housing denied even minimal access to disabled people. Lifetime homes, on the other hand, rest on the much more challenging philosophy of sustainability, flexibility and adaptability of design which caters for the changing needs of the population throughout their life course, and enables older and disabled people to 'stay put' as and when their mobility needs change (Milner and Madigan, 2001). Box 6.2 sets out what is still often presented as the main design criteria for lifetime homes and it should be noted that even their full implementation would fail to deliver full access to all living areas within a home for wheelchair users. For example, recent research by the Northern Ireland Housing Executive shows that standard specifications relate to self-propelled wheelchair users and are not spacious enough either for those in electric wheelchairs or for those who need to be pushed by others (NIHE, 2006).

The response by government to the growing debate about life-time homes and access standards was to implement changes in building regulations to meet visitability rather than lifetime standards for all new housing (Brewerton and Darton, 1997). This decision not to implement a 'lifetime approach' reflected concerns about cost as well as the resistance of the building industry (Milner and Madigan, 2001). The high emphasis placed by the government on ensuring all homes in the social rented sector are 'decent homes' has also created opportunities for housing associations to update adaptation standards within their existing stock at the same time. However, recent research suggests that the mindset remains helping individuals with 'special adaptation needs' rather than improving accessibility standards across the overall stock (Ormerod and Thomas, 2006).

This means that the vast majority of older and disabled people will continue to depend on adaptations to their existing homes if they are to 'stay put'. The main public subsidy for adaptation work is through the disabled facilities grant. Such grants not only have the capacity to transform the lives of older and disabled people (see Box 6.3) but also the capacity to do this in a cost-effective way. Research by Heywood (2001) is crucial in this respect. She coordinated teams of professionals working with two disabled researchers to assess the long-term effectiveness of work carried out through the disabled facilities grant. Drawing upon interviews with 104 recipients of major adaptations and 162 postal questionnaires, she was able to demonstrate how:

- minor adaptations (grab rails, handrails and so on) produced a range of lasting, positive consequences for nearly

> **BOX 6.2   Definition of a lifetime home**
>
> Access
>
> 1. Where car parking is adjacent to the home, it should be capable of enlargement to attain 3.3 metres width.
> 2. The distance from the car parking space to the home should be kept to a minimum and should be level or gently sloping.
> 3. The approach to all entrances should be level or gently sloping. (Gradients for paths should be the same as for public buildings in the Building Regulations.)
> 4. All entrances should be illuminated and have level access over the threshold, and the main entrance should be covered.
> 5. Where homes are reached by a lift, it should be wheelchair accessible.
>
> Inside the home
>
> 6. The width of the doorways and hallways should accord with the Access Committee for England's standards.
> 7. There should be space for the turning of wheelchairs in kitchens, dining areas and sitting rooms and adequate circulation space for wheelchair users elsewhere.
> 8. The sitting room (or family room) should be at entrance level.
> 9. In houses of two or more storeys, there should be space on the ground floor that could be used as a convenient bed space.
>
> →

all recipients (for example, 62 per cent felt safer from the risk of an accident such as a fall);

- major alterations such as bathroom conversions and stair-lifts were seen by most as having transformed their lives.

Home adaptation through disabled facilities grants (DFGs), therefore, meets the core community care objectives of the government and yet DFGs are widely acknowledged to suffer from a huge range of deficiencies. These include the lack of overall funds made available for DFG work; the complexity of the whole system; tensions between housing and social services over

10. There should be a downstairs toilet, which should be wheelchair accessible, with drainage and service provision enabling a shower to be fitted at any time.
11. Walls in bathrooms and toilets should be capable of taking adaptations such as handrails.
12. The design should incorporate provision for a future stair-lift and a suitably identified space for potential installation of a house lift (through-the-floor lift) from the ground to the first floor, for example to a bedroom next to the bathroom.
13. The bath/bedroom ceiling should be strong enough, or capable of being made strong enough, to support a hoist at a later date. Within the bath/bedroom wall, provision should be made for a future floor-to-ceiling door, to connect the two rooms by a hoist.
14. The bathroom layout should be designed to incorporate ease of access, probably from a side approach, to the bath and WC. The wash basins should also be accessible.

Fixtures and fittings

15. The living room window glazing should begin at 800 mm or lower, and windows should be easy to open/operate.
16. Switches, sockets and service controls should be at a height usable by all (i.e. between 600 mm and 1,200 mm from the floor).

Source: Cobbold (1997) p. 2.

how best to proceed; delays in obtaining an assessment; a shortage of occupational therapists; the unfairness of the tough means test; and the restrictive maximum grant (Heywood *et al.*, 2002). The government did commission a major review of the disabled facilities grant by Heywood *et al.* (2005) which made a wide range of recommendations including the need to increase the maximum grant from £25,000 to £50,000. This recommendation has not been accepted although the government continues to promote DFGs as a key mechanism for improving the lives of disabled people (Prime Ministers Strategy Group, 2005) and elderly people (HM Government, 2005). Its response to criticism

---

BOX 6.3   Using adaptations to support people in the community: case study

Mr and Mrs Grey

HIA staff explained that last year Mr Grey's parents had returned from Montserrat where their home had been destroyed by the volcano. Both are physically disabled; his father has to use a wheelchair and his mother suffers from dementia, said to have been brought on as a reaction to the shock of the volcano.

Their son has given up his job to care for them but hopes to return to work once a ground floor bathroom, recommended by the OT, has been installed. He would like to move his aunt in, as their carer. Understandably he wants to retain the living room for his exclusive use – he needs to feel that he still has a life of his own.

To give his parents and aunt a living room, the HIA is drawing up plans for a small extension. This will mean that a kitchen/diner can be fitted in as well as the shower room. The disabled facilities grant will pay for the shower and an increase in the mortgage will cover the rest.

The HIA said it saw itself as having a duty to consider the well-being of the carer as well as the person suffering from dementia.

Source: McClatchey *et al.* (2001) p. 22.

---

about complexity, bureaucracy and delay, has been to stress the potential to give clients direct control over how their DFG is spent as part of the more general move to direct payments and individual budgets (Department of Health, 2005a), a key policy development which is discussed in detail in the next chapter.

Concluding comments: towards an integrated response

This chapter has emphasised the importance of the housing dimension of community care, and hence the need to draw housing agencies and housing professionals into the centre of community care. However, as was outlined in Chapter 5, there are obstacles to effective joint working because of conflicts over roles and responsibilities, a lack of knowledge of each other's networks and a tendency for professionals to hold stereotypical images about each other. Many of these difficulties exist with respect to housing and social services as illustrated by the following two quotations from an article by Winchester and Leason (2004). The first presents the view of a housing professional about social workers:

> Social workers give people too much rope and allow them to build up arrears and take time. This is against housing practice, law, fiscal reality, potential balance and probity (p. 27).

The second outlines the negative view of a social worker about housing:

> Housing often lacks knowledge about the legislation that applies to social services and they rarely show much interest in finding out more (p. 27).

In terms of roles and responsibilities there are clear tensions at both the strategic and operational levels in areas such as homelessness and supported housing. At the centre of this tension lies the issue of who should provide and fund the care of people whose housing and support difficulties are not so great, as to ensure they meet the priority criteria for care management and a care package (see Chapter 3). Thus, housing may define a single homeless person as in priority need on the grounds of old age, mental health problems, learning difficulties or a physical impairment but be concerned that this individual will fail to retain any tenancy offered and drift into homelessness unless provided with care support from social services. However, social services will often feel unable to respond, and hence housing workers and housing agencies feel they are being 'dumped upon' (Means *et al.*, 1997; Heywood *et al.*, 2002).

A number of studies in the mid-1990s pointed to a failure to develop fully the housing dimension of community care (Arblaster *et al.*, 1996; Lund and Foord, 1997) and this problem has continued to be identified in the following decade (Cameron *et al.*, 2001). The government's own study of community and housing/homelessness in the mid-1990s devoted a chapter to joint assessment and found that:

although housing agencies are beginning to be engaged in community care implementation, housing solutions for people with 'special' needs and homeless people are still being developed in isolation, and links between community care and housing assessment procedures are rare. (Department of Health, 1994)

A decade on from this report from the Department of Health, we have seen how the review of *Supporting People* by the Office of the Deputy Prime Minister (2005) pointed to almost identical problems – arguments over what is 'housing support' and 'what is community care' linked to concerns about which government department will pay rather than a focus on meeting the holistic needs of the service user.

However, the late 1990s did see considerable efforts by government to move forward the integration of housing into the community care agenda through the encouragement of joint working between the Department of the Health and the then Department of the Environment. *Housing and Community Care: Establishing a Strategic Framework* was a joint circular designed 'to provide a framework to help housing, social services and health authorities to establish joint strategies for housing and community care so that at a strategic level the necessary co-ordination between housing, health and social services is achieved' (Department of Health/Department of the Environment, 1997, p. 1). This was backed up by operational guidance supported by both central departments through the publication of *Making Partnerships Work in Community Care: A Guide for Practitioners in Housing, Health and Social Services* (Means *et al.*, 1997). This argued the need for field-level staff to increase their knowledge and confidence about what each could contribute to community care.

Much more recently, the government has produced an excellent report on *A Sure Start to Later Life: Ending Inequalities for Older People* (ODPM, 2006) which demonstrated their appreciation of how supporting an older person to remain independent in their home requires an integrated input from a wide range of services that span housing and social services (see Figure 6.1). A very similar argument is developed in *Improving the Life Chances of Disabled People* (Prime Minister's Strategy Unit, 2005) while both the Green Paper on social care (Department of Health, 2005a) and the White Paper on 'out of hospital services'

FIGURE 6.1   *Supporting independence in later life*

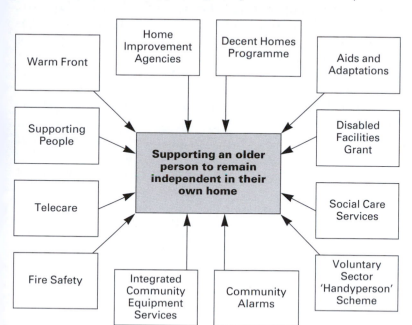

Source: Office of the Deputy Prime Minister (2006) p. 74.

(Department of Health, 2006a) stressed the importance of housing issues. And finally, the government has committed itself to a massive investment to improve housing conditions and has recognised the central importance of good quality mainstream housing to the majority of elderly and disabled people.

Despite all of this, there are reasons to be extremely careful about concluding this chapter on a positive note. Previous chapters have illustrated how community care is now driven at the local level by health/primary care rather than by social services. We have seen how primary care and the NHS is undergoing massive upheaval and how, at the time of writing, the full extent of the funding crisis in the NHS is becoming apparent. Staff are being made redundant from NHS Trusts and grants to underpin preventative services are being drastically cut back. In Wiltshire alone two indebted Primary Care Trusts suddenly withdrew £3million from community-based housing support and care schemes on 31 March 2006 on the grounds that they lacked the resources to follow through promised funding for 2006–07 (*Community Care*, 6–12 April 2006, p. 8). Foord (2005) has recently spoken of 'a new landscape of precariousness' (p. 2) for housing in the context of community care and health care changes. Heywood *et al.* (2002) probably remain accurate in their concern that 'housing organisations may struggle to keep housing high on the agenda of primary care and public health in the next few years' (p. 68).

Chapter 7

Community Care: User Empowerment

Introduction

The preceding chapters have charted significant policy developments and shifts in the main community care sectors in the period since the reforms of the early 1990s. Presented with complex, interlocking and overlapping policy initiatives, combined with continuing organisational turbulence, even experienced care practitioners may be unable to keep abreast of developments outside their immediate sphere. A far greater challenge is faced by users and carers, many of whom negotiate their way through the intricacies of care provision with little prior experience and at a crisis point in their lives. One solution, from the perspective of users and policy-makers alike, is increasing user empowerment. User empowerment, to enable service users to provide a counterweight to provider interests, has been part of the rhetoric of reform from the beginning. However, under New Labour, the development and embedding of strategies for user empowerment is an increasingly prominent policy aspiration.

This chapter examines the idea of user empowerment and charts its uneven progress in relation to different care groupings. It begins with a reminder of how the reforms sustained the disadvantaged position of users and carers within a rhetoric of user empowerment. This leads to a discussion of empowerment and of the social model of disability which locates the oppression of disabled people in social organisations and structures. The disability movement has used this model to powerful effect in its demands for independent living and for legally based rights for disabled people. The chapter also considers the perspectives of groups other than younger physically disabled people, who may face different forms of oppression and be unable or unwilling to adopt a 'disabled identity'. Understanding and engaging with the diversity of service users and carers and the oppressions they may experience is, it is argued, a precondition for empowerment. Practitioners, who may be seen as complicit with the oppression of disabled people, offer a rather different perspective on a system which may frustrate the development and use of their skills whilst failing service users. The chapter ends with a brief look at changing understandings of 'care' and 'care giving', in response to user and carer critiques.

User participation: the developing agenda

A recurrent theme in the discussion so far has been the tension at the heart of the community care reforms between two central, and potentially conflicting, policy objectives: to limit public expenditure and to create 'needs-led' services. How this tension in the negotiations between practitioners and service users would be managed on the ground became clear only after the publication of the policy guidance (Department of Health/Social Services Inspectorate, 1991a; 1991b). The needs of service users were to be identified through a process of assessment in which the practitioner would pay particular attention to the views of the user, but would alone be responsible for defining the user's needs. The power to define what counts as 'need' would rest not with the practitioner but with the local authority, whose role is to provide services to individuals with needs which fall within published eligibility criteria (1991a, p. 53).

Ensuring professional and agency control over the definition of need provides a neat solution to the problem of potentially limitless demand for 'needs-led' services, but one that sits uneasily alongside the consumerist rhetoric of the reforms. *Caring for People* had stressed that its proposals were intended to promote 'choice and independence' (Department of Health, 1989a, p. 4). The policy guidance went further, declaring that:

> the rationale for this reorganisation is the *empowerment* of users and carers. Instead of users and carers being subordinate to the wishes of service providers, the roles will be progressively adjusted. In this way, users and carers will be enabled to exercise the same power as consumers of other services.

(Department of Health/Social Services Inspectorate, 1991a, p. 9, emphasis added)

As the practitioner's control over resources means that the relationship with service users 'will never be totally equal', practitioners are advised to correct this imbalance by sharing information and encouraging users and carers to play a full part in decision-making (p. 16).

This emphasis on information sharing and on user participation has greatly increased under New Labour, for whom user involvement is a vital lever to reform in the public services (Cabinet Office, 1999; Clarke, 2005). Consultation with users and user participation of various kinds are now required, by legislation or government directive, in many areas of health and social care (Carr, 2004). The result has been a rapid development in the opportunities for users and carers to participate at different levels and in different contexts. As well as taking part in decisions about their own use of services, users may be involved at a strategic level in the planning and development of services and in other arenas, such as in professional training and in the design and conduct of research (Braye, 2000). Service users have also been appointed to senior positions in the new social care bodies: the General Social Care Council, the Social Care Institute for Excellence and the Commission for Social Care Inspection.

This strategy of extending user choice and increasing user influence through participation has been described as a 'consumerist' approach to empowerment, as it focuses on the ability of individuals to exercise choice and to exert influence, within pre-defined service systems (Starkey, 2003). Despite the growth in consultation with, and participation by, service users, little evidence has emerged of user involvement exercising a routine influence on the development and delivery of care services (CSCI, 2005a). Research into the process, impact and outcomes of user involvement is limited. Nevertheless, it is already apparent that a lack of organisational commitment, to participation as a process and to changes in response to users views, is a significant factor undermining successful service user involvement (Carr, 2004; McLaughlin *et al.*, 2004; Hodge, 2005). Such problems reflect the power differentials between service users and professionals, which raises the question of whether access to information and participation in decision-making is a realistic strategy for empowering users and carers. Can it provide an effective counterbalance to the power wielded by agencies and practitioners? To answer this we need to look briefly at what is meant by user empowerment.

What is empowerment?

There is no simple answer as to what does and what does not represent user empowerment, since it is a contested concept. However, most would argue that it involves users taking or being given more power over decisions affecting their welfare and hence it probably involves taking at least some power away from service providers, although some writers (Servian, 1996; Pease, 2002) draw upon the work of Foucault to stress that power is a relational concept rather than a zero-sum game.

Any discussion of empowerment has to consider the concept of power. Lukes (1974), in his illuminating analysis of this concept, outlines three main perspectives. The one-dimensional concept of power focuses on observable conflict and seeks to study whose preferences prevail. The two-dimensional view is more subtle in that it takes into account the way in which the powerful mobilise bias so as to ensure that the rules of the game operate in their favour so that they can keep some sources of conflict or potential conflict off the political agenda. However, Lukes argues the need to develop this perspective one stage further into a three-dimensional view of power which:

> allows for consideration of the many ways in which potential issues are kept out of politics ... What one may have here is a latent conflict, which consists in a contradiction between the interests of those exercising power and the real interests of those they exclude. These latter may not express or even be conscious of their interests. (p. 25)

In other words, the victims of non-decision-making may not always be aware that they are victims because they do not always appreciate their real interests. This perspective, if accepted, has major implications for the empowerment debate in community care. It suggests that creating opportunities for greater participation, dialogue and even control over services will not be enough, since many service users and potential service users will not be fully aware of their real interests. It suggests that empowerment requires a general raising of awareness about how society discriminates against and oppresses older people and disabled people.

The social model of disability and the case for disability rights

Understanding of the ways in which society oppresses and discriminates against disabled people has increased substantially with the growth of the disability movement in Britain and elsewhere. Campbell and Oliver (1996) provide an excellent account of the development of the movement in Britain. They chart the growth of traditional voluntary organisations such as the Royal National Institute for the Blind, which were dominated by professionals and other non-disabled people, and the formation of single-issue pressure groups such as the Disablement Income Group. Both approaches seemed ineffective in terms of improving the situation of disabled people, who began to appreciate the need to establish organisations that they controlled and that would focus on the causes, rather than the symptoms, of their disadvantaged position in society. The Union of Physically Impaired Against Segregation (UPIAS), a radical forum which explored and redefined disability as a concept, emerged in the early 1970s. Equally significant was the creation in 1981, the International Year of Disabled People, of the British Council of Organisations of Disabled People as a national campaigning body. Renamed the British Council of Disabled People (BCODP) in 1998, and subsequently the United Kingdom's Disabled People's Council, by 2007 it represented some 70 disabled-led groups with an overall membership of about 350,000 disabled people (UKDPC, 2007). Alongside this has been the development of user-controlled services, in the vanguard of which were the pioneering Centres for Independent Living (CILS) offering a range of disability-related services (Barnes, 2002).

The theoretical starting point of the UK disability movement is their commitment to a social model of disability. This model is highly critical of previous definitions of disability because of their tendency to individualise and medicalise, so that disability is seen as ultimately reducible to the functional limitations of disabled individuals (Oliver, 1996). In contrast to this, the social model of disability is based on the following distinction:

- *Impairment*: lacking part or all of a limb, or having a defective limb, organism or mechanism of the body;
- *Disability*: the disadvantage and restriction of activity caused by a contemporary social organisation which takes no or little account of people who have physical impairments and thus excludes them from the mainstream of social activities. (quoted in Oliver, 1990, p. 11)

Such an approach recognises that people have impairments but argues that it is society which disables them. This is through its imposition of, for example, segregated special schools rather than mainstream education; income maintenance benefits rather than access to the labour market; care management rather than direct payment schemes; and inaccessible housing rather than lifetime homes. The way forward is for disabled people to take control of their lives by gaining sufficient resources to decide how best to meet their own personal assistance needs rather than being expected to live on poverty benefits and to receive care services under the control of welfare professionals or family members. Disability thus becomes a political issue in which disabled people are invited to campaign collectively for their right to be full citizens of the society in which they live (Campbell and Oliver, 1996).

In adopting a rights-based approach, the disability movement is arguing not just for a right to fair treatment and consideration (often called procedural rights) but for legally based enforceable rights as an essential precondition for full citizenship.

Campaigning for rights

By raising awareness of the social injustices experienced by disabled people the disability movement has made significant progress in the campaign for legally based rights for disabled people (Barnes, 2002). Despite the opposition of successive Conservative governments to the granting of such rights, sustained campaigning by nationwide disabled organisations resulted in the passing of the Disability Discrimination Act 1995. Although limited in scope, and open to varying interpretation, the Act enshrined in law the notion of disability rights. The incoming New Labour Government was more sympathetic to the movement's demands, promising in its manifesto to 'support comprehensive, enforceable civil rights for disabled people against discrimination in society or at work' (Labour Party, 1997). In subsequent years the phased extension of the Disability Discrimination Act increased disability rights in the areas of employment, access to services, education, transport and housing. A renewed commitment to extending rights and opportunities for disabled people by Labour in their 2001 manifesto (Labour Party, 2001) led in turn to the passing of the Disability Discrimination Act 2005. This amended the earlier Act so as to include more groups as disabled (people with HIV, multiple sclerosis and cancer) and to extend the range of organisations with duties under the Act. Another significant step under New Labour was the creation of the Disability Rights Commission, a body with wide responsibilities for promoting the interests of disabled people and advising the government on the working of disability legislation. The Commission started work in 2000 and besides campaigning to raise awareness of disability issues and to strengthen legislation, it mounted a series of successful legal actions on behalf of individuals who had experienced discrimination (Disability Rights Commission, 2005). To the dismay of many disability campaigners, who feared dilution of the disability rights agenda, the Disability Rights Commission was replaced in 2007 by a new single equality body, the Commission for Equality and Human Rights (Sayce and O'Brien, 2004; BCODP, 2005a). However, the Commission has been welcomed by campaigners for older people, as a step towards making human rights a reality for a group who have had only limited protection from discrimination under existing legislation (Age Concern, 2005; Harding, 2005).

The passing of the Human Rights Act 1998, which incorporated the European Convention on Human Rights (ECHR) into United Kingdom law, provided a further opportunity for the pursuit of rights-based demands, with pressure groups such as Help the Aged urging older people and their advocates to use the Act to ensure social equality and to end discrimination (Hunt, 2001). In particular it was hoped that the Act could be used to extend user rights in areas such as health and social care provision that were not covered by the disability legislation.

At first attention focussed on the Act as a way for individuals to challenge the workings of the care system by seeking redress through the courts, as in the case of one high profile issue, the closure or transfer in ownership of residential care homes. After several well publicised deaths of care home residents shortly after an enforced move, a series of cases were brought against local authorities on the basis that closures and changes in ownership threaten residents' physical and social well-being, in breach of the protocols governing the right to life, to protection against degrading or inhuman treatment and respect for family life (articles 2, 3 and 8 of ECHR) (Harding and Gould, 2003). Despite rulings which confirmed the need to establish procedures for consultation with residents, no consensus has emerged on whether authorities are required to assess the impact on residents before or after the decision to close or transfer a home (Age Concern, 2005). The position with respect to independent sector homes, as only public authorities fall automatically within the scope of the Human Rights Act, is also problematic. In a landmark case, residents of Le Court, a home owned by the Leonard Cheshire Foundation, challenged the Foundation's decision to close the home in the courts. The ruling that independent sector providers are not subject to the terms of the European Convention on Human Rights, even when residents have been placed there by the local authority, meant that the closure decision could not be reviewed by the courts (Revans, 2002). This ruling, confirmed by the House of Lords, placed significant limits on the use of the Human Rights Act and effectively excludes service users in the independent care sector from the legal protection afforded to users of publicly provided services, and to users of other independent sector bodies, such as private hospitals which are regarded as public authorities for the purposes of the Act (Age Concern, 2005). Subsequent attempts through the courts to bring independent sector providers within the scope of the Act were unsuccessful. A case brought on behalf of an 84-year-old woman, who had been threatened with eviction from the private care home in which she had been placed by her local authority, resulted in a further ruling by the House of Lords in 2007 confirming their earlier 'Leonard Cheshire' decision. At the time of writing, there are indications that as a consequence of this ruling the government may introduce legislation to ensure that the Human Rights Act is extended to the independent sector (Hunter, 2007).

Mental health service users have had more success with actions under the Human Rights Act. For example, the Act was used by seven patients detained under the Mental Health Act 1983 to mount a successful appeal against repeated delays in hearings before the mental health review tribunal (Livesey, 2002). In 2002 a ruling by the European Court of Human Rights established that a man with autism, who had been held as an inpatient in Bournewood Hospital in his own 'best interests' under common law, had been unlawfully detained under Article 5, which relates to liberty and security, of the European Convention. The ruling in the 'Bournewood' case was significant as it exposed the absence of legal safeguards for patients who lack mental capacity and are detained under common law, compared with the safeguards in place for patients detained for treatment under the Mental Health Act (Hartrick, 2005). Further safeguards, to close the 'Bournewood gap', have been included in the Mental Health Bill 2006, although their likely effectiveness has been widely questioned (Taylor *et al.*, 2006).

As legal actions are costly and the outcomes uncertain, attention has also focussed on how public authorities might adopt a more pro-active and preventative approach to the Human Rights Act. An Audit Commission inquiry into the impact of the Act found signs of positive changes, but also evidence that public authorities tended to respond defensively rather than embracing the opportunity for reform by placing the principles of dignity and respect for individual rights at the centre of the policy agenda. More than half the authorities surveyed had not yet developed a human rights strategy (Audit Commission, 2003). Butler (2005) looks forward to the new Commission for Equality and Human Rights, which is charged with supporting public authorities in complying with the Act, to promote awareness of the positive obligations of public authorities to protect human rights.

Independent living

Whatever the long-term possibilities of the Human Rights Act for the disability movement, the limited rights of disabled people in the area of social and health care provision remain a key factor in preventing their full participation in society. The problem is summarised by Morris (2004):

> Disabled people have the same human and civil rights as non-disabled people but we are different from non-disabled people in that we have *additional requirements*, such as mobility needs, communication assistance, personal assistance and so on. A legislative framework that confers human and civil rights will not be effective for disabled people unless we also have entitlements to these additional requirements. (p. 428, emphasis in original)

The way forward, it is argued, is to establish a right to 'independent living' in order to ensure that the additional requirements of disabled people are met. This view was supported by the Disability Rights Commission which adopted 'a basic enforceable right to independent living for all disabled people' as a central policy aim in 2002. The Commission described independent living as follows:

> The term independent living refers to all disabled people having the same choice, control and freedom as any other citizen – at home, at work, and as members of the community. This does not necessarily means disabled people 'doing everything for themselves', but it does mean that any practical assistance people need should be based on their own choices and aspirations. Independent living is not the name of a particular type of service but it should be the purpose of all services. (Disability Rights Commission, 2002, p. 1)

In seeking to extend the rights of disabled people in the area of health and social care, the campaign for independent living challenges fundamental assumptions that underpin the community care reforms. Independence, in the context of the reforms, is about maintaining people in their own home, whereas independent living is about user choice and control (Campbell and Hasler, 2001; Morris, 2004). If disabled people are to receive 'assistance' that reflects their choices and is under their control, this brings into question the role of politicians and managers in determining what kinds of need are eligible for help, the role of practitioners in making decisions about individual need and the whole notion of 'care'.

The legislative framework established under the community care reforms presents significant barriers to independent living. Five fundamental problems are identified by Morris (2004):

- It places duties on local authorities to provide services, rather than gives rights to individuals to receive support;
- there is no entitlement to live at home instead of in institutional care;
- it does not adequately cover assistance to participate in leisure activities, work, have relationships, or look after children or other family members;
- there is no entitlement to advocacy;
- enforcement of existing entitlements involves negotiating an inaccessible legal system with inadequate support. (p. 429)

Although the community care reforms strengthened the rights of service users, and later carers, to an assessment of their needs (Roberts, 1992), access to services, or to cash as direct payments, remains severely circumscribed. Access depends not only on a person's level of need, as defined by the eligibility framework *Fair Access to Care Services*, but on the particular local authority's decision about which levels of need are eligible for support (Department of Health, 2003a) (see Chapter 4). Even then the local authority has the right to withdraw services or cash allocated. This was confirmed in a landmark ruling by the House of Lords which upheld the decision by Gloucestershire County Council to withdraw services, provided to the complainants after an assessment of need, on the grounds of budgetary constraints (Thompson, 1997). Another problem, noted by Morris, is the lack of entitlement to live at home instead of in institutional care, which is a particular issue for older people as the costs of a home care package may easily exceed the relatively low costs of residential care for this group.

The campaign for a right to independent living made an important step forward with the publication of the Government's Disability Strategy (Prime Minister's Strategy Unit, 2005). This contains an explicit commitment to the 'promotion of independent living' (section 4.1), using the definition from the Disability Rights Commission quoted above. Its proposals to support independent living include the introduction of individual budgets and the development of a user-led centre for independent living in every local authority to provide advocacy and support services of various kinds. The strategy was broadly welcomed by the disability movement, although the lack of any specific attention to the needs of older people, the largest disabled group, was seen as a significant omission (BCODP, 2005b).

Direct payments and individual budgets

Another milestone in the campaign for disability rights was the Community Care (Direct Payments) Act 1996 (see Chapter 3). Described as 'potentially one of the most significant developments in British social policy since the establishment of the modern welfare state' (Barnes, 2002, p. 312), direct payment schemes, which enabled people to purchase their own care, are seen as one of the cornerstones for independent living. The schemes were extended to include people aged 65 and over, from February 2000, and subsequently carers were also included. Changes introduced under the Health and Social Care Act 2001 made direct payments mandatory, which means that local authorities are now required to offer them to all eligible individuals. By 2006, 32,000 people in England were in receipt of direct payments (CSCI, 2006b, p. 23).

Evidence suggests that direct payment schemes are well received by service users, with the benefits of increased flexibility, choice and control outweighing the additional administrative burden (Stainton and Boyce, 2004). The experience of Jackie Gelling, one of the first people in the country to receive direct payments, is typical:

> The difference it has made to my life … was nothing short of miraculous. I have three carers and a driver, as needed. Being able to choose my days and times, where and when I wanted to and best of all being able to choose when and where we went for respite. (Gelling, 2006, p. 129)

Initially excluded from direct payment schemes, older people have also welcomed the opportunity to exercise choice and control: 'it's the freedom that you have, you choose who to have.

You choose what the person should do. How to do it. How she should do it. When she should do it' (Clark *et al.*, 2004, p. 36).

Substantial differences persist in the take-up of direct payments between different user groups, so that younger adults with physical or sensory impairments are far more likely to receive direct payments than all other groups (CSCI, 2005a; 2006b). People with learning difficulties are likely to require additional support, not only with managing the practicalities but also with providing initial consent (Williams and Holman, 2006). A lengthy process of supported decision-making may be necessary to satisfy the legal requirement for consent, described as 'a major stumbling block for people with learning difficulties' seeking access to direct payments (p. 68). More intensive support, for instance with recruiting personal assistants (PAs), may also be needed by older people (Clark *et al.*, 2004). Recruitment is also an issue for mental health service users who, whilst valuing the opportunity to employ someone they trust as a PA, are likely to experience difficulties in finding people willing to work short hours and to undertake tasks very different from those of a personal care assistant (Spandler and Vick, 2006).

Wide variations are also reported in the development and take-up of direct payments between different local authorities. A service user in Sunderland, for example, is 16 times more likely to receive direct payments than one who lives in Bracknell (CSCI, 2005a, p. 50). The attitude of care managers is seen as pivotal here, as users are more likely to accept direct payments if the care manager is knowledgeable and confident about how they work (Lomas, 2006). Both Lomas and Clark *et al.* (2004) found care managers who were enthusiastic about working with direct payments, whilst others had only a limited grasp of how they work and were sceptical about whether they were suitable for older people.

Despite the very real benefits to service users, and the commitment of both government and the disability movement to extending their use, direct payments have attracted controversy, particularly in matters relating to the employment of personal assistants. The question of how to balance the freedom of service users to employ someone of their choice, with concerns about their safety, has attracted particular attention. For instance, a proposal that direct payments recipients should be required to check prospective employees against a list of people barred from working with vulnerable adults was strongly rejected by disability campaigners who saw this as placing the mitigation of risk above choice and independence for disabled people (Brody, 2006a). In spite of this, increased regulation would seem inevitable in the longer term given plans by the General Social Care Council to establish a register for personal assistants employed directly by service users. There are also concerns about the supply and training of suitable people (Scourfield, 2005) and about the potential for exploitation of workers, fuelled by evidence that direct payments and other European 'cash for care' schemes, are heavily dependent on low-paid, often migrant, labour (Ungerson, 2004). The finding by Leece (2006) that stress may be lower and job satisfaction higher amongst personal assistants than amongst home care workers employed by a local authority, in spite of poorer pay and conditions, only confirms that complex factors are at work here.

For Spandler (2004) all these tensions stem from the conflicting agendas that underpin direct payments as a policy. As in the case of the wider community care reforms, direct payments are about increasing user choice and control but also about using market mechanisms to achieve cost reductions. In principle, by shifting administrative costs to the service user, resources may be freed up to purchase additional care. However, operating as isolated individuals within a care market, service users and personal assistant alike may be disempowered. Spandler argues for the use of collective strategies, such as service user and worker cooperatives to strengthen the position of both groups. In a response to Spandler's analysis Lyon (2005) highlights the need to consider the impact of direct payments on the whole social care sector. She points, in particular, to the potential for direct payments to create long-sought changes in the assessment process:

> Direct payments continue to play a key role in ongoing improvement of assessments, both because they encourage the assessor to focus on the individual rather than a menu of potential service provisions and also because they highlight inconsistencies in social care provision – it being much easier to make comparisons of cash awarded than of services being provided. (p. 246)

The idea of individual budgets, as proposed in the disability strategy and the subsequent Green Paper *Independence, Well-being and Choice* (Department of Health, 2005a), may be seen as vindicating Lyon's argument. Comprising existing separate funding streams, these offer service users the transparency and control provided by direct payments but without the responsibility for managing the budget or of acting as an employer. Individual budgets have been welcomed by the disability movement, but the detailed implementation of this policy has still to be developed and evaluated (Taylor, 2005). A consequence of the transparency of individual budgets is that issues of equality between different user groups may arise, as older people are likely to have access to a narrower range of funding streams than younger adults (Glendinning and Means, 2006).

Rights: difficulties and dilemmas

The rights of disabled people in certain areas, such as employment and access to services have increased significantly, yet progress in other respects is mixed. In particular, there has been limited success in securing legally based rights for service users in health and social care. Although sympathetic to the demands of the disability movement, various critics have pointed to difficulties that follow from adopting a rights-based approach to empowering disabled people.

Drewett (1999) acknowledges the symbolic importance of rights as a campaigning tool, but doubts their effectiveness as a strategy for effective change and identifies a number of weaknesses in the rights-based approach. First, the discussion of rights in the disability literature lacks a systematic theoretical basis, to the extent that even fundamental questions about the source and status of rights claims have been ignored. Second, she is critical of the distinction drawn in this literature between needs-based and rights-based approaches. The concepts of need and of rights are, she argues, often linked as a 'belief in the existence of universal needs often underpins support of rights' (p. 123). Third, it is unclear how rights-based approaches would translate into practice and how they would be administered differently. Finally, Drewett is doubtful about the possibility of establishing legal rights to social goods, such as social care, as historically the law has endorsed only a basis and limited view of needs and rights.

In a further contribution to this debate, Handley (2000) pursues Drewett's concerns about needs and rights and the question of how rights-based approaches would translate into practice. His critique focuses on the suggestion by Oliver, a prominent disability theorist, that the allocation of resources should be based on self-defined need, not on ascribed need (that is, need defined by experts) as at present: 'it is rights to appropriate [welfare services to meet] *their own self-defined needs* that disabled people are demanding, not to have their needs defined and met by others' (Oliver, 1996, p. 74, quoted in Handley, 2000, p. 317, emphasis added).

This reliance on self-defined need is, Handley argues, problematic as it is hard to see how self-defined needs could form the basis for rights claims given the difficulty of distinguishing between self-defined needs and wants and preferences:

> If everyone is demanding the satisfaction of their self-defined needs by right, then how are we to sort out the almost inevitable conflicts that this will generate? How are we to prioritise all of these competing claims, and who will arbitrate between them? (p. 318).

Such was the dilemma highlighted by Birmingham's Assistant Director of Social Services, after care home resident Flossie Hands unsuccessfully sought an injunction under the Human Rights Act against Birmingham City Council's plans to privatise or close their homes for older people. If the action had been successful, he suggested, the expenditure on the local authority's homes to raise them to the standards required for registration under the Care Standards Act would have a devastating impact on other services (Winchester, 2001). Such responses serve as a reminder that enacting rights through the courts does not solve the problem of how to allocate scarce resources equitably.

Young and Quibell (2000) introduce another angle to the rights debate with a discussion of the failure of rights-based strategies to ensure justice for people with learning disabilities. They question whether such strategies alone can bridge the gap between the lived experience of the learning disabled and the failure of the 'able-minded' to understand their situation. The problem, they suggest, is that the concept of rights as developed in Western societies is essentially mechanical and individualistic and linked to the notion of autonomy. Despite its symbolic power, it provides a questionable basis for determining relations between the powerful and the powerless and for facilitating understanding between them:

> 'rights' are often unsuccessful simply because people still do not know how to treat others who are different; they are not aware of the variety of social institutions or practices necessary for particular 'entitlements', or even that such 'entitlements' are necessary. The irony is that *it is the conception of human nature which the notion of 'rights' promulgates that reinforces this situation,* where individual autonomy and the force of law take precedence over the necessary ability of humans, as social animals, to understand each other. (p. 758, original emphasis)

Young and Quibell do not reject the call for rights, rather they propose a reconceptualisation of the notion to incorporate understanding of the disadvantaged, primarily through access to their stories. Understanding, they suggest, is a necessary condition for any advance in rights:

> *They do not understand us, but once we are understood, we can finally have justice. We have the right to be understood.* (p. 761, original emphasis)

It is the relative powerlessness of many service users that leads Ellis (2005) to question the disability movement's focus on civil and human rights, to the neglect of social rights. Although civil rights are protected by law, they confer essentially negative rights such as freedom from discrimination or oppression. By contrast, social, or welfare, rights confer positive rights to resources. This implies a redistribution of resources from the well off, which is essential, Ellis argues, if the disadvantaged position of many user groups is to be effectively addressed. Social rights have become discredited amongst disability campaigners for reasons that include: the lack of progress over many years in extending social rights; the stigma associated with the process of determining eligibility; and the conditions that are often attached to benefits. Nevertheless, Ellis makes the case for a more strategic approach which mobilises different kinds of rights that are mutually reinforcing.

Who is disabled?

The disability movement argues that the way forward is for disabled people to organise together and hence to act as capable agents rather than passive victims. Above all, the focus is upon their common experience of discrimination by society which means they have a common interest in fighting for their civil rights to meet their common needs. However, from the outset the movement has been led by younger physically disabled people and thus, as Campbell and Oliver (1996) have acknowledged, cannot claim to be a mass movement when other groups, especially older disabled people, participate hardly at all. Although the increasing demand for rights amongst different user groups points to a strategic convergence of some kind, the shared discourse of rights may conceal quite different perspectives as Young and Quibell's analysis suggests.

To what extent, therefore, does the disability movement articulate the needs and concerns of other user groups? In principle, the social model of disability provides the basis for an inclusive understanding of the ways in which social factors shape experiences of impairment. However, both the rhetoric of the disability movement and the social model itself have been accused of ignoring the diversity of disabled experience. The 'disabled' identity itself is at issue as users with, for example, age-related illnesses or mental health problems differ in the extent to which they perceive themselves as 'disabled'. Similarly the disability movement's rejection of the traditional 'private tragedy' model of disability can be seen as an implicit denial of the pain and suffering many users and carers experience.

The experiences of De Wolfe (2002), a long-term ME sufferer, illustrate these difficulties. The discourse of disability activism seemed irrelevant to her needs until, faced with an access problem, she drew on the social model to argue her case. However, her pain and fluctuating energy levels leave her distanced from a movement that she associates with basically vigorous people with a fixed impairment. De Wolfe locates the problem in the contested divide between disability and illness and the way in which social responsibility for those who are seen as having long-term or intractable illness is understood mainly in terms of individual health care provision and personal support. Worse still:

> The taboos that surround the topic of long-term illness, and inhibit the discussion of the experience it generates, make it hard to formulate suggestions about the social changes that would make it more tolerable. Even those with an interest in promoting such a discussion may find that they are floundering to express needs and concerns for which they are unable to find words. (p. 263)

This reluctance to even acknowledge such experiences, which in the case of disability activists may be heightened by their concern to avoid the association of impairment with personal tragedy, may leave the chronic sick feeling powerless and stigmatised. They are excluded both from a society that is intolerant of illness and from the positive images of impairment presented by the disability movement.

De Wolfe's analysis is also relevant to the largest disabled group, those with age-related impairment and disease, who may have difficulty in identifying with people who have been disabled from childhood or early adulthood and are further disadvantaged by negative attitudes towards ageing and older people. Paralleling the development of the social model of disability, there is now a considerable literature examining ways in which dependence in old age is socially constructed (Phillipson and Walker, 1986; Estes *et al.*, 2003). In particular, work has been done on the links between poverty and retirement and pension policies and on the impact of the dominant medical model of ageing (Estes and Binney, 1989). Here the emphasis on technologically advanced treatments is compared with the relative neglect of rehabilitation services and the lack of social support for those with chronic disease in old age.

Whilst disabled people themselves have been largely responsible for the theoretical advances in the understanding of disability, older people have played no such role in the study of ageing and thus have been distanced not only from the insights of the disability movement but from equivalent developments relating to old age. This is likely to change, however, as older people become unwilling simply to accept their disadvantaged status as an inevitable consequence of growing older, thus increasing the possibility of links with disability activists. A study by Priestley and Rabiee (2001) of local voluntary organisations serving older people in one large metropolitan area begins to unravel some of the complex and often contradictory understandings that may promote or impede such an alliance. Their informants' responses revealed a 'medico-functional model of disability with apparently little awareness of the social model', but there was evidence of 'social model thinking in the definition of barriers facing older people with impairments' (p. 10). The interviews also uncovered divergent understandings of old age, of disability and of the relationship between the two. The respondents were divided between those who considered as disabled anyone with a significant impairment, regardless of age or of the cause of impairment, and those who saw age-related impairment differently. The latter were likely to describe older people as disabled only if they were functioning in a way that deviated from their perception of what was normal for old age. Older people were also seen as either having fewer needs than their younger counterparts, with the implication that a restricted lifestyle is more acceptable in old age, or as having more needs, for example, because they have not 'learned to live with it' (p. 11).

Proponents of the social model were also slow to engage with issues of cognitive impairment. However, its relevance for people with learning disabilities is now established (Goodley, 2001) as is its potential to deepen understanding of the ways in which people with dementia are marginalised and discriminated against in the design and delivery of services (Gilliard *et al.*, 2005).

Survivors of the mental health system are another group who do not fit easily into the disability movement. They have developed their own organisations but these have tended to engage with the mental health system in an effort to achieve reform from within, in contrast to the separatist approach of the disabled movement (Beresford *et al.*, 2002). There are uncertainties too about whether a disabled identity is appropriate in the absence of any physical impairment and a perception that 'the unintentional colonisation of survivors by the disabled people's movement' may threaten their distinct identity (Plumb, 1994, in Beresford *et al.*, 2002). Nevertheless there is growing evidence of collaboration between both groups around shared experiences of discrimination and oppression. Fruitful links are also emerging between the concepts of independent living and of 'recovery', the process for mental health service users of reasserting control over one's own life (Spandler and Vick, 2006).

Theoretical attempts to develop the social model in ways that more fully take account of the diversity of impairment, and of individual experiences, are likely to contribute to such collaboration. The extent of these developments is chronicled by Tregaskis (2002) who speaks of separate and competing strands each of which adds to an understanding of disabled people's oppression (p. 458). Marks (1999) provides an example of how such strands may be woven together to create a more holistic understanding of disability which starts from the social model but draws on psychoanalytic insights, narrative accounts of disability and physiological and sociological accounts of the body. Acknowledging the reality of the impaired body, she speaks of disability as something that is lived and experienced physically and psychologically. Disability is, she concludes, 'socially constructed, materially embodied, and invested with fears and fantasies' (p. 177).

Empowerment and diversity

Findings from research into the needs of particular user groups and the barriers to empowerment confirm the importance of a more holistic understanding of disability that takes account of the uniqueness of individual experience, the varied social and cultural contexts in which disabled people live and the interaction of disablism with other forms of oppression such as racism and sexism.

There is, for example, substantial evidence that people from ethnic minorities are particularly disadvantaged in their contact, or lack of contact, with mental health services (Watters, 1996; Bhui, 2002). Numerous studies have confirmed that Afro-Caribbean people are more likely to be compulsorily admitted to hospital and to be diagnosed as psychotic, particularly if they are male (Bebbington *et al.*, 1994; Davies *et al.*, 1996). A national census of mental health inpatients in 2005 found that hospital admission rates were three times higher for Black African and Caribbean people and that these groups were up to 44 per cent more likely to be detained under the Mental Health Act (Healthcare Commission, 2005).

The complexity of the difficulties facing users, carers and service providers is addressed in a landmark review of the relationship between African and Caribbean communities and mental health services by the Sainsbury Centre for Mental Health (2002). The report speaks of services in which prejudice, cultural ignorance and a fear of violence influence assessment and lead to treatment that relies heavily on medication and restriction. This increases the reluctance of service users to ask for help, and to comply with treatment, which in turn reinforces the fear and prejudice of staff. These 'circles of fear' in which staff see service users as potentially dangerous and service users perceive services as harmful (p. 8) prevent black people from engaging with services. Once they do engage they may find a system which:

> reproduces the individual and institutionalised racism of society, often exacerbating and compounding our distress as, for example, we get defined in terms of Eurocentric norms and our cultural differences (in particular our culturally determined expressions of emotional distress) get pathologised. This may then drive us into a vicious circle of racism, distress, more racism, more distress, which is only likely to be broken if the true issues are acknowledged and addressed. (Trivedi, 2002, p. 78)

Trivedi, a black user of mental health services, calls for service providers to work with users in empowering ways, which enable them to see how racism (both internal and external) contributes to mental distress.

The Sainsbury Centre report concludes that change is needed in the experience of service users at each point in the care pathway. It proposes a programme of action to cover every aspect of service development and delivery, the main aims of which would be to:

- ensure that Black service users are treated with respect and that their voices are heard;

- deliver early intervention and early access to services to prevent escalation of crises;
- ensure that services are accessible, welcoming, relevant and well integrated with the community;
- increase understanding and effective communication on both sides including creating a culture which allows people to discuss race and mental health issues;
- deliver greater support and funding from the statutory sector to services led by the Black community. (Sainsbury Centre for Mental Health, 2002, p. 76)

The lack of appropriate community-based services for black users is a particular concern, so an important element in the proposed strategy for reform would be the development of 'gateway agencies', to build bridges with statutory agencies, whilst advocating for black service users (p. 76).

A landmark report by the Social Services Inspectorate on care services for black and minority ethnic older people also uncovered significant evidence of disadvantage. The inspectors found there was little choice in the services available to these groups and the ethnocentric nature of service provision often meant they had difficulty in getting their needs met (Department of Health/Social Services Inspectorate, 1998). Older people with mental health needs face particular difficulties, as revealed in a study of Asian older people in Kent (Seabrooke and Milne, 2004). Cultural lack of awareness of dementia and other mental health issues, combined with a reluctance to seek help, means that such problems are often hidden. If and when services become involved, the lack of professional interpreters and of culturally appropriate assessment and provision may result in an inadequate response to people's needs.

Cultural and faith traditions have an important role to play in the empowerment of black and minority ethnic disabled people, as described in a report on four grassroots projects sponsored by the Joseph Rowntree Foundation (Singh, 2005). Such traditions provided inspiration and focus for the projects and helped to build trust with participants and the wider community. Amongst the issues highlighted in the report is the importance of recognising that black disabled people are not a homogeneous group but individuals with multiple identities in terms of age, class, gender, faith, family role and other factors. A reductionist approach, focussing only on ethnicity and disability, cannot successfully draw on the complexity of people's experiences and resources or relate to their diverse needs.

Recognising the diversity within an apparently homogeneous group is essential if user involvement is to be genuinely inclusive, that is enabling participation by the most marginalised as well as the most powerful representatives of any group. This is illustrated in an account of a consultation exercise by social services with the local deaf community (McLaughlin *et al.*, 2004). The initial consultation strategy, a one-off questionnaire intended to gather service user opinions, produced few responses and was succeeded by a more extensive programme of outreach designed to foster the involvement of different sections of the deaf community. The result was a redefining of the purpose of the consultation and the active participation of different interest groupings within the deaf community in identifying and articulating issues of concern to them.

A particular challenge for services is how to promote the involvement of people who have both cognitive impairments and communication difficulties. This issue has been central in the *Valuing People* agenda for people with learning disabilities (see Chapter 4), but it is equally significant for other groups such as people with brain injury or dementia. Bringing all these groups together under the label 'people with complex needs', Clare and Cox (2003) look at how inclusion might be promoted in the design and delivery of services. They identify four current strands of thinking, from research and practice, which support the process of inclusion and offer ways in which it may be put into practice for people with complex needs.

The first of these, *the valuing of individual experience*, is apparent in the increasing focus on the subjective experiences of people with cognitive impairments and in the recognition that engaging with the service user's perspective makes it more likely that the services provided will increase or maintain quality of life. A second strand is concerned with developing ways of *enhancing choice and well-being* for people with very severe impairments. These include non-verbal and arts-based approaches to fostering effective communication, observational and indirect methods for monitoring well-being and techniques for assistive and augmentative communication such as the use of Makaton signing with people with learning disabilities. A third strand *shifting the balance of power in research* relates to the growing interest in the use of participatory and emancipatory styles of research in this field. Finally, work on *negotiating meaning* provides helpful insights into the interactions between professionals and people with severe impairment, and how these may promote or inhibit user involvement.

Empowering practitioners?

Underpinning much of the critique by the disability movement of community care policy and practice is the charge that the community care system is designed to serve the interests of welfare professionals from the statutory and independent sectors rather than those of community care clients (Oliver, 1990). Very similar criticisms have been made by several of those writing within the political economy of ageing tradition with Estes (1979) in particular referring to 'the ageing enterprise' as operating to the advantage of both welfare professionals and commercial interests (drug companies, private residential homes and so on). The free market policies of recent decades are perceived as intensifying these trends (Vincent, 1999; Estes *et al.*, 2003).

Previously in this chapter we referred to Lukes's three dimensions of power. Drawing on the work of Foucault (1979), Servian (1996) describes a fourth dimension of power in which power is no longer a thing to be won or lost but rather a process by which the identities of individuals are socially constructed, often by welfare professionals and welfare institutions. Such 'disciplinary' power has often been forged through the use of institutions such as school, prison and hospital with discipline in these institutions being made possible by the application of surveillance techniques. The movement of people out of closed institutions into broader society has required the development of micro-techniques of power and surveillance for those in the community, such as assessment, diagnosis, screening, codification and categorisation, all of which serve to help define the client, and the nature of his or her problems, in technical, legislative and bureaucratic terms. Such mechanisms of control may function in subtle ways, as Kaufman (1994) demonstrates from her study of a community-based multidisciplinary geriatric assessment service in the United States. Referral to the service was likely to result in increased surveillance and interventions designed to minimise risk and, as far as possible, to preserve autonomy in spite of functional limitations. However, the interaction between competing discourses of risk avoidance and autonomy, both of which are central to American and other Western societies, has paradoxical results. In order to retain their independence and avoid institutional care, older people may be required to make lifestyle changes that leave them feeling trapped by the solutions proposed for problems that others have defined.

The continuing power of professionals and agencies has been an enduring feature of community care under the new arrangements and Chapter 3 included evidence of how this power has been exercised. Implementation of the reforms saw the development of bureaucratic procedures through which access to assessment, and to services intended to promote independence, has been linked to risk and to the need for assistance with personal care. The chapter also explored the growth of what has been called the audit culture (Power, 1997) with its heavy emphasis on the direction and surveillance of local agencies by central government. Together these developments have led to changes in the practitioner role and unease amongst many practitioners. A particular concern is the impact of these changes on relationships with service users, on the exercise of professional judgement and decision-making and on the overall focus of their work. There is a perception that professional autonomy has been reduced but that power has shifted to senior management and central government agencies rather than to service users and carers (Lymbery, 1998; Harrison and Smith, 2004).

The transformation of social workers into care managers, with responsibilities for assessing needs and for designing, purchasing and monitoring care packages, is a symbol of the changing culture within care agencies and of its uncertainties. From the outset, it was unclear whether care management was simply a reframing of the social work task, reflecting the language and the separation of functions of the new managerialism in the public sector, or something entirely different. The policy guidance (Department of Health/Social Services Inspectorate, 1991a; 1991b) did not address this question. However, a case was made for continuity which rested on the argument that the skills required for care management are identical or very similar to those required for social work (Payne,

1995; Sheppard, 1995). An implication of this argument was that in traditionally low-status sectors, such as work with older people where social work skills were underdeveloped, the introduction of care management could lead to improvements in practice. However, this would depend on the way in which care management is utilised and, as Hugman (1994) observed, the development of an administrative rather than a client-centred model would be unlikely to result in an increase in either professional status or skills. As Hugman predicted, the dominant interpretation of the care management role that emerged from the reforms has emphasised the administrative aspects of the process, such as the completion of forms and the application of eligibility criteria, rather than human relations skills (see Chapter 3).

Administrative activities, which are essential to the allocation, purchasing and monitoring of care services, serve not only to categorise and control the client but also to gather data on which to judge the quality of the service. The latter, as we argued in Chapter 4, has been a key element in New Labour's plans for modernising public services. However, the consequence of all this has been a 'mechanistic approach to the assessment and planning of care in the community' and a move 'away from quality time with clients to a notion of quality bound up with the monitoring of interventions' (Gorman, 2000, p. 153). For practitioners, performance indicators and meeting government targets have become the focus of attention rather than the welfare of service users (Munro, 2004; Bradley, 2005).

Postle (2002), who studied care managers working with older people, describes them as working within an overall context of uncertainty and change. Particular aspects of this context were significant: the restricted resources; the need to operate within a market for care; and the increasing emphasis on risk. They gave rise, Postle argues, to five positions of tension and ambiguity in the care management role:

- restricted resources to meet needs: emphasis on assessment of needs;
- focusing on the minutiae of financial assessments: dealing with the person;
- spending time on paperwork and IT: taking time to develop a relationship;

- increasingly complex work: more reductionist processes such as checklists;
- concern about all aspects of risk: speed of work throughput increasing risk. (From Postle, 2002)

Whereas in the past bureaucratic tasks had appeared secondary to direct work with service users, now such tasks could not be delayed if systems were to work effectively. Elsewhere, Postle warns against the easy assumption of a false dichotomy between social work and care management. Unfavourably contrasting care management with social work runs the risk of ignoring the lack of clarity and the inherent ambiguity of the social work role, most notably in the tension between care and control which has characterised social work from the outset (Postle, 2001b). And, in the case of social work with older people, there is a danger that the contrast will be with an idealised practice that was seldom found (Marshall, 1989; Hugman, 1994) (see Chapter 2). Nevertheless, as Postle suggests, the difficulties the care managers faced in reconciling the differing aspects of their role were likely to have contributed to the decrease in job satisfaction reported by most of them and to the high levels of stress-related illness in the department where they worked (Postle, 2002). A similar picture emerges from a nationwide survey investigating attitudes to work and experiences of employment amongst front-line mental health social workers (Huxley *et al.*, 2005). The volume of work and the pressures to complete mounds of paper-work had resulted in long working hours, which were associated with high levels of stress.

Findings from research into care processes suggest that increasing bureaucratisation has done little to empower vulnerable service users in their negotiations with practitioners. For example, an ethnographic study of the process of needs assessment for older people found a focus on *agency-centred* agendas which, by distracting attention from the user's perspective, increased the risk of inappropriate or unwelcome intervention and the neglect of pressing needs (Richards, 2000). Tailoring the assessment process to engage with problems as defined by service users and with their ideas about how these might be addressed requires highly developed listening and communication skills. However, the quantity of routine information required to determine eligibility, and for agency information systems, encouraged a mechanistic approach to the assessment task. The problem is compounded by the use of assessment tools that focus on physical needs and diagnostic categories, to the neglect of psychosocial aspects of the older person's situation (Taylor and Donnelly, 2006). Given the vulnerability of older people in crisis and the complex psychological and social factors which may precipitate or prevent admission to long-term residential care, there is an urgent need for an approach to assessment that facilitates the older person's participation in decision-making and upholds their rights (Dwyer, 2005). Theoretical understandings of the ageing process and of the position of older people in society can contribute to this way of working. However, it would seem that practitioners in old age settings may be unable to draw on such knowledge to support their practice (Richards *et al.*, 2007).

Martin *et al.* (2004), in a study of access to social care for older people in six local authorities, looked specifically at the impact of the reforms on practitioner motivation and behaviour. Their findings point to a situation in which 'organisational priorities subsume the interests of individual service users' (p. 481). This stems in part from the pressures on practitioners to act as custodians of social services resources, which exceed those to advocate on behalf of service users. At the same time the top-down implementation of community care means than practitioners have become 'pawns whose responsibility it is to ensure that the will of the department is carried out' through all aspects of the care process (p. 482). A similar conclusion is drawn by Foster *et al.* (2006), from their analysis of the assessment process for disabled adults. Despite the willingness of practitioners to exercise discretion in a way that positively supports the service user's wishes, the complexities and contradictions inherent in the process make it difficult for service users to exercise choice and thus for the system to deliver personalised social care. Implementing a person-centred approach with service users who have long-term needs is also difficult if the user does not have continuing access to care management, as highlighted in a study of the state of care management in learning disability and mental health services 12 years after implementation of the reforms. The research found that often users were connected with care management only at points of major life change, and in some sites care management for people with learning disabilities was available only to those with additional needs such as a physical disability or mental health problem (Cambridge *et al.*, 2005).

Organisational agendas are sustained even in the context of initiatives designed to foster user involvement. Hodge (2005) draws on discussions within a service-led mental health forum to illustrate how power is used discursively to exclude challenging perspectives, to legitimise the status quo and to reinforce existing power relations between officials and service users. The eventual fate of the consultation exercise with the deaf community, reported earlier in this chapter, is also instructive. Having achieved its goal of a successful consultation, the local authority subsequently failed to ensure that the process of consultation would be sustained and embedded. This was a loss for the deaf community and it also compromised the position of the specialist social worker who had played a vital role in enabling and promoting discussion between the community and the authority:

> lack of ongoing dialogue after such a promising beginning seriously affected the credibility of the social worker amongst the community with which she had established the rapport and trust that had been the necessary precondition of consultation in the first place. (McLaughlin *et al.*, 2004, p. 161)

Care and empowerment

Establishing understanding and trust with service users and carers, who may be experiencing crisis and loss or be 'hard to reach', is essential to an effective helping relationship. This is skilled work that is also emotionally demanding. However, for many practitioners the emotional aspects of practice appear neglected or undervalued:

> In the shift from social work to care management the significance of the emotional labour within caring work may have become lost within the administrative and managerial process that dominates it. (Gorman, 2000, pp. 154–5)

At the same time, the growing influence of the social model of disability poses a challenge to notions of care and caring work.

As we have seen, for many disabled people 'care' is demeaning, and should be replaced by 'support' and 'assistance', concepts that imply choice and control for the service user.

A negative view of 'care' is also apparent in the early feminist critiques of community care policies as a source of exploitation of women in their role as unpaid or low-paid carers (Finch and Groves, 1983; Ungerson, 1987). By highlighting the demands of the caring role, and the way in which caring may exclude women from active participation in the labour market, this work contributed to the campaigning of carers' organisations and thus helped to raise the profile of carers on the policy agenda. However, it was also criticised for ignoring the diversity of carers and caring roles (Arber and Ginn, 1991; Fisher, 1994) for failing to recognise the satisfactions of caring as well as the costs (Nolan *et al.*, 1996), and for creating a misleading dichotomy between carer and cared for, as many disabled people are involved in active caring roles (Morris, 1993). By largely ignoring the experiences of those receiving care, many of whom were women, and the reciprocity of the caring relationship, it also contributed to 'polarised constructions of the disabled person as a burden and the informal carer as an oppressed woman' which do an injustice to the experiences of women (Lloyd, 2001, p. 721).

Such criticism has been central to the development of an account of informal care which more accurately represents the diversity of experience amongst disabled and non-disabled women. Through their struggle to access and fulfil traditional female roles, Lloyd argues, disabled women have contributed to a reconceptualisation of 'care' and 'care-giving', in three distinct ways:

- by legitimising the perspective that *caring is something that women might want to do*, or at the very least would not want someone else to do when it is their own intimate relationships which are involved;
- by demonstrating, through their own situation, that the *caring role is not synonymous with the caring function*;
- by re-establishing, through their position as both givers and receivers of care, that *informal caring takes place within a relationship*, and is thus likely to be mutual and reciprocal. (Based on Lloyd, 2001, pp. 721–5)

In questioning the assumptions in the early literature on caring, disabled feminists and other users also present a challenge to the 'conflict between attention to the needs of carers, and specifically women as informal carers, and the rights and needs of users which is at the core of much of community care policy and practice' (Orme, 2001b, p. 31).

More positive understandings of care and the caring relationship have also contributed to a developing critique of the disability movement's 'masculine' emphasis on autonomy and independence, and of its failure to recognise the universal nature of dependency and the significance of emotion, which echoes Gorman's critiques of trends in practice above:

> In developing a masculinist approach to care, the DPM (i.e. Disabled People's Movement) seeks to promote autonomy for disabled people but eliminates emotion from the caring process by transforming it into a formal, contractual, exchange relationship. (Hughes *et al.*, 2005, p. 271)

Fine and Glendinning (2005) chart the rediscovery of care as a mutual relationship-based activity, which 'is both an ideal and a daily reality'. Although care is a complex concept that resists definition, it is helpful as 'a normative, aspirational guide' even if as a daily reality it often falls short of the ideal (p. 617). Highlighting the relational nature of care also draws attention to the centrality of power issues in such relationships and the need to attend to the rights of all those involved in caring relationships (Fine and Glendinning, 2005). In the context of professional practice, where inequalities in power relationships are readily apparent, interest has been growing in the idea of 'an ethics of care' as a way of rehabilitating care, as an ideal and as a reality, and of making explicit the positive link between care and empowerment of the most marginalised. For instance, Lloyd (2006a) proposes a model for an ethic of care by Tronto (1993) as a possible framework for empowering practice by social workers working with frail older people. In doing so, Lloyd seeks to demonstrate that the five stages of the model, *attentiveness, responsibility, competence, responsiveness* and *integrity,* are not only core professional values but also essential elements in the attempt to give voice to the vulnerable and excluded.

Concluding comments

In certain respects the community care reforms of the 1990s represented a significant change from the past. Funding for care packages in the community, the introduction of care management and assessment and the transformation of local authorities from their role as service providers to that of purchasers and enablers within a social care market were all important new developments. However, despite a commitment to user empowerment, the power of professionals and agencies was maintained over what is often the most crucial stage for the service user or carer – the assessment of his or her needs. Also underpinning the reforms were the continuing assumptions that people with impairments or chronic illness would normally be cared for by family or other unpaid carers and that additional needs could be met through individualised care packages.

The renewed focus on user empowerment and the growing acceptance of a social model of disability have been important developments under New Labour. The social model of disability in particular highlights the need to rethink fundamental assumptions about *disability* and *care* and to design systems that enable people with different kinds of impairments to access the assistance and support they require. The conception of independent living proposed by the disability movement challenges not just welfare professionals but society as a whole to consider the ways in which disabled people are disempowered and socially excluded. The campaign for legally based rights by disabled activists points towards a very different vision of community care (assistance) from that which currently exists, yet as a strategy it has important weaknesses that are as yet unresolved. Service users are not a united movement; they are still widely categorised by age and pathology and there are differences relating to race and gender which are not easily subsumed within a single identity, yet there is evidence of convergence through a growing awareness of shared interests.

Critiques of the community care reforms from a practitioner perspective have also emerged. These have focused on the shift to a managerial culture in care services and on the growing burden of administration which detracts, in their view, from the quality of work with users and carers. The rediscovery of care, both formal and informal, as a mutual and relational activity may signal further shifts in professional practice and in the demands of users and carers. Whatever the aspirations of users, carers and practitioners, the possibilities for change may be determined elsewhere through the workings of a globalised economy. The next chapter looks at developments in the organisation of community care in other post-industrial societies and their influence on developments in the UK.

International Perspectives on Community Care: Lesson Drawing or Policy Learning?

Introduction

The focus of this chapter is on the practice of community or social care activities in other 'first world' countries followed by illustrations of their influence on developments in policy and practice in the United Kingdom. Hill (2006, pp. 140–52) outlines how difficult it is to compare social care policies between different societies, so this chapter confines itself to a few examples of transfer of policy and practice. It can take a number of different forms. The literature is wide ranging and attempts to provide overviews have drawn on notions such as policy convergence, policy diffusion, policy learning and lesson drawing (Dolowitz and Marsh, 1996; Evans and Davies, 1999). For the purpose of this chapter, it is assumed that community care is broadly a 'low politics' activity whereby policy learning and lesson drawing are more germane than policy convergence or diffusion.

The scrutiny of the practice of community care in other countries is structured round the themes of the earlier chapters of this book, namely the role of the family in caring; cost pressures and the role of institutional care; cost containment and collaboration; care management; and user empowerment. Examples of these themes are drawn from some EU member states, Australia and the USA. They reflect different models of social care and raise the question whether policy learning or lesson drawing takes place more easily between similar welfare regimes as opposed to crossing welfare regime boundaries.

There are several contested typologies of welfare states (see Abrahamson, 1999b; Arts and Gelissen, 2002; Hill, 2006 for overviews). The categorisation used in this chapter is that acknowledged by Abrahamson (1999a), which broadly reflects the four models of social care outlined by Anttonen and Sipilä (1996) with the four types of welfare state each reflecting a particular kind of welfare regime. The *rudimentary welfare state* (or Catholic social policy) is associated in the European Union with Latin Rim countries, such as Spain and Portugal. This tradition emphasises philanthropic solutions to welfare provision by traditional institutions such as the church, family and private charity, with limited public welfare institutions and policies developing alongside. The *residual welfare state* (or liberal social policy) has been associated in recent years with Australia, the USA and the UK. As outlined in earlier chapters of this book, this is characterised by rolling back the boundaries of the welfare state and by public services being contracted out to the independent sector. The state may be the principal funder, but it is a safety net and a regulator rather than a primary provider. The *institutional welfare state* (or corporatist social policy in the Bismarckian tradition) has been linked in particular to Germany. This tradition puts emphasis on labour market solutions to social issues, such as unemployment, sickness or old age. Those outside the labour market are likely to be dependent on local charity. The *modern welfare state* (or social democratic policy) is associated with Scandinavian countries. This is characterised by wide provision of good quality publicly provided services, with the private and voluntary sectors becoming increasingly involved in the welfare mix.

The role of the family in caring

The family has remained the main supporter of those needing care in America, Australia and much of the European Union. As already noted, the idea of personal responsibility and the family being the predominant provider is strongly entrenched in the American tradition, so care for people with longer-term care needs is provided in the main through informal care, starting with family members. The formal 'system' of providing care emphasised 'the promotion of a reasonable division of labour between informal and formal support systems' (US Department of Health and Human Services (DHHS) 1980, quoted in Davies and Challis, 1986, p. 88). However, a strategy for providing support to family carers (as opposed to users) seemed to be underplayed in the America of the 1970s and the 1980s, even though evidence (see below) indicated that informal care by family members was enhanced 'when adequate publicly funded formal services were available to complement their efforts' (Christianson, 1988; Kemper, 1992 quoted in Shaver and Fine, 1995, p. 18). For instance, care plans were defined by the DHHS as 'agreements between clients and workers about problems, goals, services and charges. The plans were to ... relate to ... the expected participation of informal supports' (Davies and Challis, 1986, p. 119), though there was passing reference to the consent of informal carers to care plans (op. cit., p. 144). The importance placed on the role of the family in supporting elderly relatives in the USA has to be set against the trend of a diminishing proportion of elderly people living with their children. The percentage more than halved from 33 to 15 per cent between 1950 and the late 1980s (Sutherland Report, 1999b, p. 158). Nevertheless, about three-quarters of the main carers of frail elderly people were relatives living in the same household (op. cit., p. 164).

In Australia, the provision of informal care came to be recognised as a key feature of social policy (Shaver and Fine, 1995, p. 1), so official support for carers also became a central concern of social policy, not least in the context of changing demographic and labour market pressures, which were thought could lead to a lowering of the availability of informal carers, particularly family based carers. In a 1995 report on families supporting older or disabled people, the Australian Bureau of Statistics noted that in 1993 over 60 per cent of people with a handicap received informal care only, just over 30 per cent received both formal and informal care and under 10 per cent were supported by formal services only (quoted in Shaver and Fine, 1995, p. 7). The introduction of community care policies did not herald the replacement of unpaid informal care-giving by the provision of formal services. Informal and formal care were seen as complementary rather than as substitutes (ibid.). Indeed, the development of community based services increased the role of informal caregivers 'as advocates and representatives of dependent clients and as clients in their own right' (op. cit., p. 16). Official responses have included the development of a national carers' strategy, which includes the provision of respite care, information and advice and a carer's pension scheme (Sutherland Report, 1999b, pp. 175, 204). 'Informal care provided by spouses, partners and other family members, remains by far the most prevalent form of support in the early twenty-first century ... [though] new forms of "shared care", in which formal services work hand in hand with family carers, suggest the distinction between public and private responsibilities is increasingly blurred' (Fine, 2001, pp. 1, 10).

The role of the family was not a central feature of the administratively orientated 2004 policy document on community care in Australia, though it did recognise that the recent developments in community care services during the ten years (1996–2006) of the centre right Commonwealth Government had been achieved 'with the considerable contribution of family carers and volunteers' (Department of Health Ageing (DOHA), 2004, p. 10). Programmes funded through DoHA provided (a) national respite for carers and (b) a carers information and support facility through Carer Respite Centres and Carelink Centres. In addition, financial support through a Carers Package was provided through the Commonwealth Department of Family and Community Services. This comprised carer payments to people whose responsibilities prevented them from holding down jobs and non-means-tested carer allowances to people who support at home on a daily basis a relation with a disability or chronic medical condition.

So much for the role of the family in caring in the *residual welfare state*. The family has remained the main supporter of those needing care across the European Union. National attitudes, behaviour and policy towards caring for adults were examined in a 16-country cross-national study on family obligations undertaken in 1994 covering the then 12 member states of the European Union and the four applicant countries of Austria, Finland, Norway and Sweden. Millar and Warman (1996) distinguished between those countries where there were legal obligations on the family to provide care (for example Germany and Greece) and those where there were no such obligations (for example Denmark). They also categorised the 16 countries into those where service provision was locally organised (such as Germany); those where it was locally organised under national regulation (Denmark); and those where it was nationally organised (Greece). Systems of care payments were divided into those made to care givers (Denmark), those made to care receivers (Germany and Greece) and those made to both (the United Kingdom). The adequacy of payments was, however, another matter. In other words, the picture was one of great variety. The role of the family in caring covered a wide spectrum ranging from systems 'where the family provides virtually all the support to situations where family care is an optional extra to state services' (p. 43) and there was no trend towards a common pattern of provision. Work undertaken towards the end of the 1990s suggested no major changes in family care-giving for older people in nine EU countries and Poland (Philp, 2001).

The family continues to hold a central position in *rudimentary welfare states*. 'Although the urbanisation and modernisation of Greek society in the 1970s and 1980s has influenced the already changing social structure of the Greek family, the family continues to play a central role' (Marinakou, 1998, p. 244). Triantafillou and Mestheneos (2001) pointed out that discussion on the need for public policy to support carers had started towards the end of the 1980s but 'very little priority has been given to this issue and as yet [referring to 1998] support for family carers has not been incorporated on a systematic basis into public policy' (p. 77). Symeonidou (1997) made the point that in Greece women are the basic prop of the family and have internalised their role as carers. This role transmutes into 'compulsory altruism' which can have a 'negative impact on the carer's physical and/or mental health, especially in more severe cases (such as mental handicap)' (pp. 355, 356).

The family has also been expected to play a central role in the *institutional welfare state*, particularly for those outside the labour market, creating a major responsibility for and strain on relatives, where they exist. In Germany until the mid-1990s the provision of income support could be made only after a comprehensive examination of the circumstances of family members, following the principle of subsidiarity, a Roman Catholic social doctrine whereby society should provide help to its weaker members whilst taking care to preserve their self-respect and autonomy, so the state intervenes only when family or civil society are not able to offer support. One of the consequences of this was that many adult children in Germany struggled to mobilise the resources necessary to carry out caring tasks. Support for carers was a central focus of the reforms of the mid-1990s (see below), providing they were spending at least 14 hours a week on home care. 'Giving benefits is meant to strengthen the already existing family care potential ... However, the insurance scheme gives also the option to widen the range of possible "care persons" away from family relatives to neighbours and other informal care persons willing to perform care on a regular basis' (Kondratowitz *et al.*, 2002, p. 241). Evers and Sachsse (2003, p. 73) comment that the new scheme encouraged to some extent 'traditional and female dominated forms of caring'.

The *modern welfare state* has also been under pressure, but here the thrust is to involve the voluntary and private sectors more, rather than require the family to take on the caring role. The argument in Denmark is that the family is not in a position to provide care. Munday (1996) drew on the 1992 Danish report to the European Commission Observatory on Social Exclusion to point out that the institution of the family had weakened substantially in the last 30 years, so care functions were taken over by the state. Research Volume 1 of the Royal Commission on Long Term Care (Sutherland Report, 1999b) noted that in Denmark the proportion of women in paid employment rose from 49 per cent in 1965 to 78 per cent in 1988–89 (p. 159). However, children do care about their older relatives; this takes the form of advocacy and pressure on the professionals. The main burden of informal care in Denmark falls upon spouses or partners, leading Jamieson (1991) to argue that 'perhaps these are the ones who pay the highest price for a welfare system which is geared towards state provided professional solutions to health and social problems' (p. 120).

Salvage (1995) examined future prospects for the family care of older people in the EU over the 20-year period to 2015. She concluded that governments needed to make urgent plans based on the recognition of the current overdependence on informal care. Four options were put forward (pp. 68–76):

- reducing demand for care by improving older people's health and independence;
- stimulating supply by making it easier for families to support older relatives;
- developing new ways of providing support, including surrogate families and intergenerational housing schemes;
- improving the image and experience of residential care.

The European Commission's study of social protection for dependency in old age (Pacolet *et al*., 1999) argued that the distinction between formal and informal care might be of less relevance in the future 'since informal carers will receive training and become more professional in their work and to some degree even be paid for their work' (p. 28). Daly (2002) concluded that there was an 'increasing willingness of welfare states to pay for private/family care – a good which was formerly generated free in the family' (p. 268). This has to be encouraging news for those who are both carers and work in the formal labour market. The first annual report on the social situation in the EU published by Eurostat (2000) stated that 5 per cent of men and 9 per cent of women who held down a job of at least 30 hours a week also put in up to four hours per day in caring for a dependent adult.

In conclusion, therefore, it is no exaggeration to underline the point that the family is the basis for care in all welfare systems, but there are increasing uncertainties (and cautious responses to these uncertainties) about the ability of family-based informal carers to sustain this role in the future. Any UK government would benefit from scrutiny of policy responses in other states and other welfare regimes, in the light of rapidly changing socio-economic contexts.

Cost pressures and institutional care: the examples of Germany and Denmark

In a number of European countries with different welfare state traditions, the policy trend since the mid-1970s has been away from institutional provision, particularly for elderly people. The prime reason for this policy shift has been the cost to the public purse, supported by what were seen as inappropriate admissions of people who could live in (cheaper) non-institutional settings. Another factor has been the preferences of disabled and older people themselves. These preferences were shared by the vast majority of the general public in the European Community who thought that older people should be helped to stay in their own homes. This consensus extended across virtually the whole of the age group and was shared by both sexes (Eurobarometer Survey, 1993, p. 29). By the end of the 20th century Ackers and Dwyer (2002) were able to report, using the results of a six-country study of Greece, Italy, Portugal, the UK, Ireland and Sweden, that there was 'some evidence of convergence in relation to state-provided institutional care (with a general retrenchment)' (p. 78). This retrenchment had been brought about in part by pressures to reduce social expenditure. Fiscal measures were required to ensure compliance with the convergence criteria in relation to monetary union (p. 105).

In institutional welfare states such as Germany, the policy trend in the 1980s was fuelled by the need to cut costs (Kondratowitz *et al.*, 2002, p. 241), and involved increased day care and domiciliary services at the expense of residential provision. In 1984 the social assistance law gave community services priority over care in institutions (Tester, 1996, p. 18). Residential care for elderly people had in the main been provided by the non-statutory sector and in 1999 served about 5 per cent of the older population of whom 16 per cent were in public institutions (Evers and Sachsse, 2003, pp. 59, 60). This was because the principle of subsidiarity applied not only to the responsibilities of families for their needy members but also to the relationship between statutory and voluntary bodies. Conditional priority had to be given to a small number of leading voluntary non-profit organisations which wished to provide such social help. They were described as forming a 'virtual cartel' in local welfare markets (Schunk, 1998, p. 30).

The financial responsibility of the family to support an elderly relative often meant that the parent moved in with the children rather than entering residential care. However, as in Greece and elsewhere, there was concern that the capability of the family to provide care was lessening because of changes in society and the increasing numbers of older people (Lawson, 1996, p. 40).

Problems also existed in the health care system. In the 1980s, about 30 per cent of all beds in acute hospitals had been occupied by elderly patients with an average length of stay as high as 40 days. The extent of hospital care was related to a shortage of domiciliary and day care services. It was officially estimated that some 20–30 per cent of hospital patients over the age of 65 were long-term patients who could be better supported through day clinics, rehabilitation centres or residential/nursing homes. The problem was made more acute by the then social insurance system in Germany which drew a distinction between sickness (covered by insurance) and general frailty (perceived as a personal risk). Alber (1991) explained that this meant that 'prolongation of the stay in acute hospitals is the only way to prevent older patients from having to foot the bill for delivery into nursing homes which they can rarely afford' (p. 25).

Despite the expenditure cutbacks associated with unification in 1990, a major new element in the German care insurance scheme was introduced in the mid-1990s. Home care benefits were payable from April 1995 and institutional care benefits from July 1996. This policy development had an impact on the major social welfare organisations. 'Germany's care insurance scheme has ... reduced the power of the well-established cartel of home service providers' (Glendinning, 2002b, p. 311). After many years of privilege, the leading not-for-profit providers of residential and domiciliary care found themselves under pressure 'to improve efficiency to survive in competition with commercial providers in the social services market developing under the new Care Insurance' (Leisering, 2001, p. 169). Individuals in need of long-term domiciliary care were entitled to choose between payments for care and services in kind bought on their behalf by the insurance funds. The monetary value of the hours of help was greater than the alternative cash payment in order to discourage misuse of funds (Baldock and Ely, 1996, p. 211). By 1999, about two million people were receiving benefits from the scheme, just under 1.5 million in private households and just over half a million in care institutions. More than half were over 80 (Kondratowitz *et al.*, 2002, p. 240) and two-thirds were women (Evers and Sachsse, 2003, p. 59). By 2003, the long term care insurance scheme had halved the number of older people living in nursing homes who were dependent on means-tested benefits to pay for their care. Waiting lists had virtually disappeared (Glendinning, 2003, p. 13).

The interim judgement is that a good new scheme was introduced which had a number of deficiencies, including lack of advocacy and counselling for potential users, a less than comprehensive assessment system and a lack of coordination between service deliverers as well as between different sources of funding (Kondratowitz *et al.*, 2002, pp. 244–5). The excluding assessment system was modified in part by the passing of the Dementia Care Act 2002, which provided additional benefits for people with cognitive impairments (Glendinning, 2003, p. 13).

It is not likely that the UK government is going to introduce in the near future an insurance scheme of this kind, but attempts to overcome some of the deficiencies identified in the German scheme could be of relevance in the ongoing debate in Britain about the more effective use of scarce resources, as it seems to be the case that additional funds for social care are not a high priority in the spending review discussions taking place in the mid-2000s.

It is of interest to note that Denmark, as a *modern welfare state* with an emphasis on universality, has traditionally had a comparatively high rate of institutional care for older people (Walker, 1992). The principle of universality covers both health and social care in Denmark and is based on citizenship rather than insurance rights. The services are both financed and provided by the public sector (counties and municipalities), leaving the voluntary sector to provide advocacy and act as pressure groups. The home help service was merged in the mid-1990s with domiciliary health care to overcome the conflicts between health and social care staff (Walker and Maltby, 1997, p. 94). Denmark has continued to provide a high level of free home care provision 'with over 20% of those aged 67 + receiving some service [and] from July 1996, there was a legal requirement on local authorities to offer consultations to all those aged 80+ in their homes'. This was extended in July 1998 to those aged 75 or over (Sutherland Report, 1999b, p. 180).

Earlier, in the 1960s, both domiciliary and residential care services for older people had been expanded, but there was no intention to replace institutional care. Rather, the range of services was to relieve families of the caring role and attempt to improve the quality of life for older people. However, in the 1980s there was a growing critique of institutional care, which resulted in major legislative reform in 1987. Deinstitutionalisation was based on an expectation of economic savings as well as philosophies of enhancing self-realisation, increased choice and autonomy (Pedersen, 1998, p. 83). In brief, the principle underpinning the legislation was that the care available to people should not be linked to the kind of accommodation they were living in. The 1980s legislation stopped the building of nursing homes and provided for the building of special dwellings for older people who would be supported, where necessary, by a 24-hour home care service, which focused more on personal domestic help (see Giarchi, 1996).

The point of the reform was that every older person, whatever kind of care he or she needed, had the right to independent housing and care according to his or her needs. The impact of these legal changes was affected by professional resistance, local politics and the economic disruption caused by the recession (Abrahamson, 1991, p. 56). However, in general, care policies have proved popular and have been well resourced. Denmark does have a practice of fining local authorities if they are slow in providing appropriate accommodation and services for elderly people ready for discharge from hospital (Pedersen, 1998, p. 96). The level of investment in local services means that this is not seen as an unreasonable burden.

Through the Community Care (Delayed Discharge) Act 2003, the UK has already taken on board the idea of fining local authorities for being laggardly in providing for people deemed to be ready for discharge from hospital. What was not transferred from the Scandinavian practice was the level of investment in local government so that yet another central government initiative created additional pressures on financially stretched local authority services.

Cost containment and collaboration: the example of Australia

Problems of collaboration between health and social care abound in the literature on service planning and provision. In Australia long-term funding was separated from health funding as early as the 1960s (Glendinning *et al.*, 2004, p. 18), so it was argued that the former was protected from the processes and demands of the latter, underpinned by the power of the medical profession. The longer term consequence of this ring-fencing of long-term care funding was the creation of difficulties in collaboration between health and social care services, vividly illuminated by a study of discharge planning (Fine, 1998). 'Problems often arise when ongoing care is being planned, because services provided to those at home are currently organised and financed separately to those within hospitals' (p. 113). Following the development of community-based services in the 1980s and the 1990s, the fragmentation of health and social care was seen as a major difficulty (Fine, 1995). 'Accusations of cost-shifting between State and Commonwealth funded programmes and between private and public service providers are still rife, and evidence of serious imbalances and misallocations in the use of resources has continued to mount' (Fine, 1998, p. 111).

One of the attempts to overcome this problem using capped pooled budgets and the use of case managers in the late 1990s was through Commonwealth-led coordinated care trials and aged care assessment teams. A series of local trials in each State covered 'frail older people, people with chronic mental health problems, specific disease groups (such as cancer) and aboriginal populations with high levels of health needs ... the reforms were intended to promote the co-ordination of different types of services, allowing acute hospitals to work closely with primary care and community support services' (Fine, 1998, pp. 121–2). The aim was to get the best outcomes per dollar for each patient. However, critics of this 'managed competition' approach argued that previously ring-fenced monies for social care might be diverted to financially stretched health services and that the trials could become 'medicalised' because of the key role played by health service personnel. Fine (1998, pp. 122–3) commented that, as a consequence of these kinds of concerns, the trials 'appear to have taken on a more collaborative and less competitive approach' and his conclusion in the late 1990s was that it was not at the time possible 'to speak of a single Australian model for integrating care services across the different sectors'. Problems of coordination were built into the range of community services developed in the 1980s and 1990s (Fine, 1999). The problems have subsequently deepened with advances in acute medical interventions which 'have led to attempts to seek solutions by using long-term care services as cheaper substitutes, through the creation of an "integrated" system of coordinated care. With this, the separate character of aged care services and the problems experienced with co-ordination have been intensified' (Fine, 2001).

This theme of coordination, collaboration and partnership was a central concern of the 2004 policy document on the way forward for community care in Australia, based on the view that effective linkages between the various services relevant to the needs of frail older people and other groups requiring care in the community would help to control the costs of provision. The Foreword to the document stated that the review leading up to the policy paper was to focus on interlinked care programmes which should result in 'an appropriate continuum of care in the community, that is of high quality, affordable and accessible' (DoHA, 2004, p. 2). Consistency and coordination were to be developed in assessment processes, access to services, eligibility criteria, fee levels, financial reporting, quality assurance, performance outcomes, data collection on service users and planning. The outcome was to be a 'streamlined and better co-ordinated community care system' (op. cit., p. 4) ensuring that limited resources would be directed at those most in need (op. cit., p. 26). In part, there was to be enhanced collaboration in respect of community care between the Commonwealth and State governments, and in part closer coordination at the regional/local levels within States to be able to use scarce resources more effectively in the delivery of services. At the time of writing, the jury was still out on whether the twin aims of closer collaboration and good cost control had been achieved. 'Attempts to link informal care, community care, primary health care, acute hospital and specialist care and long-term residential aged care into a seamless, integrated system has come at a time of pressures to reduce costs and to make it increasingly self-funding' (Fine, 2006, p. 2). Whilst there is little doubt that the demand for more and better quality community care will increase, the key issue is how the expansion is to be funded – by government or by users. Bruen (2005, p. 131) argues that this 'will definitely become a major topic of debate, including issues of fiscal policy, ideology and politics'.

Perhaps the most likely example of lesson drawing for the UK from developments in Australia is the introduction of coordinated care trials, together with the subsequent problems of implementation. The UK Royal Commission on Long Term Care recommended close examination of the relevance for Britain of the aged care assessment teams as a possible model of effective collaboration (Sutherland Report, 1999b, pp. 208–9).

Care management

The neo-liberal American version of the welfare state has exhibited in full the mixed economy of welfare with its 'mixture of corporate, philanthropic and public sources of welfare provision' (Clarke and Piven, 2001, p. 261) though there was 'evidence of a clear preference for market mechanisms and market incentives to deal with the problems at hand' (Heffernan, 2003, p. 145). Important features of the US tradition include individual rather than socialised insurance arrangements linked to working in the formal labour market, and a marked preference for private insurance rather than public assistance to support those in need. The reforms of the 1960s and 1970s, the 'war on poverty', did extend the range of services available to the disadvantaged, but the distinction between insurance and assistance schemes was not removed, reflecting old poor law ideas of the deserving and undeserving poor (Heffernan, 2003, pp. 157–9). As with some other post-industrial societies, the widespread recession from the 1970s created a backlash, an attack on welfare dependency, which was seen to make the economy less competitive. The shift from the welfare to the competition state (Cerny, 1992) took dramatic form, shifting from the war on poverty to a war on welfare. This was encapsulated during the Clinton administration with the passing of the Personal Responsibility Act in 1996. It focussed on the traditional notion of work rather than welfare as the basis of personal and familial independence and, according to Clarke and Piven (2001, p. 38), 'did indeed mark "the end of welfare as we know it", representing the culmination of neo-conservative and neo-liberal attacks on "welfare" that had been developing since the late 1970s'. Whether it was a culmination in the light of the policies of the Bush administration of the early 21st century is a matter of opinion (Waddon and Jaenicke, 2006).

The provision of home and community-based care in the USA reflects the broader picture of the American welfare state. Care for people with longer term needs is provided primarily through informal care, whether the family, neighbours, friends or community organisations. 'It is important to point out that the family and other informal systems remain the norm in giving social care in the United States' (Heffernan, 2003, p. 147). In addition, there are formal services, paid for either from private or public funds, which provide care in the home or in community-based settings and nursing homes offering specialised medical, nursing or social care services. There is a variety of funding sources to cover nursing home and or community care costs: public monies, personal expenditure and private long-term care insurance. In the early 1990s, it was estimated that the total spent each year in the USA on long-term care added up to 50 billion dollars, 20 per cent for community care and 80 per cent for nursing homes (Clark, 1991). Of the ten billion dollars spent on community care, 41 per cent of the income came from personal payments, 25 per cent from the federal health insurance programme for elderly people (Medicare), 12 per cent from the federal welfare programme for low income people regardless of age (Medicaid) and 10 per cent from private long-term insurance. The remaining 12 per cent came from individual state programmes or other federal funding, such as the Older Americans Act 1965.

It was under this latter legislation that there was an expansion of case management and other supportive services for frail elderly people. Goodman (1981, quoted in Davies and Challis, 1986, p. 98) stated that case management 'means that a single worker deals with multiple client needs and mobilises a range of services ... case managers can be seen as an intervening structure between the individual and the complex array of bureaucracies providing programs'. The role is essentially one of coordination rather than direct provision of services (a brokerage model) and covers care planning, arranging for services to be delivered and monitoring provision to allow for reassessment. However, the caseloads appeared at times to be such that it raised doubts about the effectiveness of case management work. One programme (Assessment for Community Care Services, ACCESS) was reported to have a load of 200 clients per manager in 1982 (Eggert and Williams, 1982, p. 1, quoted in Davies and Challis, 1986, p. 124). This administrative approach to case management did not allow for flexibility on the part of case managers or the agencies within the local care environment, though there were some models of care management that did integrate services from a variety of sources, such as the programme of All-inclusive Care for the Elderly (Glendinning *et al.*, 2004, p. 17).

Davies and Challis (1986, ch. 3) drew on the American experience of the case management approach in developing a long-term model for community care in Britain. In particular, they looked at local initiatives that preceded the 'channelling' projects commissioned by the US Department of Health and Human Services (DHHS) in the 1980s. By 'channelling' was meant 'arrangements required to match services (if not resources) to needs in long-term care' (Davies and Challis, 1986, p. 87). The point being made was that the projects were aimed at using existing resources more effectively. Channelling was built round 'the improved performance of case management tasks by managers providing continuity of oversight' (op. cit., p.88). The key issue for the mixed economy of welfare was that existing resources were to be found in a wide range of agencies. Davies and Challis (1986, p. 144) comment that in the 1980s it was 'to the Americans that we (the British) have to look for thorough, comprehensive and integrated advances in some aspects of management and organisation'. More recently, Heffernan has concluded that 'long-term care is a serious problem within the US health and social welfare system ... Solutions ... wait upon the successful reform of the whole health care system' (2003, p. 160). Meanwhile 'the growth of social care provision, delivered through varieties of the market mechanism outside of the public sector and outside of the informal sector, is certain to continue' (op. cit., p. 164). The apparent paradox is that much of the funding for formally provided social care services comes from the government, the public sector, through cash transfers to recipients who pay for the services or through contracts with providers to deliver services to specified groups of clients. Private long-term care insurance has not proved a popular option, even in the US (Sutherland Report, 1999b, pp. 166–8; Fine and Chalmers, 2000, pp. 19–20; Glendinning *et al.*, 2004, p. 5).

In terms of policy learning, yet again the likelihood of success in developing an insurance-based system in the UK would defy evidence from round the world, including the USA. What is undoubtedly clear is that the idea of case management in America did have a major influence on the community care debate in Britain in the 1980s, not least as a result of the innovative work by staff at the Personal Social Services Research Unit of the University of Kent (Davies, 1986). A more recent US import underpins the UK government's initiative in addressing long term conditions (see Chapter 5). An evaluation of the Evercare approach to the case management of frail elderly people in nine primary care trusts in England concluded that radical system redesign would be needed to reduce the level of hospital admissions (Gravelle *et al.*, 2006). The lesson to be drawn from this project is to ensure that the circumstances in the country of origin are replicated in the country of receipt. 'In the United States, Evercare substantially reduced hospital admissions among residents in nursing homes, but the US version of Evercare was markedly different to the version in the United Kingdom as the former included intensive domiciliary nursing care of patients when they became ill' (ibid.).

User and carer empowerment

In the previous chapter, the influence of the proponents in the UK of the social model of disability and the case for disability rights was outlined. Developments in America played a part in this process, not least flowing from visits in the 1970s and 1980s to innovative projects by people from the UK with physical or learning disabilities (Hurst, 2005; Smith, 2005). In the USA, Frankfather and Caro (1981) described a consumer-orientated disability model of channelling and contrasted it with a 'professional/medical' model. It was in essence a voucher model, an income support strategy rather than a professionally led coordination strategy (a brokerage model). However, Davies and Challis (1986, p. 95) commented that there was little evidence about the effects of such a scheme and argued that vouchers were 'alien to the assumptive world of British health and social care policy'. As earlier chapters of this book show, the idea of direct payments or individualised budgets, if not vouchers as such, has in recent years become a central plank of the strategy for UK adult social care. The notion of user empowerment was not very visible in the Davies and Challis 1986 overview of US strategies for community care and did not go much further than the approval of care plans by clients and their informal carers.

This relatively restricted view did not take account of user-orientated developments such as the Centre for Independent Living movement founded in California in 1970 or the People First forum of people with learning difficulties founded in 1974, let alone the more overtly mainstream political activities of the American Association of Retired Persons (founded in 1958) or even the Gray Panthers Movement founded in 1970 by Maggie Kuhn. This was a time of civil rights struggles and opposition to the Vietnam war. Davies and Challis (published in 1986) cannot be criticised for not mentioning the 1990 Americans with Disabilities Act, but the latter legislation did build on the earlier 1973 Rehabilitation Act, which did place some emphasis on the elimination of structural discrimination, reflecting a social model of disability approach. 'In the period between these two pieces of legislation the American disability movement blossomed in numbers, degree of activism, development of politically sophisticated lobbying and identification as a self-conscious political constituency. At least in part this was in explicit response to the struggle to enforce the Rehabilitation Act. This, in turn, became the crucial factor in the passage of the second, more powerful piece of legislation' (Gooding, 1994, p. 79). The 1990 Americans with Disabilities Act prohibited discrimination in the fields of employment, state and local government responsibilities (including social services), goods and services more broadly and telecommunications (Degener, 2005, pp. 97–8).

In a statement celebrating the fifteenth anniversary of the passing of the Americans with Disabilities Act, a body launched in 1995 called the American Association of People with Disabilities (2005) asserted that 'the ADA is slowly driving policy changes that have enabled more people with significant mental and physical disabilities to live independently in the community, but the ongoing institutional bias in the Medicaid program keeps too many people trapped in nursing homes and other institutions, unable to enjoy the freedoms and personal choices about where and how to live that other Americans take for granted'. Celebrating the same anniversary, the National Council on Disability (2005) referred to the 1990 Act as a 'watershed event for advancing the civil rights of people with disabilities' and described it as being 'the impetus for a revolution in the inclusion, integration and empowerment of Americans with disabilities'. In 2005, the Council conducted an ADA impact study and reported that significant strides had been made in such areas as transportation and accessible public facilities, communications systems, engagement in the political process by voting, attending post-secondary education and reduced discrimination in employment. Among the barriers still to be overcome was the lack of affordable housing for people with disabilities, but the report appeared to be silent on the issue of control over or user involvement in health and social care services.

The transfer of the notion of case management in the USA to care management in the UK (Davies, 1986) originated with influential researchers at the University of Kent. By way of contrast, the flow of ideas about user empowerment came from groups of service users drawing lessons from innovative practices in America and using the information to influence the policy debate in the UK.

Focus on carers: debates in Australia

In Australia, with the development of community-based care came some recognition of the need for new kinds of planning, managing and delivery of services. Shaver and Fine (1995, p. 16) noted that this shift increased the importance of informal caregivers as advocates and representatives of dependent users and as users in their own right. The main emphasis, however, was on making service deliverers more responsive to the needs of individual service users in a post-bureaucratic mode of organisation. They argued for a 'co-production of care' model (Wilson, 1994) in which all parties (providers, carers and users) played an active role in the tasks needed for effective home based care. 'This vision of co-production can be thought of as teamwork on a small scale, with the person receiving care, the caregiver and formal service workers actively co-operating to achieve a common goal' (Shaver and Fine, 1995, p. 24). These debates focussed more on the needs of carers than service users. 'The federal Government has promoted a series of initiatives to support carers, under the umbrella of a national carer's strategy. Carers now have a much wider range and level of available services, including respite care. There is a carer's pension to provide income support to those providing care ... There is an active advocacy organisation and local groups' (Sutherland Report, 1999b, pp. 175, 204). The UK Royal Commission also noted that, following challenges to centre-right government plans to increase user charges, organisations representing the interests of elderly people were 'drawn back into a consultation process ... The elderly advocacy groups are pretty formidable in Australia and influential in promoting standards and access in both the residential and homecare sectors' (ibid., pp. 177, 204). This is, however, still some way away from user empowerment. The 2004 community care policy document did not dwell on user empowerment, though the needs of carers were acknowledged (see above) and representatives of user groups were included as members of a National Reference Group for the Review of Community Care, whose role was to engage with the implementation of the strategies outlined in the policy paper, arguing for demonstrable improved outcomes for clients and carers and significantly increased resources for community care. The National Reference Group, whilst highlighting the important of choice, did not advocate strategies such as direct payments or individualised budgets. The voice of service user groups was muted.

Just as in the USA, cash for care strategies were less central in Australia than arguments for the closer involvement of service users (and carers) in the planning, management and delivery of services, an advocacy approach. This was picked up by the UK Royal Commission on Long Term Care, which referred to active advocacy (what other sort is there?) and the formidable nature of influential pressure groups acting on behalf of elderly people. The lesson drawing in this context could apply to similar bodies in the UK such as Age Concern England or Help the Aged. However, to repeat, this is not user empowerment.

The voice of older people: Germany and Denmark

In a study of the politics of old age in Europe, Walker and Naegele (1999) concluded that between the 1950s and the 1970s pressure groups were less interested in the political mobilisation of older people but rather focused on the representation of older people in the policy arena. However, following the fiscal crisis of the mid-1970s and increasing concern about the public expenditure implications of population ageing, a new politics of old age emerged. Walker (1999, pp. 10, 18) referred to the creation in 1975 of the Senior Protection Association in Germany. By the mid-1990s it had 15,000 members. In the 1980s the two main political parties also made special arrangements for pensioner groupings (Naegele, 1999, pp. 104–6).

In Germany, senior citizens' councils were first formed in 1972. By the beginning of 1997, there were over 700. In general, those active in the councils were people already linked to the local political system and their remit was very broad. It could cover 'active ageing' concerns, such as leisure and education, information and advice services and advocacy, and the approach was essentially consensual (for details, see Naegele, 1999, pp. 101–4). Whether these bodies, and their equivalents in other EU member states, have an influence on the social care policy process or the quality of services delivered is a moot point. How much user empowerment can be discerned in community care policy-making and practice? It was argued that the option of cash benefits in the new social insurance scheme would empower consumers and thereby guarantee competitive pricing (Schneider, 1999, p. 50) but in Germany, as elsewhere, a market approach was received with scepticism. 'Consumer empowerment will be of little use, given oligopolistic or monopolistic supply of professional care services that prevail in rural areas or small municipalities' (op. cit., p. 63).

Indeed, Evers and Olk (1991) concluded early on that for elderly people in Germany there had been a traditional strong dominance of producers' over consumers' interests and power. However, they contrasted this with the debate held by organisations of disabled people who have argued that the power of decisionmaking should be turned upside down to create a user centred culture of care (see Schneider, 1999, p. 66). In 2002 legislation was passed on the equalisation of persons with disabilities, but it focused in the main on creating barrier-free services provided by the public sector. As already noted in relation to the 1994 social insurance scheme, the cash total available is less than the maximum value of professional care that can be secured in order to avoid the misuse of funds. For frail, older people and others who could face difficulties in deciding between care or cash, and in deciding what to purchase if the cash option is preferred, the development of independent nonprofitmaking advocacy and advice centres has been an important innovation in Germany. However, a commentary on the new scheme argued that there was a 'deficit in giving independent advocacy and counselling to ... applicants in order to accompany their way successfully into the complicated system' (Kondratowitz *et al.*, 2002, pp. 244–5).

In Denmark, a new grassroots organisation, known as the C Team, was established in the early 1990s. It was distinct from existing bodies representing the interests of older people and focused on challenging proposed cuts in health and social care.

Local authorities in several EU countries have set up advisory boards or councils of older people. They include Denmark and Germany, and in Sweden they had to be created by law in all municipalities. In Denmark in 1980 there were four local senior citizens' councils; by 1995 there were 200. As well as senior citizens' councils, users' councils were also developed which could represent the interests of older users with respect to institutional, day or domiciliary care (Pedersen, 1998, p. 100).

The debate on empowerment has been muted in a *modern welfare state* like Denmark. The welfare state system is highly decentralised and there were major reforms in the provision of care in the 1990s. Access to both benefits and services is open to all as a citizen's right, so provision is not seen as stigmatising and is not conditional upon insurance contributions. The main role of pensioners' organisations has been to demand the right to negotiate the amount of pensions and to struggle against the exclusion by professionals of, for instance, elderly people participating in decisionmaking in domiciliary or institutional care. Indeed, 65 per cent of homes for elderly people had residents' councils as long ago as 1965 (Munday, 1996, p. 35).

Thus, in northern European Union countries, grassroots organisations comprising older people and their advocates increased in numbers and influences in the last quarter of the 20th century. Even so, the debate on empowerment was masked by the debate on the continuance of professional dominance and the cash-for-care option in the new insurance system in Germany, and the notion of citizens' rights in Denmark.

The voice of disabled people: Denmark, Germany and Spain

Unlike Walker and Naegele's (1999) overview of the politics of old age, there has been no similar EU-wide profile of user empowerment in respect of disabled people despite the concern at the EU level for the quality of life for people with disabilities and despite trenchant advocacy by organisations of disabled people themselves.

In Denmark, the Danish Council of Organisations of People with Disabilities (DCOPD) was established in 1934 to act as a body to negotiate with government and to represent the interests of disabled people in a variety of settings. By the 1960s it was closely involved in discussions about any legislation of relevance to disabled people. In effect, this engagement reflected the principles of the social model of disability (Bengtsson, 2000). However, by the 1980s in a difficult economic environment, interest groups such as the DCOPD became less centrally involved in policy debates.

In 1993, following parliamentary debate, an Equal Opportunities Centre for Disabled Persons was created with a brief to encourage all sectors of society to treat disabled people equally, in other words, a mainstreaming strategy. Bengtsson (2000, p. 372) comments that the Centre has used dialogue rather than setting demands, leading some organisations of disabled people to view this approach as being 'too weak and compliant' (ibid). However, he concluded that 'most of the organisations of people with disabilities are satisfied with the model of political influence represented by the Equal Opportunities Centre' and made the broad point that 'the social struggle of people with disabilities has been similar to that of workers, and the resulting institutions are best seen as corporatist bodies within the power structure' (op. cit., pp. 375–6).

It has proved difficult to develop an overview of user empowerment and disabled people in Germany. Drake (1999, p. 96) stated that there was a thriving disabled people's movement, 'that campaigns domestically and has membership of Disabled People's International'. One of the most prominent of these organisations is that concerned with people disabled by war and their families (known as VdK). It is a key member of the German Disability Council and the president of VdK also chairs the Disability Council. In 1994 the organisation was renamed and became the Sozialverband VdK Deutschland. By this time only 20 per cent of its 1.1 million members were victims of war. The rest were either people disabled for other reasons or recipients of pensions.

Today the VdK comprises 14 Länder level bodies (Berlin/ Brandenburg and Lower Saxony/Bremen had combined). There are 9,000 local organisations, 90,000 volunteers and 1,500 bodies which employ staff. The main focus of VdK is to influence the legislation at both federal and Länder level and the practices of local administrations; to advise members on benefits; to support rehabilitation of individuals; to advocate for appropriate housing and physical environments; and to support people with specific disabilities or illnesses. In addition, VdK is an anti-war body. At the end of the 20th century there were 22 centres for independent living in Germany.

In southern Europe it was in 1993 that the Spanish Council of Representatives of People with Disabilities (CERMI) was established. This advocacy body comprised the ten main disability organisations 'integrating more than 2,000 smaller associations and institutions, in total representing a community of two and a half million people with disabilities' (Verdugo *et al.*, 2000, p. 327). In recent years it has played a significant role in policy debates on employment, access, education, health and welfare at both the domestic and EU level. It represents Spain on the European Disability Forum and has been instrumental in the development of the Committee of Southern European People with Disabilities. One key initiative in the late 1990s was the agreement between CERMI and the Spanish Ministry of Labour and Social Affairs to create a National Council of People with Disabilities. It was formally established in June 1999 as a governmental organisation.

The European Union and empowerment

Despite a wide range of initiatives across the European Union, the 2006 report on Social Inclusion in Europe (European Commission, 2006) concluded that the active participation of disadvantaged people, including disabled and elderly citizens, in the compilation of National Action Plans (NAPs) to address poverty and social exclusion, had not been structured into the NAPs process. Consultation was more likely to occur with groups representing the excluded rather than the excluded themselves. Even in Sweden, it was reported that 'there is still a need to put in place a system to establish a real user cooperation at all levels of society' (p. 147). Even where involvement was recognised 'there is little evidence of a direct link between mobilisation of actors and the actual impact on policies' (ibid.). However, this 2006 report did acknowledge that 'people with disabilities tend to have the best organised representation and are accordingly most strongly present in dealings with authorities' (ibid.). The overall impression of user activity is that it is embedded within official systems in the countries of the European Union. Few, if any, lessons can be drawn on effective practices for user empowerment. It still has a long way to travel to enter fully the world of decision-making. Perhaps that should not be its direction of travel. Stronger lobbying through Brussels-based groups such as AGE and the European Disability Forum, together with their national member organisations, might have more influence on the social inclusion agenda.

Concluding comments

This chapter has not focused on direct comparison of community care policies in different countries. It has provided profiles of community care in countries that reflect different welfare regimes and, where relevant, indicates a possible influence on policy and practice in the UK. The most obvious example of impact from outside the UK is the importation of the notion of case (care) management from the USA. Both societies broadly fit into the liberal social policy (residual) welfare state model. Another example is the fines placed upon local authorities if they are deemed to be dilatory in providing appropriate accommodation and services for people, mainly older people, ready for discharge from hospital. This practice was imported from Scandinavia and perhaps illustrates the complexity of transferring a policy from one type of welfare state to another. As well as the political will to effect this kind of transfer in principle, implementation requires a similar kind of infrastructure to achieve effective results. In Scandinavia, the level of investment in local services has meant that this deterrent strategy has not been seen as an unreasonable burden. This is far from the case for local government in the UK.

More common than the direct importation of community care policies and practices from outside the UK has been examples of policy debate that draw on activities in other countries. For instance, the Royal Commission on Long Term Care included in one of its research volumes a chapter on practice in a number of first world countries (drawing on OECD (1996) studies) and, inter alia, noted that Australia's system of Aged Care Assessment Teams was worth close consideration for application in the UK. Gooding (1994) and Scott (1994), at the time working for the Royal Association for Disability and Rehabilitation, reported in detail on disability rights in the USA and the impact of the 1990 Americans with Disabilities Act (ADA). Their clear intention was to influence the debate on the forthcoming Disability Discrimination Act in the UK. Degener commented that 'the ADA has had such an enormous impact on foreign law development that one might feel inclined to say that its international impact has been larger than its domestic effect' (2005, p. 89). As part of its wide-ranging study of the UK as an ageing society, the Audit Commission (2004a) arranged for a literature review of international practices of support for carers of older people (Glendinning, 2003) and the Joseph Rowntree Foundation supported a research project on the funding of long-term care for older people, which focused on lessons from other countries (Glendinning *et al.*, 2004). This kind of contribution can influence the climate of debate.

Another indirect form of influence on the policy debate comes from recent developments in the policy process of the European Union. Member state governments have, in relation to a range of key concerns, not least in the sphere of social policy, signed up to a procedure known as the open method of coordination. This requires all member states to prepare individual papers on recent developments leading to national action plans. These are circulated to all governments for peer review and the European Commission both comment on them and prepare a synthesis report for discussion and decision by the Council of Ministers and the European Parliament. Examples of the open method of coordination include information exchange on pensions policy, health and long-term care and peer review for social protection and social exclusion, all of which are highly relevant to the debate about the future profile of community care for people with special needs.

As important as the direct transfer of policy and practices or the highlighting of interesting developments in other countries are the broad, global influences across the board on the development of community care strategies. Examples include the reduction in the extent of institution-based care, the heightened recognition for providing practical support for carers and the need for enhanced integration of health, social and other care services in response to multiple disadvantages. One of the key factors underpinning all these examples is the changing role of women in the formal labour market and another is the importance of international migration for both the caring role and the staffing of day and domiciliary care services. 'There is no research that has examined support for carers in the context of growing world-wide problems of migration' (Glendinning, 2003, p. 30). A third factor is the general pressure from rising health and insurance costs on the levels of public expenditure in all first world countries. This internationalisation of the policy debate in principle enables campaigners and policy-makers in the UK to become more aware and make use of illuminating policies, practices and procedures in community care in other countries. However, the context in which interesting developments are located is as important for full understanding of their potential transferability as the policies and practices themselves.

Chapter 9

Community Care: New Directions and Old Challenges

Our central concern has been the modernisation agenda for public policy of Labour Governments since 1997 and how this has impacted upon community care policy and practice. This final chapter draws the key threads together to reflect upon achievements and failures so far as well as likely future directions.

A new world of welfare provision?

There is little doubt that the Labour Government has had a vision of a new world of welfare provision for the traditional community groups, namely older people, people with mental health problems, people with learning disabilities and physically and sensory disabled people. We would argue that this has four main components, namely a stress on well-being and fitness; getting people into paid work; user empowerment; and the extensive use of assistive technology. Each of these will now be considered in turn.

First, there is a new mantra around fitness and well-being, especially in later life. Prevention is back in vogue. The government is already producing reports (Department of Health, 2006d) on progress against the goals of the White Paper on Community Services (Department of Health, 2006a) which included 'better prevention and early intervention for improved health, independence and well-being' (p. 13). The plethora of new initiatives listed in the progress report in relation to this goal included NHS Life Checks (with 1,200 trainers in post by early 2007 to help those at risk), psychological therapies and partnerships for older people projects (POPPs). The NHS Life Checks will target people at certain points in their life cycle including at 50 years of age. The clear intention of government is to improve the fitness of older people so that they will in due course make dramatically reduced demands on health and social care services. A distinction has often been made between a third age with the potential for self-fulfilment and expression in later life (Laslett, 1989; Gilleard and Higgs, 2000; 2005) and a fourth age of declining health and dependency. The aim of government is to push back the boundaries of the third age and ideally to remove the need for any fourth age for many people. At the extreme end of genetic and medical research this is leading a minority to seek 'the key' to everlasting life (Harper, 2006; Vincent, 2006), while in the mainstream science of ageing there is growing knowledge about how diet, lifestyle and environment can be combined to improve health and well-being at the end of the life course (Kirkwood, 1999).

The second component impacts upon all the main community groups, namely a sustained attempt to get people into, or back into, the labour market despite their care and support needs. This was absolutely central to the Prime Minister's Strategy Unit (2005) report on *Improving the Life Chances of Disabled People*. The growing emphasis upon older people remaining in work has received wide publicity especially since it is under-pinned by the Employment Equality (Age) Regulations 2006 which makes it unlawful to discriminate against workers on the grounds of age. Rather less well profiled has been the pathways to work initiative designed to help people on incapacity benefit (IB) to get back to work. The pilots provide health rehabilitation services, tailored job advice and work placements and the government has felt able to present a positive picture of how this is enabling IB claimants to re-enter the labour market (Department for Work and Pensions, 2005)

Such 'success' has encouraged the government to release a Green Paper on *A New Deal for Welfare: Empowering People to Work* (Department for Work and Pensions, 2006a). The Green Paper included a commitment to get one million older workers into jobs. It also announced the replacement of IB and income support for incapacity from 2008 for new claimants and its replacement with a new system of employment and support allowances to include a higher rate for people with a serious condition and financial penalties for claimants who do not coop-erate. Not all are convinced of such reforms with Leason (2006) pointing out that four in ten people claiming IB have a mental health problem. The health of such individuals could easily be worsened if they felt coerced into work or work-related activity with which they are simply not well enough to cope. Against this, Layard (2006) has called for a massive expansion of psychological therapy services as the best way to reduce the incidence of depression and anxiety disorders and hence to get large numbers of adults back to work.

For people with learning disabilities, the emphasis has also been upon increasing their involvement in the labour market (Prime Minister's Strategy Unit, 2005) with mainstream and 'special needs' schools expected to provide work placement experiences (Department for Work and Pensions, 2006b). For those who will still not be able to find employment in the open market, a number of schemes have been established to provide subsidised forms of employment such as the Supported Employment Programme (SEP) and its successor WORKSTEP. However, this is yet another example (see below on 'modernisation muddles') of a large gap between rhetoric and reality. Unlike SEP, WORKSTEP is only available to those working 16 or more hours per week, thus excluding many people with learning disabilities wishing to work fewer hours.

But what of those who will never be able to work in the formal (or subsidised) labour market because of their high levels of frailty or impairment? Here the whole thrust of government policy is to stress user choice and user empowerment on the grounds that services should be driven by the needs of service users rather than professionals (see Chapter 7). The next section considers the limits to this drive.

The final component of 'the new world of welfare provision' relates to releasing the power of assistive technology to support people in the community and in institutional settings. This was another strong element of the Prime Minister's Strategy Unit (2005) report on *Improving the Life Chances of Disabled People*. It is, of course, sensible for all governments to explore the potential and cost-effectiveness of assistive technology in a range of settings. However, there are tensions between its capacity to empower through enabling older and disabled people to 'remain in control' and its potential to act as a form of intrusive surveillance. For example, Percival and Hanson (2006) have explored Telecare which delivers health and social care services in people's own homes through the use of technology which can monitor activities and provide information and reminder systems (e.g. to take your medicine). The more elaborate versions can also provide virtual home visits. Telecare will only represent a new world of welfare provision if properly resourced, recognises the importance of human contact, offers user choice and is well integrated into other support systems.

There are dangers in any 'new world of welfare provision' and some of these have already been alluded to in this section. Perhaps the biggest of these is the narrowness of some of the thinking. We have seen how the White Paper on Community Services (Department of Health, 2006a) stresses early intervention for improved health, independence and well-being. However, the central focus seems to be on fitness in order to save on community care and health costs in the future rather than upon quality of life which is more likely to relate to social networks, social participation and the pursuit of meaningful activities than fitness per se (Raynes *et al.*, 2001). The failure to address quality of life concerns from an holistic perspective is an issue for all the main community care groups. Thus, Murray (2002a; 2002b) researched how young disabled teenagers, and especially those with learning difficulties, tended to be excluded from 'normal' everyday leisure activities. Leisure was usually organised through the family when the teenagers wanted to be with other young people, doing things that young people do. Badlan's (2006) sample of young people with cystic fibrosis did manage to immerse themselves in such activities but subsequent chosen lifestyles were often in conflict with the 'staying healthy' advice from health and social care professionals.

Overall, however, this 'new world of welfare provision' does at least have the potential to generate a very creative and positive agenda if some of the main pitfalls can be avoided. The first of these is the growing gap between the vision and the practicalities of public finance. Not only are there significant financial pressures upon the public sector in the short term but all the indicators are that this will continue for the period 2008–11 as a result of the next comprehensive spending review. Two of these pitfalls will now be considered in turn. The first is the limits of user empowerment and choice and the second is the element of policy chaos which has descended across the public policy reform agenda.

The limits of user empowerment and choice

The proposals contained in the Government's disability strategy (Prime Minister's Strategy Unit, 2005) and the adult social care Green Paper, *Independence, Well-being and Choice* (Department of Health, 2005a) have reaffirmed New Labour's commitment to extending opportunities for user choice and control in service provision. These include the acceptance of the idea of independent living, as defined by the disability movement, the promotion of direct payments and the introduction of individual budgets. At the same time, the development of the role of care broker, working in partnership with service users to facilitate choice and service procurement, signals changing expectations for local authority adult services. Whilst it is too early to predict the impact of these proposals, important barriers to the extension of user choice and empowerment have still to be addressed.

First, a central plank of the community care reforms, the power of local authorities to define need, and therefore to control access to resources, remains firmly in place. Whilst the civil rights of disabled and older people have increased in certain areas, under legislation such as the Disability Discrimination Act and the Human Rights Act, there has been little extension of service users' rights in the social care arena (see Chapter 7). Widening access and other rights to social care requires a willingness by government and society at large to increase the scope of funded social care provision.

Second, enabling meaningful user participation, at an individual or organisational level, requires considerable commitment and effort. Practitioners and the agencies responsible for arranging and providing social care are faced with many competing demands. Social workers, for example, may lack sufficient time because of high caseloads to develop a full understanding of the wishes of service users with complex needs. Similarly, managers are unlikely to initiate a fundamental redesign of services in response to criticisms from service users, unless this accords with other priorities such as the need to meet government targets or to balance the budget. The growing interest in the feminist ethics of care, and the rediscovery of care, as a morally based activity that is central to human relationships, offers a potentially fruitful bridge between practitioners and users and one that may be empowering for both (Lloyd, 2006a).

Third, although the social model of disability is increasingly influential, doubts persist about whether or not it is effective in promoting the interests of all service users. For many disabled activists, it is key to advances in the position of disabled people and in our understanding of disability, whilst others, as reported in Chapter 7, are unconvinced. A powerful case for a more sophisticated disability model has recently been made by Shakespeare (2006). Central to his argument is the charge that the social model 'downplays the role of impairment in the lives of disabled people' (p. 50). For Shakespeare, issues of embodiment mean that disabled people are inevitably disadvantaged, and he calls for new ways of conceptualising disability which do not rely on an over-simplistic dichotomy, such as that between the medical and social models.

Modernisation muddles

Chapters 4 to 7 all explored the implications of the modernisation of the welfare state for community care. In doing this, the continued complexity and range of policy changes and reforms have become apparent.

The emphasis placed by the government upon partnership in this modernisation process was the key to achieving joined-up government and was called both 'the new mantra' (Heywood *et al.*, 2002, p. 142) and 'New Labour's big idea' (Clark, 2002, p. 107). In terms of health and social care, the argument for the importance of this was presented in a clear and decisive way:

> people want and deserve the best public services ... It is the responsibility of government, local government and the NHS to ensure that those justifiable expectations are met. People care about the quality of the services they get – not how they are delivered or who delivers them. We all need to ensure that service quality does not suffer because of artificial rigidities within and between service deliverers. (DoH/DETR, 1999)

It is, therefore, quite clear that the government aspired to a much more coherent and flexible approach in which a range of agencies work together in the interests of service users and carers.

However, as explained in Chapter 5, theories of joint working indicate the difficulty in achieving this in practice. In addition, Clark (2002) pointed out the tension in New Labour approaches between emphasising community orientation and participation as the key to joined-up working at the local level and a desire to impose joined-up working and hence improve performance through centralised indicators which require very specific forms of partnership to be demonstrated.

Indeed, in Chapters 4, 5 and 6 we have demonstrated the lack of even incremental progress in joined-up working let alone a modernisation revolution in joined-up government. Instead, what was found was modernisation muddles, in which managers and field-level staff struggle to keep pace with the demand for policy change and the ever increasing flood of directives, guidelines and indicators.

However, the response of government has not been to reduce the speed of change in order to allow the gap between policy and its implementation to be reduced. Instead, these earlier chapters have demonstrated how what Pressman and Wildavasky (1973) called 'implementation deficit' has been blamed by central government upon weakness in initial policy proposals and shortcomings in the local leadership of change. More specifically, the heavy reliance on partnership working has been reduced with a growing belief in markets and competition as the only ways to ensure efficiency and user responsiveness. In Chapter 5 we illustrated how much of this is being driven through as a result of further major reform in health care policy (payment by results, foundation hospital trusts, support for the growth of private care providers, etc.). It is too early to assess the impact of these major quasi-market reforms upon health care let alone the 'knock-on' consequences for social care; although Propper *et al.* (2006) have recently argued that there is neither strong theoretical nor empirical support for competition in health care. However, it is now clear that modernisation muddles are much more than just a temporary phenomenon that will have very little salience by the time of the next general election. It is clear that Labour's record in office with regard to the National Health Service (and to a lesser extent community care) will feature as a high profile campaign issue with David Cameron as the leader of the Conservative Party already making clear his intention to do this.

The response of the Labour Government has been yet more of

what Appleby and Coote (2002) called 'relentless, almost hyper-active intervention' (p. 5). What is the cause of this hyperactivity? The temptation is to see this as flowing rather narrowly from 'Blairism' or 'New Labour'. However, Sennett (2006) in *The Culture of the New Capitalism* profiles how the information revolution across the private and public sectors has centralised power in the hands of senior executives and prompted their belief that they know enough to command immediate change from the top. Furthermore, he argues that in this 'MP3 kind of institution' (p. 172), with its focus on immediacy, staff become overwhelmed by a mixture of information and instruction made all the worse by the tendency of such technology to disable 'the craft of communication' (p. 173). Added to this is the speed of innovation and change in modern capitalism with obsolescence and uselessness faced by many staff and not just those with the least skills and education.

Sennett believes New Labour fell into the trap of embracing the MP3 culture in its public reform agenda without recognising all its limitations in terms of maintaining commitment from staff and the trust of the public. Interestingly, he is able to show how work policies show the same frenetic pattern as those for community care:

> The initial policies about work were good: job training and counselling, industrial safety, work-family issues all squarely addressed. Each year, however, there were more policies, or different policies which reformed the previous policies which reformed the mess Labour had inherited. As the policies kept coming, the public trust in them eroded. Within the councils of government, the manufacture of ever-new policies appeared as an effort to learn from the actions previously taken; to the public, the policy factory seemed to indicate the government lacked commitment to any particular course of action. (p. 174)

It is equally impossible to criticise many of the aspirations of the Labour Government for health and social care. For example, Box 9.1 outlines the five key elements of older people's care which policy change is intended to achieve. Few would feel able to disagree with these hoped for outcomes – the problem lies with the messy reality on the ground.

BOX 9.1   Key elements of older people's care

1. Early intervention and assessment of old age conditions;
2. long-term conditions management in the community integrated with social care and specialist services;
3. early supported discharge whenever possible delivering care closer to home;
4. general acute hospital care whenever you need it combined with quick access to new specialist centres;
5. partnerships built around the needs and wishes of older people and their families.

Source: Philp (2007) p. 1.

The strength of Sennett's critique is that it emphasises just how culturally embedded is policy hyperactivity by New Labour. The profusion of policy pronouncements beginning to emerge from the leader of the Conservative Party suggests that the 'New Conservatism' will be based upon similar cultural assumptions to 'New Labour'.

Despite the importance of the international trends identified by Sennett (2006) it is still important to avoid becoming completely obsessed with these contemporary critiques in assessing present day community care and practice for two reasons. First, the Sennett type of critique can cause us to see present policy directions as inevitable and yet the divergent health and social care policy directions of Wales and Scotland indicate that this does not have to be the case. If we look at Wales, it is certainly true that the same frenetic 'MP3 culture' of endless policy announcements can be found (see Box 9.2). However, the volume of policy change is not the same as the direction of policy, as already discussed in Chapter 5. The six policy documents listed in Box 9.2 place an enormous emphasis upon personalised responsive social care services, prevention strategies and on partnership working between health and social care. However, there is an almost complete lack of any reference to creating efficiency and responsiveness through creating markets of health care and social care providers. Not all are convinced. Mooney and Williams (2006) accept that 'Welsh and Scottish social policies ... are tied to particular national visions of a better Wales or a New Scotland' (p. 624).

BOX 9.2   Policy change and social care in Wales, 2003–07

- Welsh Assembly Government (2003a) *The Strategy for Older People in Wales*
- Welsh Assembly Government (2003b) *Health, Social Care and Well-being Strategies*
- Welsh Assembly Government (2005) *Designed for Life: Creating World Class Health and Social Care for Wales in the 21st Century*
- Welsh Assembly Government (2006a) *A Strategy for Social Services in Wales over the Next Decade*
- Welsh Assembly Government (2006b) *National Service Framework for Older People in Wales*
- Welsh Assembly Government (2007) *Fulfilled Lives, Supportive Communities*

However, they also argue that this is still essentially neo-liberal and largely reflective of 'New Labour UK-wide ambition' (p. 625). This would suggest that more policy change and a greater emphasis on markets will come to Welsh social care in due course.

The second reason for caution with regard to Sennett's analysis is that if community care remains in a massive muddle, some of the blame for this has deep historical roots (see Chapter 2). How to organise and fund long-term care has a much longer history than the Sutherland Report (1999a). The prioritisation of acute health care over primary care is equally long established as is the low priority accorded to community-based health and welfare services for all the main community care groups. Above all, how to distinguish health care from welfare has a long and tortuous history. Modernisation policies may be part of the present community care muddle but this muddle can be traced right back to the Poor Law.

The rediscovery of social care?

Have we reached the end of the road for social services?. At one level this has certainly occurred since the social services authorities/departments established as a result of the Seebohm Report

(1968) are no more (see Chapter 2). The decision of government to combine education and social services provision for children (see Chapter 1) resulted in their disbandment. Rather than a Director of Social Services covering both child care and community care there is now both a Director of Children's Services and a Director of Adult Social Services (DASS). The Department of Health (2006c) has argued that 'the DASS forms an integral part of the Government's strategy for adult social care ... and our vision for the modernisation of community services' (p. 5).

However, though it may have been the end of the road for social services it is not so, apparently, for local authorities in terms of community care policy and practice. There has been no takeover of the local authority role by care trusts (Glendinning and Means, 2002). Instead, the government is trying yet another relaunch of local government (Department of Communities and Local Government, 2006) with the Director of Adult Social Services playing a central role:

> The DASS should provide a specific focus on adults and this should involve a role in championing the needs and aspirations of adults and promoting well-being that goes beyond the organizational boundaries of adult social care. The DASS should also provide strong leadership and co-ordination in ensuring that local providers of mainstream public services recognize and meet the needs of individual adults with care needs and their carers. He or she should work closely with the full range of providers of community services and benefits, including Supporting People/housing support; leisure services; adult education; community safety and the independent, voluntary and community sector as well as with Primary Care Trusts (PCTs) and other NHS organisations to take a whole systems approach to providing care and support well-being. (p. 6)

The full implementation of this broad agenda by Directors of Adult Social Services would indeed deliver 'the new world of welfare provision' considered in both Chapter 6 and in the first section of this chapter. Has there been a genuine rediscovery of social care?

At first glance, this does indeed appear to be happening. Not only is there the new role for the DASS as outlined above (see also Chapters 1 and 4) but also the fact that a progress report on the White Paper on Community Services (Department of Health, 2006a) has been subtitled 'Health and Social Care Working together in Partnership' (Department of Health, 2006d). The Chancellor of the Exchequer even got into this act in his pre-budget report of December 2006 by recognising the 'significant implications' of the rising older population for the future of social care provision. This helped *Community Care* to be able to say in an editorial at the end of 2006 that 'all in all the foundations of social care look more secure now than they did at the start of the year' (14 December 2006–3 January 2007, p. 5).

However, it would be a mistake to get too carried away with this rediscovery of social care. The Chancellor may have recognised the need for increased resources but saw this as coming from efficiency savings. There seems little prospect that the government will seriously address the proposals in the Wanless Review on *Securing Good Care for Older People* in terms of developing a partnership funding model between the state and the individual where costs of care are shared for those needing care (Wanless Review, 2006). Such a model would still require major additional investment in social care by the state but this might just turn some of the rhetoric of the numerous policy reports outlined in earlier chapters into at least something of a reality. However, the opposite situation is true at the moment. More and more local authorities are in such a dire financial position that they can only meet the social care needs of those adults in crisis situations and projections suggest that this situation is likely to get worse unless more money is allocated to local authorities for social care services (Forder, 2007). The reality on the ground is becoming ever more disengaged from the rhetoric emanating from central government.

As argued in Chapter 5, the most cynical explanation for this situation is that government clings onto a commitment to local authority funded social care because such care can be charged for, unlike health care provided through the National Health Service. Cost containment in relation to the main community care groups remains a central concern. This is despite one consequence of this being the continuation of the artificial divide between 'what is social care?' and 'what is health care?' which was a focus of Chapters 2 and 5 and which was so strongly criticised by the Sutherland report (1999a) on long term care. The continuation of this divide has almost certainly been an inhibiting factor in the expansion of Care Trusts despite various attempts by government to increase financial flexibilities. It can be argued that there is no great rediscovery of social care. Rather, social care struggles on, marginalised in relation to health care, but not yet fully incorporated by it.

Frontline staff matter

The last section stressed that ideological debate is very much alive and others will see very different possibilities to those outlined so far. One possibility is the likely emergence of not just national but international providers of health and social care (Player and Pollock, 2001; Holden, 2003; Drakeford, 2006). The former cottage industry of family-run residential and nursing homes has turned into a sector dominated by a small number of national players, some of which are likely to develop international aspirations.

Holden (2003) predicts 'an increasing concentration of provision in long term care, and a deepening of internationalisation as existing large firms utilise their advantages' (p. 122). However, the reason for raising this possibility is not a desire to return to the globalization debate but rather to stress the importance of frontline staff. Governments come and go. Service provision may move from the statutory to the voluntary or the private sectors. Assessment responsibilities may move between health and social services. However, the experience of community care services by most people is defined by the quality of their contact with professional and non-professional care staff. For service users this close link between the processes and outcomes of care services exists at every stage of service planning and delivery. Thus an assessment that takes full account of the views of the service user is more likely to result in appropriate and acceptable service provision than one that does not (Richards, 2000). Process issues remain central after services are in place, as demonstrated by users of domiciliary care services whose judgements about service quality reflect the nature of the relationship with care staff and the way in which care is delivered (Henwood *et al.*, 1998; Francis and Netten, 2004).

Positive contact with service users, the belief that they are 'making a difference', has traditionally been an important source of job satisfaction for social care professionals. However, as outlined in Chapter 7, many practitioners are critical of the increase in administrative tasks and fear that the reduction in the time available for service users has had a direct impact on the quality of their interventions. The concerns of practitioners have been echoed in an inquiry by the King's Fund which found evidence of a continuing crisis of morale and a lack of appropriate training and support amongst social care staff (Henwood, 2001).

It is clear that the New Labour governments have made considerable efforts to improve the social care workforce through important initiatives such as the establishment of the General Social Care Council and the introduction of registration and of codes of conduct for social care workers (see Chapter 4). What is less certain is the long-term impact of these measures on the continuing crisis of recruitment and retention, which is widely linked to low pay, to high stress levels in the workplace and to the perception among social care workers that their skills and commitment are not valued. Worryingly, there is a widespread view that morale has deteriorated further with the increase in monitoring and regulation that has occurred throughout the public services since New Labour came to power (Jones, 2001; Huxley *et al.*, 2005). There are also concerns that the move towards a market of health and social care providers may force 'workers to identify with the needs of their organisation before the needs of service users or local communities' (Hoggett *et al.*, 2006, p. 771).

Chapter 7 showed how social care practitioners are also under pressure from another quarter, from the disability rights and other user movements. However, here at least there is a potential for fruitful alliances around strategies for user empowerment and the social model. An emphasis on user empowerment would involve a radical reframing of the practitioner role, to move away from the bureaucratic processing of service users and towards the development of skills for facilitating change with service users and their communities. Similarly, incorporating the social model into social 'care' or 'assistance' focuses attention on the way in which service users and both formal and informal care-givers are disadvantaged by negative attitudes towards impairment and illness and by a social organisation which continues to exclude people with illness or impairments from full social participation.

Concluding comments

This final chapter has focussed on policy changes and yet many would claim that the scope for change has become prescribed within very narrow limits because of the end of ideological debates about welfare. Both Labour and Conservative parties are united in their acceptance of the mixed economy of social care, their belief in the greater efficiency of the private sector and their assumption that the general public is reluctant to accept higher general taxation as the best route to fund service improvements.

Globalisation debates have tended to strengthen such perceptions from the belief that global capital and transnational corporations have placed considerable restrictions upon individual nation states. However, there is some recognition of how misleading this can be both at the level of overall welfare provision (Sykes *et al.*, 2001) and in terms of variations in approaches to community care taken by different European countries (see Chapter 8).

The work of Sennett reminds us to note how the public sector often follows the private sector in terms of organisational forum and culture and that the present international tendency is towards policy hyperactivity. There may be strong common themes (individual budgets, a mixed economy of welfare, etc.) in how many countries are tackling community care agendas but the specific policies available to such countries as the concrete expression of these themes are almost infinite. Rather than sterile debates about whether or not we are experiencing an end to ideology, we would make a plea for the next government to focus down on two agendas. First, it will need to resist the temptation to go down the road of endless policy change – the priority should rather be on reducing implementation deficit and the gap between rhetoric and reality on the ground. Second, there needs to be a clear settlement on how social care is to be funded including a clear response to the options offered by the Wanless Review (2006). The organisation of social care and the continuation of the health and social care divide should not be driven from a desire to contain social care costs especially when policy objectives increasingly bear no relationship to the monies available to deliver them. As argued by Glasby (2006), what is needed is a national debate about 'what should we receive free of charge from state and what should we expect to pay for?' (p. 196). After all, a fundamental principle argued for by the Griffiths Report (1988) (see Chapter 3) was that the objectives set for community care should reflect the resources available for achieving them. Griffiths also argued that the way forward for community care was not massive organisational change and that a real strength of what he was reviewing was how much of community care was delivered through local authorities which were accountable to their local populations. Perhaps it is time for all of us to re-read the Griffiths Report despite the fact that it is nearly 20 years old.

Guide to Further Reading

Chapter 1: Introducing Community Care

Readers wishing to keep abreast of key debates in community care will find that the academic journal *Health and Social Care in the Community* and the professional journal *Community Care* are important sources of information. The Wanless Review (2006) on *Securing Good Care for Older People* is a valuable source of information about need and service utilisation as is *Improving the Life Chances of Disabled People* (Prime Minister's Strategy Unit, 2005).

Chapter 2: From Institutions to Care in the Community: The History of Neglect

Some readers may wish to learn more about the general development of the British welfare state and Glennerster (2006) provides a useful introduction, while Miller (2004) provides a fascinating account of key changes in how we now produce welfare. More detailed service histories can be found in Means and Smith (1998b), Dale and Melling (2007) and Thomson (1998). Thane (2005a) edits a collection on the fascinating long history of old age from the Ancient Greeks to the 20th century.

Chapter 3: Implementing the Community Care Reforms

A rich and insightful account of how local authorities tackled the challenge of implementing the reforms is provided by Lewis and Glennerster (1996). For detailed reporting and analysis on progress since the reforms see, for example, Ware *et al.* (2003) on commissioning and older people's services and Cambridge *et al.* (2005) on care management in learning disability and mental health services.

Chapter 4: Community Care and the Modernisation Agenda

Annual reports by the Commission for Social Care Inspection on the state of social care (2005a; 2006b) give a comprehensive and detailed overview of social care after nearly a decade of modernisation under New Labour. Clarkson and Challis (2006) provide a helpful analysis of the difficulties involved in assessing performance by local authorities, whilst Munro (2004) reflects on the challenge of evaluating complex professional interventions. The weekly journal *Community Care* is an excellent source of information about new policy initiatives and a guide to what is happening on the ground. In the rapidly changing world of health and social care the Department of Health website (www.dh.gov.uk) and the websites of other social care bodies are invaluable resources.

Chapter 5: Health and Social Care: From Collaboration to Incorporation?

Key government modernisation policies towards health and social care are clearly laid out in the White Paper, *Our Health, Our Care, Our Say* (Department of Health, 2006a). The extent of the challenge of joint working and partnership working has been spelt out by Barrett *et al.* (2005) and Sullivan and Skelcher (2002) amongst others. Means and Smith (1998b) and Means *et al.* (2002) provide detailed histories of the shifting boundaries between health and social care for older people which was also a central concern of the Royal Commission on Long Term Care (Sutherland Report, 1999a). *Community Care* is an excellent source of articles by those exploring the implications of the White Paper.

Chapter 6: Housing and Community Care

A useful overview of housing policy is provided by Lund (2006), Peace *et al.* (2006) and Clough *et al.* (2004), who provide useful introductions to debates around the meaning of home. Foord and Simic (2005) give a detailed review of supported housing policies while *Improving the Life Chances of Disabled People* (Prime Minister's Strategy Unit, 2005) is an important source of information around housing and disability issues.

Chapter 7: Community Care: User Empowerment

Morris (2004) presents a helpful analysis of the limitations of the community care reforms from the perspective of the disability movement and the campaign for independent living. A fascinating picture of direct payments as experienced by users, personal assistants and practitioners is contained in the edited collection by Leece and Bornat (2006). For an insightful discussion of different approaches to empowerment, see Starkey (2003), whilst Carr (2004) and SCIE (2007) provide an overview of developments in user participation and examples of different models of participation in practice. Fine and Glendinning (2005) and Hughes *et al.* (2005) examine the shifting meanings of key concepts such as care and dependency.

Chapter 8: International Perspectives on Community Care

For a recent comparative social policy text that has specific chapters on health services and social care, see Hill (2006). An overview of social policy in the European Union is provided by Hantrais (2007). The issue of care in the human services in the 21st century, drawing on literature from the USA, Australia and the UK is thoughtfully addressed by Fine (2007). Examples of policy and practice in the field of learning disabilities in a range of countries can be found in Welshman and Walmsley (2006). A dated but still illuminating book offering a comparative perspective on community care for older people is Tester (1996).

Chapter 9: Community Care: New Directions and Old Challenges

The White Paper on Community Services *Our Health, Our Care, Our Say* (Department of Health, 2006a) and the Green Paper on social care (Department of Health, 2005a) are the most detailed outlines of government intentions for community care. Sennett (2006) provides a key critique of policy hyperactivity while Shakespeare (2006) calls for a more sophisticated disability model that is not based on a dichotomy between social and medical models. The Wanless Review (2006) sets out the main funding options for social care.

References

Abberley, P. (1991) 'The significance of the OPCS disability surveys', in M. Oliver (ed.), *Social Work, Disabled People and Disabling Environments* (London: Jessica Kingsley), pp. 156–76.

Abbott, P. and Sapsford, R. (1987) *Community Care for Mentally Handicapped Children* (Milton Keynes: Open University Press).

Abrahamson, P. (1991) 'Welfare for the elderly in Denmark: from institutionalisation to self-reliance', in A. Evers and I. Svetlik (eds), *New Welfare Mixes in Care for the Elderly, Vol. 2, Austria, Denmark, Finland, Israel, Netherlands* (Vienna: European Centre for Social Welfare Policy and Research), pp. 35–61.

Abrahamson, P. (1999a) 'The welfare modelling business', *Social Policy and Administration*, vol. 33, no. 4, pp. 394–415.

Abrahamson, P. (1999b) 'The Scandinavian model of welfare', in D. Bouget and B. Palier (eds), *Comparing Social Welfare Systems in Nordic Europe and France, vol. 4, France-Nordic Europe* (Paris: MIRE), pp. 31–60.

Abrams, P. (1977) 'Community care: some research problems and priorities', *Policy and Politics*, vol. 6, no. 2, pp. 125–51.

Ackers, L. and Dwyer, R. (2002) *Senior Citizenship? Retirement Migration and Welfare in the European Union* (Bristol: Policy Press).

Adams, S. (2006) *Small Things Matter: The Key Role of Handy Person Services* (Nottingham: Care & Repair).

Age Concern (2005) *Human Rights: Policy Position Paper* (London: Age Concern).

Alber, J. (1991) *The Impact of Public Policies on Older People in the Federal Republic of Germany*, Konstanz, Spring (submission to the EC Observatory on Older People).

Alzheimer's Society (2007) *Dementia UK* (London: Alzheimer's Society).

American Association of People with Disabilities (2005) *Statement of Solidarity on 15th Anniversary of Americans with Disabilities Act* (http://www.aapd-dc.org/News/adainthe/solidarityada.html accessed on 23 June 2006).

Andrews, G.J. and Phillips, D.R. (2000) 'Private residential care for older persons: local impacts of care in the community reforms in England and Wales', *Social Policy and Administration*, vol. 34, no. 2, pp. 206–22.

Andrews, G.J. and Phillips, D.R. (eds) (2005) *Ageing and Place: Perspectives, Policy, Practice* (Abingdon: Routledge).

Anttonen, A. and Sipilä, J. (1996) 'European social care services: is it possible to identify models?', *Journal of European Social Policy*, vol. 6, no. 2, pp. 87–100.

Appleby, J. and Coote, A. (2002) *Five-Year Health Check: A Review of Government Health Policy, 1997–2002* (London: King's Fund).

Appleton, N. (2002) *Planning for the Majority: The Needs and Aspirations of Older People in General Housing* (York: Joseph Rowntree Foundation).

Arber, S. and Ginn, J. (1991) *Gender and Later Life: A Sociological Analysis of Resources and Constraints* (London: Sage).

Arblaster, L., Conway, J., Foreman, A. and Hawtin, M. (1996) *Asking the Impossible? Inter-Agency Working to Address Housing, Health and Social Care Needs of People in Ordinary Housing* (Bristol: Policy Press).

Arksey, H. (2002) 'Rationed care: Assessing the support needs of informal carers in English social services authorities', *Journal of Social Policy*, vol. 31, no. 1, pp. 81–101.

Arts, W. and Gelissen, J. (2002) 'Three worlds of welfare capitalism or more? A state-of-the-art report', *Journal of European Social Policy*, vol. 12, no. 2, pp. 137–58.

Askham, J., Nelson, H., Tinker, A. and Hancock, B. (1999) *To Have and to Hold: The Bond between Older People and the Homes They Own* (York: York Publishing Services).

Association of Directors of Social Services (ADSS) Cymru (2005) *Social Work in Wales: A Profession to Value* (www.allwalesunit.gov.uk/garthwaitereport).

Association of Directors of Social Services (ADSS) (2005) *Pressures on Learning Disability Services* (London: ADSS).

Atkin, K. (1996) 'An opportunity for change: voluntary sector provision in a mixed economy of care', in W. Ahmad and K. Atkin (eds), *'Race' and Community Care* (Buckingham: Open University Press), pp. 144–60.

Atkinson, D. (1988) 'Residential care for children and adults with mental handicap', in I. Sinclair (ed.), *Residential Care: The Research Reviewed* (London: HMSO), pp. 125–56.

Audit Commission (1985) *Managing Social Services for the Elderly More Effectively* (London: HMSO).

Audit Commission (1986) *Making a Reality of Community Care* (London: HMSO).

Audit Commission (1992) *Community Care: Managing the Cascade of Change* (London: HMSO).

Audit Commission (1994) *Finding a Place: A Review of Mental Health Services for Adults* (London: HMSO).

Audit Commission (1996) *Balancing the Care Equation: Progress with Community Care* (London: HMSO).

Audit Commission (1997) *The Coming of Age: Improving Care Services for Older People* (London: HMSO).

Audit Commission (1998) *Home Alone: The Role of Housing in Community Care* (London: Audit Commission).

Audit Commission (2002) *Recruitment and Retention: A Public Service Workforce for the 21st Century* (London: Audit Commission).

Audit Commission (2003) *Human Rights: Improving Public Service Delivery* (London: Audit Commission).

Audit Commission (2004a) *Older People – Independence and Well-being, The Challenge for Public Services* (www.audit-commission-gov.uk/ older people, accessed 29 June 2006).

Audit Commission (2004b) *Supporting Frail Older People: Independence and Well-Being 3* (London: Audit Commission).

Audit Commission (2005a) *CPA – The Harder Test: Single Tier and County Councils' Framework for 2005* (London: Audit Commission).

Audit Commission (2005b) *Housing Market Renewal* (London: Audit Commission).

Audit Commission (2006) *CPA – The Harder Test Framework for 2006* (London: Audit Commission).

Aves, G. (1964) 'The relationship between home and other forms of care', in K. Slack (ed.), *Some Aspects of Residential Care of the Elderly* (London: National Council of Social Service), pp. 11–17.

Badlan, K. (2006) 'Young people living with cystic fibrosis: an insight into their subjective experience', *Health and Social Care in the Community*, vol. 14, no. 3, pp. 264–70.

Baldock, J. and Ely, P. (1996) 'Social care for elderly people in Europe: the central problem of home care', in B. Munday and P. Ely (eds), *Social Care in Europe* (Hemel Hempstead: Prentice-Hall), pp. 195–225.

Balloch, S. and McLean, J. (2000) 'Human resources in social care', in B. Hudson (ed.), *The Changing Role of Social Care* (London: Jessica Kingsley), pp. 85–102.

Balloch, S., Banks, L., Hill, M., Smith, N. and Szanto, C. (2004) *East Sussex Brighton and Hove Social Care Workforce Mapping Study* (Brighton University: Health and Social Policy Research Centre).

Barclay, P. (1982) *Social Workers: Their Role and Tasks* (London: Bedford Square Press).

Barnes, C. (1996) 'Theories of disability and the origins of the oppression of disabled people in western society', in L. Barton (ed.), *Disability and Society: Emerging Issues and Insights* (Harlow: Longman), pp. 43–60.

Barnes, C. (2002) 'Introduction: disability, policy and politics', *Policy and Politics*, vol. 30, no. 3, pp. 311–18.

Baron, S. and Haldane, J. (eds) (1992) *Community, Normality and Difference: Meeting Social Needs* (Aberdeen: Aberdeen University Press).

Barrett, G., Sellman, D. and Thomas, J. (2005) *Interprofessional Working in Health and Social Care: Professional Perspectives* (Basingstoke: Palgrave).

Bartlett, P. and Wright, D. (eds) (1999) *Outside the Walls of the Asylum: The History of Care in the Community, 1750–2000* (London: The Athlone Press).

Barton, P., Bryon, S., Glasby, J., Hewitt, G., Jagger, C., Kaambwa, B., Martin, G., Nancarrow, S., Parker, H., Parker, S., Regen, E. and Wilson, A. (2006) *A National Evaluation of the Costs and Outcomes of Intermediate Care for Older People*, Health Services Management Group (Birmingham: University of Birmingham) and Leicester Nuffield Research Unit (Leicester: University of Leicester).

Bauld, L., Chesterman, J., Davies, B., Judge, K. and Mangalore, R. (2000) *Caring for Older People: An Assessment of Community Care in the 1990s* (Aldershot: Ashgate).

Beattie, A., Daker-White, G., Gilliard, J. and Means, R. (2004) 'How can they tell? A qualitative study of the views of younger people about their dementia and dementia care services', *Health and Social Care in the Community*, vol. 12, no. 4, pp. 359–68.

Beattie, A., Daker-White, G., Gilliard, J. and Means, R. (2005) 'They don't quite fit the way we organise our services – results from a UK field study of marginalised groups and dementia care', *Disability and Society*, vol. 20, no. 1, pp. 67–80.

Bebbington, P., Feeney, S., Flannigan, C., Glover, G., Lewis, S. and Wing, J. (1994) 'Inner London collaborative audit of admissions in two health districts. II: Ethnicity and the use of the Mental Health Act', *British Journal of Psychiatry*, vol. 165, pp. 743–9.

Bell, D. and Bowes, A. (2006) *Financial Care Models in Scotland and the UK* (York: Joseph Rowntree Foundation).

Bengtsson, S. (2000) 'A truly European type of disability struggle: disability policy in Denmark and the EU in the nineties', *European Journal of Social Security*, vol. 2, no. 4, pp. 363–77.

Beresford, P., Harrison, C. and Wilson, A. (2002) 'Mental health service users and disability: implications for future strategies', *Policy and Politics*, vol. 30, no. 3, pp. 387–96.

Bernard, M., Bartram, B., Biggs, S. and Simms, J. (2004) *New Lifestyles in Old Age: Health, Identity and Well-Being in Berryhill Retirement Village* (Bristol: Policy Press).

Better Regulation Task Force (2004) *Bridging the Gap – Participation in Social Care Regulation* (www.brtf.gov.uk).

Beveridge Report (1942) *Social Insurance and Allied Services* (London: HMSO).

Bhui, K. (ed.) (2002) *Racism and Mental Health* (London: Jessica Kingsley).

Bosanquet, N. (1978) *A Future for Old Age* (London: Temple Smith).

Bovell, V., Lewis, J. and Wookey, F. (1997) 'The implications for social services departments of the information task in the social care market', *Health and Social Care in the Community*, vol. 5, no. 2, pp. 94–105.

Bowl, R. (1986) 'Social work with old people', in C. Phillipson and A. Walker (eds), *Ageing and Social Policy* (Aldershot: Gower), pp. 128–45.

Boyne, G. (2000) 'External regulation and Best Value in local government', *Public Money and Management*, July–September, pp. 7–12.

Bradley, G. (2005) 'Movers and stayers in care management in adult services', *British Journal of Social Work*, vol. 35, pp. 511–30.

Bradley, G. and Manthorpe, J. (eds) (2000) *Working on the Fault Line* (Birmingham: Venture Press).

Braye, S. (2000) 'Participation and involvement in social care. An overview', in H. Kemshall and R. Littlechild (eds), *User Involvement and Participation in Social Care* (London: Jessica Kingsley), pp. 9–28.

Brenton, M. (2001) 'Older people's co-housing communities', in S. Peace and C. Holland (eds), *Inclusive Housing in an Ageing Society* (Bristol: Policy Press), pp. 169–88.

Brenton, M., Heywood, F. and Lloyd, L. (2002) *Housing and Older People: Changing the Viewpoint, Changing the Results* (London: London and Quadrant Housing Trust).

Brewerton, J. and Darton, D. (eds) (1997) *Designing Lifetime Homes* (York: Joseph Rowntree Foundation).

British Council of Disabled People (BCODP) (2005a) *British Council of Disabled People's Manifesto: The voice of disabled people still fighting for full rights* (http://www.bcodp.org.uk, accessed 12 April 2007).

British Council of Disabled People (BCODP) (2005b) *Improving the Life Chances of Disabled People; a response from the British Council of Disabled People* (http://ww.bcodp.org.uk, accessed 25 November 2005).

British Medical Association (1992) *Priorities for Community Care* (London: British Medical Association).

Brody, S. (2005a) 'Housing providers struggle under impact of budget cuts', *Community Care*, 16–22 June, pp. 16–17.

Brody, S. (2005b) 'Anxiety among the plaudits for Supporting People upheaval', *Community Care*, 24–30 November, pp. 18–19.

Brody, S. (2006a) 'Mandatory checks plan "denies choice"', *Community Care*, 27 April–3 May, pp. 18–19.

Brody, S. (2006b) 'Cornish abuse findings expose "lack of understanding" of rights', *Community Care*, 6–12 July, p. 6.

Brown, D. (2002) 'New care standards body to be axed in favour of merged inspectorate', *Community Care*, 25 April–1 May, p. 16.

Bruen, W. (2005) 'Aged care in Australia: past, present and future', *Australian Journal on Ageing*, vol. 24, no. 3, September, pp. 130–3.

Burgner Report (1996) *The Regulation and Inspection of Social Services* (London: Department of Health).

Butler, F. (2005) *Improving Public Services; Using a Human Rights Approach* (London: IPPR).

Byrne, L. (2006) 'Speech at Local Government Conference', 8 March, (www.dh.gov.uk).

Cabinet Office (1999) *Modernising Government* (London: The Stationery Office).

Callaghan, D. (2006) 'Northern Ireland – super for some', *Community Care*, 26 October–1 November, pp. 30–1.

Cambridge, P. (1992) 'Case management in community services: organisational responses', *British Journal of Social Work*, vol. 22, no. 5, pp. 495–517.

Cambridge, P., Carpenter, J., Forrester-Jones, R., Tate, A., Knapp, M., Beecham, J. and Hallam, A. (2005) 'The state of care management in learning disability and mental health services 12 years in community care', *British Journal of Social Work*, vol. 35, pp. 1039–62.

Cambridge, P., Hayes, L. and Knapp, M. with Gould, E. and Fenyo, A. (1994) *Care in the Community: Five Years On* (Canterbury: Personal Social Services Research Unit, University of Kent).

Cameron, A., Harrison, L., Burton, P. and Marsh, A. (2001) *Crossing the Housing and Care Divide* (Bristol: Policy Press).

Cameron, A. and Lart, R. (2003) 'Factors promoting and obstacles hindering joint working: a systematic review of the research evidence', *Journal of Integrated Care*, vol. 11, no. 2, pp. 9–17.

Campbell, J. and Hasler, F. (2001) 'Real joined-up thinking – a systematic approach to the barriers of disablement', *Critical Social Policy*, vol. 21, no. 4, pp. 531–3.

Campbell, J. and Oliver, M. (1996) *Disability Politics: Understanding our Past, Changing our Future* (London: Routledge).

Care Services Improvement Partnership (CSIP) (2005) *Everybody's Business: Integrated Mental Health Services for Older Adults* (London: Department of Health).

Carlton, N., Heywood, F., Izuhara, M., Pannell, J., Fear, T. and Means, R. (2003) *The Harassment and Abuse of Older People in the Private Rented Sector* (Bristol: Policy Press).

Carr, S. (2004) *Has Service User Participation Made a Difference to Social Care Services?* SCIE Position Paper No. 3 (London: Social Care Institute for Excellence).

Cerny, P. (1992) *The Changing Architecture of Politics: Structure, Agency and the Future of the State* (London: Sage).

Cestari, L., Munroe, M., Evans, S., Smith, A. and Huxley, P. (2006) 'Fair Access to Care Services (FACS): implementation in the mental health context of the UK', *Health and Social Care in the Community*, vol. 14, no. 6, pp. 474–81.

Challis, D. (1993) 'Care management: observations from a programme of research', *PSSRU Bulletin 9* (Canterbury: University of Kent).

Challis, D., Chessum, R., Chesterman, J., Luckett, R. and Wood, R. (1988) 'Community care for the frail elderly: an urban experiment', *British Journal of Social Work*, vol. 18 (supplement), pp. 13–42.

Challis, D., Clarkson, P., Williamson, J., Hughes, J., Venables, D., Burns, A. and Weinberg, A. (2004) 'The value of specialist clinical assessment of older people prior to entry to care homes', *Age and Ageing*, vol. 33, no. 1, pp. 25–34.

Challis, D., Weiner, K., Darton, R., Hughes, J. and Stewart, K. (2001) 'Emerging patterns of care management: arrangements for older people in England', *Social Policy and Administration*, vol. 35, no. 6, pp. 672–87.

Challis, L. (1990) *Organising Public Services* (London: Longman).

Christianson, J. (1988) 'The effects of channelling on informal care', *HRS: Health Services Research*, vol. 23, no. 1, April, pp. 99–117.

Clapham, D. (2005) *The Meaning of Home: A Pathways Approach* (Bristol: Policy Press).

Clare, L. and Cox, S. (2003) 'Improving service approaches and outcomes for people with complex needs through consultation and involvement', *Disability and Society*, vol. 18, no. 7, pp. 935–53.

Clark, H., Dyer, S. and Horwood, J. (1998) *'That Bit of Help': The High Value of Low Level Preventative Services for Older People* (Bristol: Policy Press/Joseph Rowntree Foundation).

Clark, H., Gough, H. and Macfarlane, A. (2004) *It Pays Dividends: Direct Payments and Older People* (Bristol: Joseph Rowntree Foundation/Policy Press).

Clark, R. (1991) *Home and Community-based Care in the USA* (Washington, DC: Office of the Assistant Secretary for Planning and Education, US Department of Health and Human Services).

Clark, T. (2002) 'New Labour's big idea: joined-up government', *Social Policy and Society*, vol. 1, no. 2, pp. 107–17.

Clarke, J. (2005) 'New Labour's citizens: activated, empowered, responsibilised, abandoned?', *Critical Social Policy*, vol. 25, no. 4, pp. 447–63.

Clarke, J. and Glendinning, C. (2002) 'Partnership and the remaking of welfare governance', in C. Glendinning, M. Powell and K. Rummery (eds), *Partnerships, New Labour and the Governance of Welfare* (Bristol: Policy Press), pp. 33–50.

Clarke, J. and Newman, J. (1997) *The Managerial State* (London: Sage).

Clarke, J. and Piven, F.F. (2001) 'United States: an American welfare state' in P. Alcock and G. Craig (eds), *International Social Policy* (Basingstoke: Palgrave), pp. 26–44.

Clarkson, P. and Challis, D. (2006) 'Performance measurement in social care: a comparison of efficiency measurement methods', *Social Policy and Society*, vol. 5, no. 4, pp. 461–77.

Clarkson, P., Hughes, J. and Challis, D. (2005) 'The potential impact of changes in public funding for residential and nursing home care in the United Kingdom: The Residential Allowance', *Ageing and Society*, vol. 25, part 2, pp. 159–80.

Clough, R. (1990) *Practice, Politics and Power in Social Services Departments* (Aldershot: Avebury).

Clough, R., Leamy, M., Miller, V. and Bright, L. (2004) *Housing Decisions in Later Life* (Basingstoke: Palgrave).

Cobbold, C. (1997) *A Cost Benefit Analysis of Lifetime Homes* (York: Joseph Rowntree Foundation).

Cole, T. and Edwards, C. (2005) 'The 19th Century', in P. Thane (ed.), *The Long History of Old Age* (London: Thames & Hudson), pp. 211–62.

Commission for Social Care Inspection (2004) *CSCI Role and Responsibilities* (London: CSCI).

Commission for Social Care Inspection (2005a) *The State of Social Care in England 2004–05* (London: CSCI).

Commission for Social Care Inspection (2005b) *Leaving Hospital – Revisited: A Follow-up Study of a Group of Older People who were Discharged from Hospital in March 2004* (London: CSCI).

Commission for Social Care Inspection (2006a) *Performance Ratings for Adults' Social Services in England* (London: CSCI).

Commission for Social Care Inspection (2006b) *The State of Social Care in England 2005–06* (London: CSCI).

Commission for Social Care Inspection (2006c) *A New Outcomes Framework for Performance Assessment of Adult Social Care 2006–07 Consultation Document* (London: CSCI).

Commission for Social Care Inspection (2006d) *Time to Care? An Overview of Home Care Services for Older People in England* (London: CSCI).

Commission for Social Care Inspection (2006e) *Inspection of Social Care Services for Older People (Northumberland County Council)* (London: CSCI).

Commission for Social Care Inspection (2007) *Adult Performance Indicators for 2006–07 (Version 3)* (www.csci.org.uk/docs/adult_PIs_2006-07.doc).

Community Care (2005) 'Will prevention be a cure-all?', *Community Care*, 9–15 June, pp. 32–4.

Community Care (2006a) 'Services to be axed or rationed as adult social care funding is cut back', *Community Care*, 9–15 March, p. 6.

Community Care (2006b) 'Focus on Scotland', *Community Care*, 26 October–1 November, pp. 45–9.

Community Care (2007) 'Care partnership may split in two', *Community Care*, 22–28 February, p. 6.

Craig, G. and Manthorpe, J. (1996) *Wiped off the Map – Local Government Reorganisation and Community Care*, Papers in Social Research No. 5 (Hull: University of Lincolnshire and Humberside).

Crane, M. (1999) *Understanding Older Homeless People* (Buckingham: Open University Press).

Crinson, I. (2005) 'The direction of health policy in New Labour's third term', *Critical Social Policy*, vol. 25, no. 4, pp. 507–16.

Croucher, K., Hicks, L. and Jackson, K. (2006) *Housing with Care for Later Life: A Literature Review* (York: Joseph Rowntree Foundation).

Crowther, M. (1981) *The Workhouse System, 1834–1929: The History of an English Social Institution* (London: Methuen).

Cutler, T. and Waine, B. (2003) 'Advancing public accountability? The social services "star" ratings', *Public Money and Management*, vol. 23, no. 2, pp. 125–8.

Dale, P. (2007) 'Tensions in the voluntary-statutory alliance: lay professionals and the planning and delivery of mental deficiency services, 1917–45', in P. Dale and J. Melling (eds), *Mental Illness and Learning Disability since 1850: Finding a Place for Mental Disorder in the United Kingdom* (London: Routledge), pp. 154–78.

Dale, P. and Melling, J. (eds) (2007) *Mental Illness and Learning Disability since 1850: Finding a Place for Mental Disorder in the United Kingdom* (London: Routledge).

Dalley, G. (1996) *Ideologies of Caring: Rethinking Community and Collectivism* (Basingstoke: Macmillan).

Daly, M. (2002) 'Care as a good for social policy', *Journal of Social Policy*, vol. 31, part 2, April, pp. 251–70.

Davies, B. (1986) 'American lessons for British policy and research on long-term care of the elderly', *Quarterly Journal of Social Affairs*, vol. 2, pp. 321–55.

Davies, B. (1992) 'On breeding the best chameleons', *Generations Review*, vol. 2, no. 2, pp. 18–21.

Davies, B. and Challis, D. (1986) *Matching Needs to Resources in Community Care* (Aldershot: Gower).

Davies, S., Thornicroft, G., Leese, M. *et al.* (1996) 'Ethnic differences in risk of compulsory psychiatric admission among representative cases of psychosis in London', *British Medical Journal*, vol. 312, no. 7030, pp. 533–7.

Davies Report (1995) *Report of the Inquiry into the Circumstances Leading to the Death of Jonathan Newby (A Volunteer Worker) on 9th October 1993* (Oxford: Oxfordshire Health Authority).

Deakin, N. (1995) 'The perils of partnership: the voluntary sector and the state, 1945–1992', in J. Davis Smith, C. Rochester and R. Hedley (eds), *An Introduction to the Voluntary Sector* (London: Routledge), pp. 40–65.

Degener, T. (2005) 'Disability discrimination law: a global comparative approach', in A. Lawson and C. Gooding (eds), *Disability Rights in Europe: From Theory to Practice* (Oxford: Hart Publishing), pp. 87–106.

Department for Work and Pensions (2002) *Building Choice and Responsibility: A Radical Agenda for Housing Benefit* (London: Department for Work and Pensions).

Department for Work and Pensions (2005) *Incapacity Benefit Reforms – Pathways to Work Pilots Performance and Analysis* (London: Department for Work and Pensions).

Department for Work and Pensions (2006a) *A New Deal for Welfare: Empowering People to Work* (London: Department for Work and Pensions).

Department for Work and Pensions (2006b) *Improving Work Opportunities for People with a Learning Disability* (London: Department for Work and Pensions).

Department of Communities and Local Government (2006) *Strong and Prosperous Communities: The Local Government White Paper* (London: The Stationery Office).

Department of Health (1989a) *Caring for People: Community Care in the Next Decade and Beyond* (London: HMSO).

Department of Health (1989b) *Working for Patients* (London: HMSO).

Department of Health (1990) *Community Care in the Next Decade and Beyond: Policy Guidance* (London: HMSO).

Department of Health (1994) *Implementing Caring for People: Housing and Homelessness* (London: Department of Health).

Department of Health (1995a) *NHS Responsibilities for Meeting Continuing Health Care Needs* (London: Department of Health).

Department of Health (1995b) *Building Bridges: A Guide to Arrangements for Inter-Agency Working for the Care and Protection of Severely Disabled People* (London: Department of Health).

Department of Health (1995c) *An Introduction to Joint Commissioning* (London: Department of Health).

Department of Health (1995d) *Practical Guidance on Joint Commissioning* (London: Department of Health).

Department of Health (1995e) *Moving Forward: A Consultation Document on the Regulation and Inspection of Social Services* (London: Department of Health).

Department of Health (1997) *The New NHS: Modern, Dependable* (London: The Stationery Office).

Department of Health (1998a) *Modernising Social Services: Promoting Independence, Improving Protection, Raising Standards* (London: The Stationery Office).

Department of Health (1998b) *Modernising Mental Health Services: Safe, Sound and Supportive* (London: Department of Health).

Department of Health (1999a) *Saving Lives: Our Healthier Nation* (London: The Stationery Office).

Department of Health (1999b) *A National Service Framework for Mental Health* (London: The Stationery Office).

Department of Health (1999c) *Fit for the Future? National Required Standards for Residential and Nursing Homes for Older People – Consultation Document* (London: Department of Health).

Department of Health (1999d) *Caring about Carers: A National Strategy for Carers* (London: Department of Health).

Department of Health (1999e) *Better Care, Higher Standards: A Charter for Long Term Care* (London: Department of Health).

Department of Health (2000a) *A Quality Strategy for Social Care* (London: Department of Health).

Department of Health (2000b) *A Quality Strategy for Social Care: Executive Summary* (London: Department of Health).

Department of Health (2000c) *Shaping the Future NHS: Long Term Planning for Hospitals and Related Services: Consultation Document on the Findings of the National Beds Inquiry* (London: The Stationery Office).

Department of Health (2000d) *The NHS Plan: A Plan for Investment, A Plan for Reform* (London: The Stationery Office).

Department of Health (2000e) *Managing Dangerous People with Severe and Dangerous Personality Disorder* (London: The Stationery Office).

Department of Health (2000f) *No Secrets: Guidance on Developing and Implementing Multi-agency Policies and Procedures to Protect Vulnerable Adults from Abuse* (London: Department of Health).

Department of Health (2001a) *Valuing People: A New Strategy for Learning Disability for the 21st Century* (London: The Stationery Office).

Department of Health (2001b) *Fit for the Future? National Required Standards for Residential and Nursing Homes for Older People – Summary of Responses* (London: Department of Health).

Department of Health (2001c) *Care Homes for Older People: National Minimum Standards* (London: The Stationery Office).

Department of Health (2001d) *Nothing About Us Without Us: The Report from the Service Users Advisory Group* (London: Department of Health).

Department of Health (2001e) *Family Matters: Counting Families In* (London: Department of Health).

Department of Health (2001f) *Learning Difficulties and Ethnicity* (London: Department of Health).

Department of Health (2001g) *National Service Framework for Older People* (London: The Stationery Office).

Department of Health (2001h) *Shifting the Balance of Power within the NHS: Securing Delivery* (London: Department of Health).

Department of Health (2001j) *Building Capacity and Partnership in Care* (London: Department of Health).

Department of Health (2002) *National Minimum Standards for Care Homes for Older People/National Minimum Standards for Care Homes for Younger Adults (18–65): Proposed Amended Environmental Standards* (London: Department of Health).

Department of Health (2003a) *Fair Access to Care Services: Guidance on Eligibility Criteria for Adult Social Care (revised)* (London: Department of Health).

Department of Health (2003b) *Domiciliary Care: National Minimum Standards* (London: Department of Health).

Department of Health (2004) *The NHS Improvement Plan: Putting People at the Heart of Public Services* (London: Department of Health).

Department of Health (2005a) *Independence, Well-being and Choice; Our Vision for the Future of Social Care for Adults in England* (London: The Stationery Office).

Department of Health (2005b) *The National Service Framework for Long-Term Conditions* (London: Department of Health).

Department of Health (2005c) *Supporting People with Long-Term Conditions: An NHS and Social Care Model to Support Local Innovation and Interpretation* (London: Department of Health).

Department of Health (2005d) *Gershon Efficiency Programme 2004–2008: Efficiency Technical Note* (London: Department of Health).

Department of Health (2005e) *The Government's Annual Report on Learning Disability 2005* (London: The Stationery Office).

Department of Health (2006a) *Our Health, Our Care, Our Say: A New Direction for Community Services* (London: The Stationery Office).

Department of Health (2006b) *The NHS in England: The Operating Framework for 2006/07* (London: Department of Health).

Department of Health (2006c) *Best Practice Guidance on the Role of the Director of Adult Social Services* (London: Department of Health).

Department of Health (2006d) *Our Health, Our Care, Our Say: Making it Happen* (London: Department of Health).

Department of Health (2007) *Commissioning Framework for Health and Well-being* (London: Department of Health).

Department of Health (website) www.dh.gov.uk/en/Policyandguidance/Healthandsocialcaretopics/Socialcare/Vulnerableadults/DH_4118919

Department of Health and Ageing (DoHA) (2004) *A New Strategy for Community Care: The Way Forward* (Canberra: Commonwealth of Australia).

Department of Health and Social Security (1971) *Better Services for the Mentally Handicapped* (London: HMSO).

Department of Health and Social Security (1975) *Better Services for the Mentally Ill* (London: HMSO).

Department of Health and Social Security (1977) *Priorities in the Health and Social Services: The Way Forward* (London: HMSO).

Department of Health and Social Security (1978a) *A Happier Old Age* (London: HMSO).

Department of Health and Social Security (1978b) *Collaboration in Community Care: A Discussion Document* (London: HMSO).

Department of Health and Social Security (1981) *Growing Older* (London: HMSO).

Department of Health/Department for Education and Skills (2006) *Options for Excellence: Building the Social Care Workforce of the Future* (London: Department of Health).

Department of Health/Department of the Environment (1997) *Housing and Community Care: Establishing a Strategic Framework* (London: Department of Health).

Department of Health/Department of the Environment, Transport and the Regions (DoH/DETR) (1999) *Health Act 1999 – Modern Partnerships for the People,* Letter to health and social care agencies, 8 September (London: DoH/DETR).

Department of Health/Social Services Inspectorate (1991a) *Care Management and Assessment: Practitioners' Guide* (London: HMSO).

Department of Health/Social Services Inspectorate (1991b) *Care Management and Assessment: Managers' Guide* (London: HMSO).

Department of Health/Social Services Inspectorate (1991c) *Care Management and Assessment: Summary of Practice Guidance* (London: HMSO).

Department of Health/Social Services Inspectorate (1995) *Social Services Departments and the Care Programme Approach: An Inspection* (London: Department of Health).

Department of Health/Social Services Inspectorate (1998) *'They Look After Their Own, Don't They?' Inspection of Community Care Services for Black and Ethnic Minority Older People* (London: Department of Health).

Department of Health/Social Services Inspectorate (1999) *Still Building Bridges* (London: The Stationery Office).

Department of Health/Social Services Inspectorate (2000) *A Modern Social Service: 9th Annual Report of the Chief Inspector of Social Services* (London: Department of Health).

Department of the Environment, Transport and the Regions (1998) *Modernising Local Government: Improving Local Services through Best Value* (London: DETR).

Department of the Environment, Transport and the Regions (with Department of Health) (2001) *Quality and Choice for Older People's Housing: A Strategic Framework* (London: DETR).

Department of the Environment, Transport and the Regions (2001) *Private Sector Renewal: A Consultation Paper* (London: DETR).

Department of Transport, Local Government and the Regions (2001a) *Strong Local Leadership: Quality Public Services* (London: The Stationery Office).

Department of Transport, Local Government and the Regions (2001b) *Supporting People: Policy into Practice* (London: DTLR).

Deputy Prime Minister (1998) *Modern Local Government: In Touch with the People* (London: The Stationery Office).

De Wolfe, P. (2002) 'Private tragedy in social context? Reflections on disability, illness and suffering', *Disability and Society,* vol. 17, no. 3, pp. 255–67.

Digby, A. (1978) *Pauper Palaces* (London: Routledge & Kegan Paul).

Disability Rights Commission (2002) *Policy Statement on Social Care and Independent Living* (London: Disability Rights Commission).

Disability Rights Commission (2005) *Disability Rights Commission: 5 Years of Progress* (London: Disability Rights Commission).

Dolowitz, D. and Marsh, D. (1996) 'Who learns what from whom? A review of the policy transfer literature', *Political Studies*, vol. 44, pp. 345–57.

Douglas, A. (1998) 'Motherhood and apple pie', *Community Care*, 3–9 December, p. 12.

Dowling, B., Powell, M. and Glendinning, C. (2004) 'Conceptualising successful partnerships', *Health and Social Care in the Community*, vol. 12, no. 4, pp. 309–17.

Drake, R. (1996) 'A critique of the role of the traditional charities', in L. Barton (ed.), *Disability and Society: Emerging Issues and Insights* (Harlow: Longman), pp. 147–66.

Drake, R. (1999) *Understanding Disability Policies* (Basingstoke: Macmillan).

Drakeford, M. (2006) 'Ownership, regulation and the public interest: the case of residential care for older people', *Critical Social Policy*, vol. 26, no. 4, pp. 932–44.

Drewett, A. (1999) 'Social rights and disability: the language of "rights" in community care policies', *Disability and Society*, vol. 14, no. 1, pp. 115–28.

Duffy, S. (2006) 'The implications of individual budgets', *Journal of Integrated Care*, vol. 14, no.2, pp. 3–10.

Dwyer, S. (2005) 'Older people and permanent care; whose decision?', *British Journal of Social Work*, vol. 35, pp. 1081–92.

Easterbrook, L. (2002) *Healthy Homes, Healthier Lives* (Nottingham: Care & Repair).

Eggert, G. and Williams, T. (1982) *Direct Assessment versus Brokerage: A Comparison of Care Management Models* (Rochester, NY: Monroe County Long-term Care Program Inc).

Ellis, K. (2005) 'Disability rights in practice: the relationship between human rights and social rights in contemporary social care', *Disability and Society*, vol. 20, no. 7, pp. 691–704.

Emerson, E. and Hatton, C. (1996) *Moving Out: The Impact of Relocation from Hospital to Community on the Quality of Life of People with Learning Disabilities* (London: HMSO).

Estes, C.L. (1979) The *Aging Enterprise* (San Francisco, CA: Jossey-Bass).

Estes, C., Biggs, S. and Phillipson, C. (2003) *Social Theory, Social Policy and Ageing* (Maidenhead: McGraw Hill/Open University Press).

Estes, C.L. and Binney, E.A. (1989) 'The biomedicalisation of aging: dangers and dilemmas', *The Gerontologist*, vol. 29, no. 5, pp. 587–96.

Eurobarometer Survey (1993) *Age and Attitudes: Main Results from a Eurobarometer Survey* (Brussels: Commission of the European Communities, Directorate-General V, Employment, Industrial Relations and Social Affairs).

European Commission (1996) *Equality of Opportunity for People with Disabilities: A New European Community Disability Strategy* (Luxembourg: Office for Official Publications of the European Communities).

European Commission (2006) *Social Exclusion in Europe 2006* (Luxembourg: Office for Official Publications of the European Communities).

Eurostat (2000) *The Social Situation in the European Union* (Luxembourg: Office for Official Publications of the European Communities).

Evans, M. and Davies, J. (1999) 'Understanding policy transfer: a multi-level, multi-disciplinary perspective', *Public Administration*, vol. 77, no. 2, pp. 361–85.

Evans, S. and Means, R. (2007) *Balanced Retirement Communities? A Case Study of Westbury Fields* (Bristol: St Monica Trust).

Evers, A. and Olk, T. (1991) 'The mix of care provisions for the frail elderly in the Federal Republic of Germany', in A. Evers and I. Svetlik (eds), *New Welfare Mixes in Care for the Elderly, Vol. 3, Canada, France, Germany, Italy, United Kingdom* (Vienna: European Centre for Social Welfare Policy and Research), pp. 59–100.

Evers, A. and Sachsse, C. (2003) 'The pattern of social services in Germany: the care of children and older people', in A. Anttonen, J. Baldock and J. Sipilä (eds), *The Young, the Old and the State: Social Care Systems in Five Industrial Nations* (Cheltenham: Edward Elgar), pp. 55–79.

Eyden, J. (1965) 'The physically handicapped', in D. Marsh (ed.), *An Introduction to the Study of Social Administration* (London: Routledge & Kegan Paul), pp. 161–74.

Finch, J. and Groves, D. (eds) (1983) *A Labour of Love: Women, Work and Caring* (London: Routledge & Kegan Paul).

Fine, M. (1995) 'Community based services and the fragmentation of provision', *Australian Journal of Social Issues*, vol. 30, no. 2, pp. 143–61.

Fine, M. (1998) 'Acute and continuing care for older people in Australia: contesting new balances of care', in C. Glendinning (ed.), *Rights and Realities: Comparing New Developments in Long-Term Care for Older People* (Bristol: Policy Press), pp. 105–26.

Fine, M. (1999) 'Coordinating health, extended care and community support services: reforming aged care in Australia', *Journal of Aging and Social Policy*, vol. 11, no. 1, pp. 67–90.

Fine, M. (2001) 'Aged care, ethics and public policy', *Contemporary Nurse*, vol. 11, nos. 2/3, December, pp. 109–14.

Fine, M. (2006) *Contesting Prospects: Aged Care for a Longevity Society* (unpublished paper), January.

Fine, M. (2007) *A Caring Society? Care and the Dilemmas of Human Service in the 21st Century* (Basingstoke: Palgrave).

Fine, M. and Chalmers, J. (2000) ' "User pays" and other approaches to the funding of long-term care for older people in Australia', *Ageing and Society*, vol. 20, part 1, January, pp.5–32.

Fine, M. and Glendinning, C. (2005) 'Dependence, independence or inter-dependence? Revisiting the concepts of "care" and "dependency" ', *Ageing and Society*, vol. 25, no. 4, pp. 601–21.

Finkelstein, V.G. (1993) 'Disability: a social challenge or an administrative responsibility?', in J. Swain, V. Finkelstein, S. French and M. Oliver (eds), *Disabling Barriers – Enabling Environments* (London: Sage), pp. 34–43.

Fisher, M. (1990–91) 'Defining the practice content of care management', *Social Work and Social Services Review*, vol. 24, no. 6, pp. 659–80.

Fisher, M. (1994) 'Man-made care: community care and older male carers', *British Journal of Social Work*, vol. 24, no. 6, pp. 659–80.

Fiske, A. and Jones, R. (2005) 'Depression', in M. Johnson (ed.), *The Cambridge Handbook of Age and Ageing* (Cambridge: Cambridge University Press), pp. 245–51.

Foord, M. (2005) 'Introduction: supported housing and community care: towards a new landscape of precariousness', in M. Foord and P. Simic (eds), *Housing, Community Care and Supported Housing – Resolving Contradictions* (Coventry: Chartered Institute of Housing), pp. 2–19.

Foord, M. and Simic, P. (2001) 'A sustainable approach to planning housing and social care: if not now, when?', *Health and Social Care in the Community*, vol. 9, no. 3, pp. 168–76.

Foord, M. and Simic, P. (eds) (2005) *Housing, Community Care and Supported Housing: Resolving Contradictions* (Coventry: Chartered Institute of Housing).

Forder, J. (2007) 'The pressure's on', *Community Care*, 8–14 February, pp. 30–1.

Forrest, R., Kennett, P. and Leather, P. (1994) *Home Owners with Negative Equity* (Bristol: SAUS Publications).

Foster, M., Harris, J., Jackson, K., Morgan, H. and Glendinning, C. (2006) 'Personalised social care for adults with disabilities: a problematic concept for frontline practice', *Health and Social Care in the Community*, vol. 14, no. 2, pp. 125–35.

Foucault, M. (1967) *Madness and Civilisation* (London: Tavistock).

Foucault, M. (1979) *Discipline and Punish: The Birth of the Prison* (Harmondsworth: Penguin).

Francis, J. and Netten, A. (2004) 'Raising the quality of home care: A study of service users' views', *Social Policy and Administration*, vol. 38, no. 3, pp. 290–305.

Frankfather, D. and Caro, F. (1981) *The Aggregate Costs of Home Care: Regulating Demand and Controlling the Costs of Production* (Community Service Society, NY: Institute for Social Welfare Research).

Frazer, R. and Glick, G. (2000) *Out of Services: A Survey of Social Services Provision for Elderly and Disabled People in England* (London: Needs Must).

Friend, J., Power, J. and Yewlett, C. (1974) *Public Planning: The Intercorporate Dimension* (London: Tavistock).

Fyson, R. and Ward, L. (2004) *Making Valuing People Work: Strategies for Change in Services for People with Learning Disabilities* (Bristol: Policy Press).

Gates, B. (2001) 'Valuing People: long awaited strategy for people with learning disabilities for the twenty-first century in England', *Journal of Learning Disabilities*, vol. 5, no. 3, pp. 203–7.

Gelling, J. (2006) 'Being a guinea pig for direct payments', in J. Leece and J. Bornat (eds) *Developments in Direct Payments* (Bristol: Policy Press), pp. 128–30.

Gershon, P. (2004) *Releasing Resources for the Frontline: Independent Review of Public Sector Efficiency* (London: HM Treasury).

Giarchi, G. (1996) *Caring for Older Europeans: Comparative Studies in 29 Countries* (Aldershot: Arena).

Gibbons, J. (1988) 'Residential care for mentally ill adults', in I. Sinclair (ed.), *Residential Care: The Research Reviewed* (London: HMSO), pp. 157–97.

Gilleard, C. and Higgs, P. (2000) *Cultures of Ageing: Self Citizen and the Body* (Harlow: Prentice-Hall).

Gilleard, C. and Higgs, P. (2005) *Contexts of Ageing: Class, Cohort and Community* (Cambridge: Polity Press).

Gillen, S. (2006) 'Inquiry into staff roles in England to mirror Scottish and Welsh reviews', *Community Care*, 26 October–1 November, p. 8.

Gilliard, J., Means, R., Beattie, A. and Daker-White, G. (2005) 'Dementia care in England and the social model of disability', *Dementia*, vol. 4, no. 4, pp. 571–86.

Gladstone, D. (1996) 'The changing dynamic of institutional care', in D. Wright and A. Digby (eds), *From Idiocy to Mental Deficiency* (London: Routledge), pp. 134–61.

Glasby, J. (2004) 'Discharge responsibilities? Delayed hospital discharges and the health and social care divide', *Journal of Social Policy*, vol. 33, no. 4, pp. 593–604.

Glasby, J. (2005) 'The future of adult social care: lessons from previous reforms', *Research, Policy and Planning*, vol. 23, no. 2, pp. 61–70.

Glasby, J. (2006) 'Bringing down the Berlin Wall: partnership working and the health and social care divide', *Health and Social Care in the Community*, vol. 14, no. 3, pp. 195–6.

Glasby, J. and Littlechild, R. (2004) *The Health and Social Care Divide: the Experiences of Older People* (Bristol: Policy Press).

Glendinning, C. (2002a) 'A charge too far', *Community Care*, 11–17 July, pp. 34–5.

Glendinning, C. (2002b) 'European policies on home care services compared', in B. Bytheway, V. Bacigalupo, J. Bornat, J. Johnson and S. Spurr (eds), *Understanding Care, Welfare and Community: A Reader* (London: Routledge), pp. 292–312.

Glendinning, C. (2003) *Support for Carers of Older People – Some Intranational and International Comparisons* (http://www.audit-commission.gov.uk/olderpeople/olderpeopleliterature.asp, accessed 29 June 2006).

Glendinning, C., Davies, B., Pickard, L. and Comas-Herrera, A. (2004) *Funding Long Term Care for Older People: Lessons from Other Countries* (York: Joseph Rowntree Foundation).

Glendinning, C., Hudson, B. and Means, R. (2005) 'Under Strain?: Exploring the troubled relationship between health and social care', *Public Money and Management*, vol. 25, no. 4, pp. 245–52.

Glendinning, C. and Means, R. (2002) 'Rearranging the deckchairs on the Titanic of long-term care? Integrating health and social services for older people in England', paper presented at the Social Policy Association conference, University of Teesside, 17–19 July.

Glendinning, C. and Means, R. (2006) 'Personal Social Services: developments in adult social care', in L. Bauld, K. Clarke and T. Maltby (eds), *Social Policy Review 18: Analysis and Debate in Social Policy 2006* (Bristol: Policy Press), pp. 15–31.

Glennerster, H. (2006) *British Social Policy* (3rd edition) (Oxford: Blackwell).

Godfrey, M., Keen, J., Townsend, J., Moore, J., Ware, P., Hardy, B., West, R., Weatherly, H. and Henderson, K. (2005) *An Evaluation of Intermediate Care for Older People*, Institute of Health Sciences and Public Health Research (Leeds: University of Leeds).

Godfrey, M., Townsend, J. and Denby, T. (2004) *Building a Good Life for Older People in Local Communities* (York: Joseph Rowntree Foundation).

Godlove, C. and Mann, A. (1980) 'Thirty years of the welfare state; current issues in British social policy for the aged', *Aged Care and Services Review*, vol. 2, no. 1, pp. 1–12.

Godsell, M. (2002) 'The social context of service provision for people with learning disabilities: continuity and change in the professional task', unpublished PhD thesis, University of Bristol.

Goffman, E. (1968) *Asylums: Essays on the Social Situation of Mental Patients and Other Inmates* (Harmondsworth: Penguin).

Gooding, C. (1994) *Disabling Laws, Enabling Acts: Disability Rights in Britain and America* (London: Pluto Press).

Goodley, D. (2001) ' "Learning difficulties" ', the social model of disability and impairment: challenging epistemologies', *Disability and Society*, vol. 16, pp. 207–31.

Goodman, C. (1981) *Natural Helping Among Older Adults* (Long Beach, CA: Department of Social Work, California State University).

Goodwin, S. (1990) *Community Care and the Future of Mental Health Service Provision* (Aldershot: Avebury).

Gorman, H. (2000) 'Winning hearts and minds? – emotional labour and learning for care management work', *Journal of Social Work Practice*, vol. 14, no. 2, pp. 149–58.

Gravelle, H., Dusheiko, M., Sheaff, R., Sargent, P., Boaden, R., Pickard, S., Parker, S. and Roland, M. (2006) 'Impact of case management (Evercare) on frail elderly patients: controlled before and after analysis of quantitative outcome data', *British Medical Journal*, (BMJ, doi = 10.1136/bmj.39020.413310.55, published 15 November 2006).

Grieg, R. (2001) 'The real challenges in *Valuing People*', *Managing Community Care*, vol. 9, no. 3, pp. 3–6.

Griffiths, S. (1997a) 'Bringing the house down', *Community Care*, 29 May–4 June, pp. 22–3.

Griffiths, S. (1997b) *Housing Benefit and Supported Housing: The Implications of Recent Changes* (York: Joseph Rowntree Foundation).

Griffiths Report (1988) *Community Care: An Agenda for Action* (London: HMSO).

Haber, C. (1983) *Beyond Sixty-Five: The Dilemma of Old Age in America's Past* (Cambridge: Cambridge University Press).

Hadley, R. and Clough, R. (1996) *Care in Chaos: Frustration and Challenge in Community Care* (London: Cassell).

Handley. P. (2000) 'Trouble in paradise – a disabled person's right to the satisfaction of a self-defined need: some conceptual and practical problems', *Disability and Society*, vol. 16, no. 2, pp. 313–25.

Hantrais, L. (2007) *Social Policy in the European Union* (3rd edition) (Basingstoke: Palgrave).

Harding, T. (2005) 'Nothing less than equality and human rights', *Community Care*, 26 October, www.communitycare.co.uk

Harding T. and Gould, J. (2003) *Memorandum on Older People and Human Rights* (London: Help the Aged).

Hardy, B., Young, R. and Wistow, G. (1999) 'Dimensions of choice in the assessment and care management process: the views of older people, carers and care managers', *Health and Social Care in the Community*, vol. 7, no. 6, pp. 482–91.

Harper, S. (2006) *Ageing Societies* (London: Hodder Education).

Harris, A. (1961) *Meals on Wheels for Old People* (London: National Corporation for the Care of Old People).

Harrison, F. (1986) *The Young Disabled Adult: The Use of Residential Homes and Hospital Units for the Age Group 16–64* (London: Royal College of Physicians).

Harrison, S. and Smith, C. (2004) 'Trust and moral motivation; redundant resources in health and social care?', *Policy and Politics*, vol. 32, no. 3, pp. 371–86.

Hartrick, A. (2005) 'Bournewood Patients; the common law is not enough', *Community Care Legal Updates*, 7 February, www.communitycare.co.uk

Hayes, D. (2004) 'Ladyman promises less bureaucracy as incentive for quality care homes', *Community Care*, 4–10 November, p. 6.

Hayes, D., Taylor, A. and Callaghan, D. (2004) 'Special Report: ADSS Spring Seminar, 21–23 April, Torquay', *Community Care*, 29 April–5 May, pp. 10–11.

Health Advisory Service (1983) *The Rising Tide: Developing Services for Mental Illness in Old Age* (London: HMSO).

Healthcare Commission (2005) *Count Me In: The National Mental Health and Ethnicity Census* (London: Healthcare Commission).

Healthcare Commission (with the Audit Commission and the Commission for Social Care Inspection) (2006) *Living Well in Later Life: A Review of Progress Against the National Service Framework for Older People* (London: Healthcare Commission).

Healthcare Commission (2007) *Investigation into the Services for People with Learning Disabilities by Sutton and Merton Primary Care Trust* (London: Commission for Healthcare Audit and Inspection).

Heffernan, J. (2003) 'Care for children and older people in the United States: laggard or merely different?', in A. Anttonen., J. Baldock and J. Sipilä (eds), *The Young, The Old and the State: Social Care Systems in Five Industrial Nations* (Cheltenham: Edward Elgar), pp. 143–66.

Help the Aged (2002) *Nothing Personal: Rationing Social Care for Older People* (London: Help the Aged).

Hendey, N. and Pascall, G. (2002) *Disability and Transition to Adulthood: Achieving Independent Living* (Brighton: Pavilion).

Henwood, M. (1994) *Hospital Discharge Workbook: A Manual on Hospital Discharge* (London: Department of Health).

Henwood, M. (2001) *Future Imperfect? Report of the King's Fund Care and Support Inquiry* (London: King's Fund).

Henwood, M. (2006) 'Effective partnership working: a case study of hospital discharge', *Health and Social Care in the Community*, vol. 14, no. 5, pp. 400–7.

Henwood, M., Lewis, H. and Waddington, E. (1998) *Listening to Users of Domiciliary Care Services: Developing and Monitoring Quality Standards* (Leeds: Nuffield Institute for Health).

Heywood, F. (2001) *Money Well Spent: The Effectiveness and Value of Housing Adaptations* (Bristol: Policy Press).

Heywood, F., Gangoli, G., Langan, J., Marsh, A., Moyers, S., Smith, R. and Sutton, E., with Hodges, M. and Hamilton, J. (2005) *Reviewing the Disabled Facilities Grant Programme* (London: Office of the Deputy Prime Minister).

Heywood, F, Oldman, C. and Means, R. (2002) *Housing and Home in Later Life* (Buckingham: Open University Press).

Heywood, F., Pate, A., Means, R. and Galvin, J. (1999) *Housing Options for Older People (HOOP): A Developmental Project to*

Refine a Housing Option Appraisal Tool for Use by Older People (London: Elderly Accommodation Counsel).

Heywood, M. (2005) 'Clearer care criteria', *Community Care*, 24 February–2 March, pp. 36–7.

Higgins, J. (1989) 'Defining community care: realities and myths', *Social Policy and Administration*, vol. 23, no. 1, pp. 3–16.

Hill, M. (2000a) 'Organisation within local authorities', in M. Hill (ed.), *Local Authority Social Services: An Introduction* (Oxford: Blackwell), pp. 158–78.

Hill, M. (2000b) 'The central and local government framework', in M. Hill (ed.), *Local Authority Social Services: An Introduction* (Oxford: Blackwell), pp. 139–57.

Hill, M. (2006) *Social Policy in the Modern World: A Comparative Text* (Oxford: Blackwell Publishing).

Hills, J. (2007) *Ends and Means: The Future Roles of Social Housing in England*, ESRC Research Centre for Analysis of Social Exclusion (London: London School of Economics and Political Science).

Hirsch, D. (2005) *Facing the Costs of Long-Term Care: Towards a Sustainable Funding System* (York: Joseph Rowntree Foundation).

HM Government (2005) *Opportunity Age: Meeting the Challenges of Ageing in the 21st Century* (London: Department for Work and Pensions).

HM Treasury (2004) *2004 Spending Review: Stability, Security and Opportunity for All: Investing for Britain's Long-term Future, New Public Spending Plans 2005–2008* (London: HM Treasury).

Hodge, S. (2005) 'Participation, discourse and power: a case study in service user involvement', *Critical Social Policy*, vol. 25, no. 2, pp. 164–79.

Hofman, A., Rocca, W. and Brayne, C. (1991) 'The prevalence of dementia in Europe: a collaborative study of 1980–1990 findings', *International Journal of Epidemiology*, vol. 20, no. 3, pp. 736–8.

Hoggett, P. (2001) 'Agency, rationality and social policy', *Journal of Social Policy*, vol. 30, part 1, pp. 37–56.

Hoggett, P., Mayo, M. and Miller, C. (2006) 'Private passions, the public good and public service reform', *Social Policy and Administration*, vol. 40, no. 7, pp. 758–73.

Holden, C. (2002) 'British government policy and the concentration of ownership in long-term care provision', *Ageing and Society*, vol. 22, no. 1, pp. 79–94.

Holden, C. (2003) 'Globalisation and welfare: a meso-level analysis', in R. Sykes, C. Bochel and N. Ellison (eds), *Social Policy Review No. 14: Developments and Debates 2001–2002* (Bristol: Policy Press), pp. 107–22.

Holland, C. and Peace, S. (2001) 'Inclusive housing', in S. Peace and C. Holland (eds), *Inclusive Housing in an Ageing Society* (Bristol: Policy Press), pp. 235–60.

Hood, C., James, O. and Scott, C. (2000) 'Regulation of government: has it increased, is it increasing, should it be diminished?', *Public Administration*, vol. 78, no. 2, pp. 283–304.

House of Commons Health Select Committee (2004) *Elder Abuse, Second Report of Session 2003–4 Vol. 1* (London: The Stationery Office).

House of Lords Library (1995) *Community Care (Direct Payments) Bill: Library Notes* (London: House of Lords).

Hoyes, L., Lart, R., Means, R. and Taylor, M. (1994) *Community Care in Transition* (York: Joseph Rowntree Foundation/London: Community Care).

Hudson, B. (1987) 'Collaboration in social welfare: a framework for analysis', *Policy and Politics*, vol. 15, no. 3, pp. 175–82.

Hudson, B. (2002) 'Interprofessionality in health and social care: the Achilles' heel of partnership?', *Journal of Interprofessional Care*, vol. 16, no. 1, pp. 7–17.

Hudson, B. (2005) 'Sea change or quick fix? Policy on long-term conditions in England', *Health and Social Care in the Community*, vol. 13, no. 4, pp. 378–85.

Hughes, B., McKie, L., Hopkins, D. and Watson, N. (2005) 'Love's Labour's Lost? Feminism, the Disabled People's Movement and an Ethic of Care', *Sociology*, vol. 39, no. 2, pp. 259–75.

Hugman, R. (1994) 'Social work and case management in the UK: models of professionalism and elderly people', *Ageing and Society*, vol. 14, no. 2, pp. 237–53.

Hunt, M. (2001) *The Human Rights Act: What are the Implications for Older People?* (London: Help the Aged).

Hunter, M. (2005) 'Eyes shut to social care', *Community Care*, 10–16 February, pp. 24–5.

Hurst, R. (2005) 'Disabled Peoples' International: Europe and the social model of disability', in C. Barnes and G. Mercer (eds), *The Social Model of Disability: Europe and the Majority World* (Leeds: The Disability Press), pp. 65–79.

Hunter, M. (2007) 'Care homes: out of the public eye', *Community Care*, 2 August, pp. 16–17.

Huws Jones, R. (1952) 'Old people's welfare – successes and failures', *Social Services Quarterly*, vol. 26, no. 1, pp. 19–22.

Huxham, C. (ed.) (1996) *Creating Collaborative Advantage* (London: Sage).

Huxley, P., Evans, S., Gately, C. Webber, M., Mears, A., Pajak, S., Kendall, T., Medina, J. and Katona, C. (2005) 'Stress and pressures in mental health social work: the worker speaks', *British Journal of Social Work*, vol. 35, no. 7, pp. 1063–79.

IBSEN (2007) *Individual Budgets Evaluation: A Summary of Early Findings* (www.ibsen.org.uk).

In Control (2006) 'In Control NOW', Newsletter of In Control, vol. 1, no. 1, Nov/Dec (www.In-Control.org.uk).

Interdepartmental Review of Funding for Supported Accommodation (1998) *Supporting People: A New Policy and Funding Framework for Support Services* (London: Department of Social Security).

Jagger, C., Brayne, C., Comas-Herrara, A., Robinson, T., Lindesay, J. and Croft, P. (2006) *Compression or Expansion of Disability? Forecasting Future Disability Levels Under Changing Patterns of Disease: Final Report*, Leicester Nuffield Research Unit (Leicester: University of Leicester).

Jamieson, A. (1991) 'Community care for older people', in G. Room (ed.), *Towards a European Welfare State?* SAUS Study 6 (Bristol: SAUS Publications), pp. 107–26.

Jerrom, C. (2002) 'Scotland blazes a trail on free personal care for older people', *Community Care*, 27 June–3 July, pp. 18–19.

Joffe, J. and Lipsey, D. (1999) 'Note of dissent', in Sutherland Report, *With Respect to Old Age: A Report by the Royal Commission on Long Term Care* (London: The Stationery Office), pp. 113–43.

Johnson, M. (1990) 'Dependency and interdependency', in J. Bond and P. Coleman (eds), *Ageing in Society: An Introduction to Social Gerontology* (London: Sage), pp. 209–28.

Johnson, P. (1987) *Structural Dependency of the Elderly: A Critical Note* (London: Centre for Economic Policy Research).

Johnson, R. (2006) 'The twain shall meet', *Community Care*, 23 February–1 March, pp. 38–9.

Jones, C. (2001) 'Voices from the front line: state social workers and new labour', *British Journal of Social Work,* vol. 31, no. 4, pp. 547–62.

Jones, K. (1972) *A History of the Mental Health Services* (London: Routledge & Kegan Paul).

Jones, K. (1993) *Asylums and After* (London: The Athlone Press).

Jones, K. and Fowles, A. (1984) *Ideas on Institutions* (London: Routledge & Kegan Paul).

Joseph Rowntree Foundation (2002) *Britain's Housing in 2022: More Shortages and Homelessness* (York: Joseph Rowntree Foundation).

Kaufman, S.R. (1994) 'The social construction of frailty: an anthropological perspective', *Journal of Aging Studies,* vol. 8, no. 1, pp. 45–58.

Kemp, P. (2006) 'Up to the job?', *Roof*, January/February, pp. 27–9.

Kemper, P. (1992) 'The use of formal and informal home care by the disabled elderly', *HRS: Health Services Research*, vol. 27, no. 4, pp. 421–51.

Kirkwood, T. (1999) *Time of Our Lives: The Science of Ageing* (Oxford: Oxford University Press).

Knapp, M., Fernandez, J.-L., Kendall, J., Beecham, J., Northey, S. and Richardson, A. (2005) *Developing Social Care: The Current Position* (London: Social Care Institute for Excellence).

Knapp, M., Hardy, B. and Forder, J. (2001) 'Commissioning for quality: ten years of social care markets in England', *Journal of Social Policy*, vol. 30, part 2, pp. 283–306.

Knapp, M., Wistow, G., Forder, J. and Hardy, B. (1993) *Markets for Social Care: Opportunities, Barriers and Implications*, PSSRU Discussion Paper 919 (Canterbury: Personal Social Services Research Unit, University of Kent).

Kondratowitz, H.-J. von., Tesch-Römer, C. and Motel-Klingebiel, A. (2002) 'Establishing systems of care in Germany: a long and winding road', *Ageing Clinical and Experimental* Research, vol. 14, no. 4, pp. 239–46.

Labour Party (1997) *New Labour: Because Britain Deserves Better* (London: The Labour Party).

Labour Party (2001) *Ambitions for Britain* (London: The Labour Party).

Laing, W. and Saper, P. (1999) 'Promoting the development of a flourishing independent sector alongside good quality public services', in Part One of *Community Care and Informal Care*, Research Volume 3, The Royal Commission on Long Term Care (London: The Stationery Office), pp. 87–102.

Langan, J., Means, R. and Rolfe, S. (1996) *Maintaining Independence in Later Life: Older People Speaking* (Oxford: Anchor Trust).

Laslett, P. (1989) *A Fresh Map of Life* (London: Weidenfield and Nicholson).

Lawson, R. (1996) 'Germany: maintaining the middle way', in V. George and P. Taylor-Gooby (eds), *European Welfare Policy: Squaring the Welfare Circle* (Basingstoke: Macmillan), pp. 31–50.

Layard, R. (2006) *The Depression Report: A New Deal for Depression and Anxiety Disorders*, Centre for Economic Performance (London: London School of Economics and Political Science).

Leason, K. (2005) 'Curtains for care homes?', *Community Care*, 7–13 April, pp. 32–3.

Leason, K. (2006) 'Cash cut or helping hand?', *Community Care*, 16–22 February, pp. 28–9.

Leat, D. (1988) 'Residential care for younger physically disabled adults', in I. Sinclair (ed.), *Residential Care: The Research Reviewed* (London: HMSO), pp. 199–239.

Le Grand, J. (2003) *Motivation, Agency and Public Policy: Of Knights and Knaves, Pawns and Queens* (Oxford: Oxford University Press).

Le Grand, J. and Bartlett, W. (eds) (1993) *Quasi-Markets and Social Policy* (Basingstoke: Macmillan).

Leece, J. (2006) 'It's not like being at work: a study to investigate stress and job satisfaction in employees of direct payments users', in J. Leece and J. Bornat (eds), *Developments in Direct Payments* (Bristol: Policy Press), pp. 189–204.

Leece, J. and Bornat, J. (eds) (2006) *Developments in Direct Payments* (Bristol: Policy Press).

Leichsenring, K. and Alaszewski, A. (eds) (2004) *Providing Integrated Health and Social Care for Older Persons: A European Overview of Issues at Stake* (Aldershot: Ashgate).

Leisering, L. (2001) 'Germany: reform from within', in P. Alcock and G. Craig (eds), *International Social Policy* (Basingstoke: Palgrave Macmillan), pp. 161–82.

Lewis, J. (2001) 'Social services departments and the health/social care boundary: players or pawns?', in I. Allen (ed.), *Social Care and Health: A New Deal?* (London: Policy Studies Institute), pp. 23–39.

Lewis, J. and Glennerster, H. (1996) *Implementing the New Community Care* (Buckingham: Open University Press).

Lipsky, M. (1980) *Street Level Bureaucracy* (New York: Russell Sage).

Livesey, B. (2002) 'Delays in mental health tribunal hearings breach human rights', *Community Care Legal Updates*, 20 May, www.community-care.co.uk.

Lloyd, L. (2006a) 'A caring profession? The ethics of care and social work with older people', *British Journal of Social Work*, vol. 36, pp. 1171–85.

Lloyd, L. (2006b) 'Call us carers: limitations and risks in campaigning for recognition and exclusivity', *Critical Social Policy*, vol. 26, no. 4, pp. 945–60.

Lloyd, M. (2000) 'Where has all the care management gone? The challenge of Parkinson's disease to the health and social care interface', *British Journal of Social Work*, vol. 30, no. 6, pp. 737–54.

Lloyd, M. (2001) 'The politics of disability and feminism: discord or synthesis?', *Sociology*, vol. 35, no. 3, pp. 715–28.

Local Government Association (2005) *Beyond the Black Hole – A Time of Opportunity and Challenge* (London: Local Government Association).

Lomas, A. (2006) 'Care managers and direct payments', in J. Leece and J. Bornat (eds), *Developments in Direct Payments* (Bristol: Policy Press), pp. 237–49.

Lukes, S. (1974) *Power: A Radical View* (London: Macmillan).

Lund, B. (2006) *Understanding Housing Policy* (Bristol: Policy Press).

Lund, B. and Foord, M. (1997) *Housing Strategies and Community Care: Towards Integrated Living?* (Bristol: Policy Press).

Lunt, N., Mannion, R. and Smith, P. (1996) 'The finance of community care', in N. Lunt and D. Coyle (eds), *Welfare and Policy: Research Agendas and Issues* (London: Taylor & Francis), pp. 78–96.

Lymbery, M. (1998) 'Care management and professional autonomy: the impact of community care legislation on social work with older people', *British Journal of Social Work*, vol. 28, no. 6, pp. 863–78.

Lyon, J. (2005) 'A systems approach to direct payments: a response to friend or foe? Towards a critical assessment of direct payments', *Critical Social Policy*, vol. 25, no. 2, pp. 240–52.

Macnicol, J. (2006) *Age Discrimination: An Historical and Contemporary Analysis* (Cambridge: Cambridge University Press).

Maher, J. and Green, H. (2002) *Carers 2000: Results from the Carers Module of the General Household Survey 2000* (London: The Stationery Office).

Malin, N., Rose, D. and Jones, G. (1980) *Services for the Mentally Handicapped in Britain* (London: Croom Helm).

Mandelstam, M. (2007) *Betraying the NHS: Health Abandoned* (London: Jessica Kingsley).

Marinakou, M. (1998) 'Welfare states in the European periphery: the case of Greece', in R. Sykes and P. Alcock (eds), *Developments in European Social Policy: Convergence and Diversity* (Bristol: Policy Press), pp. 231–47.

Marks, D. (1999) *Disability: Controversial Debates and Psychosocial Perspectives* (London: Routledge).

Marsh, A., Gordon, D., Heslop, P. and Pantazis, C. (2000) 'Housing deprivation and health: a longitudinal analysis', *Housing Studies*, vol. 15, no. 3, pp. 411–28.

Marshall, M. (1989) 'The sound of silence: who cares about the quality of social work with older people?', in C. Rojek, G. Peacock and S. Collins (eds), *The Haunt of Misery: Critical Essays in Social Work and Helping* (London: Routledge), pp. 109–22.

Martin, F. (2001) 'Evidence is the key to promise of intermediate care', *Community Care*, 26 July–1 August, pp. 18–19.

Martin, G.P., Phelps, K. and Katbamna, S. (2004) 'Human motivation and professional practice: of knights, knaves and social workers', *Social Policy and Administration*, vol. 38, no. 5, pp. 470–87.

Martin, J., Meltzer, H. and Elliot, D. (1988) *The Prevalence of Disability Among Adults*, OPCS Surveys (London: HMSO).

Martin, M. (1995) 'Medical knowledge and medical practice: geriatric knowledge in the 1950s', *Social History of Medicine*, vol. 7, no. 3, pp. 443–61.

Matthews, O. (undated) *Housing the Infirm*, published by the author and originally distributed through W.H. Smith & Son.

McClatchey, T., Means, R. and Morbey, H. (2001) *Housing Adaptations and Improvements for People with Dementia* (Bristol: University of the West of England).

McCormack, H. (2007a) 'Inquiry reveals another institutional abuse scandal involving NHS trust', *Community Care*, 18–24 January, p. 6.

McCormack, H. (2007b) 'Change can't come too soon for campus and hospital residents', *Community Care*, 25–31 January, pp. 16–17.

McEwan, P. and Laverty, S. (1949) *The Chronic Sick and Elderly in Hospital* (Bradford: Bradford (B) Hospital Management Committee).

McLaughlin, H., Brown, D. and Young, A.M. (2004) 'Consultation, community and empowerment: Lessons from the deaf community', *Journal of Social Work*, vol. 4, no. 2, pp. 153–65.

Means, R. (1986) 'The development of social services for elderly people: historical perspectives', in C. Phillipson and A. Walker (eds), *Ageing and Social Policy: A Critical Assessment* (Aldershot: Gower), pp. 87–109.

Means, R. (1996) 'From "special needs" housing to independent living?', *Housing Studies,* vol. 11, no. 2, pp. 207–31.

Means, R. (1999) 'Housing and housing organisations: a review of their contribution to alternative models of care for elderly people', in A. Tinker *et al.* (eds), *Alternative Models of Care for Older People,* Research Volume 2, The Royal Commission on Long Term Care (London: The Stationery Office), pp. 299–324.

Means, R. (2001) 'Lessons from the history of long-term care for older people', in J. Robinson (ed.), *Towards a New Social Compact for Care in Old Age* (London: King's Fund), pp. 9–28.

Means, R. (2006) 'Safe as houses? Ageing in place and vulnerable older people in the UK', *Social Policy and Administration*, vol. 41, no. 1, pp. 65–85.

Means, R., Brenton, M., Harrison, L. and Heywood, F. (1997) *Making Partnerships Work in Community Care: A Guide for Practitioners in Housing, Health and Social Services* (Bristol: Policy Press).

Means, R., Morbey, H. and Smith, R. (2002) *From Community Care to Market Care: The Development of Welfare Services for Older People* (Bristol: Policy Press).

Means, R., Richards, S. and Smith, R. (2003) *Community Care: Policy and Practice* (3rd edition) (Basingstoke: Palgrave).

Means, R. and Smith, R. (1998a) *Community Care: Policy and Practice* (2nd edition) (Basingstoke: Macmillan).

Means, R. and Smith, R. (1998b) *From Poor Law to Community Care: The Development of Welfare Services for Elderly People, 1939–1971* (Bristol: Policy Press).

Mencap (2002) *The Housing Timebomb: The Housing Crisis Facing People with a Learning Disability and Their Older Parents* (London: Mencap).

Mental Health Foundation (1994) *Creating Community Care: Report of the Mental Health Foundation Inquiry into Community Care for People with Severe Mental Illness* (London: Mental Health Foundation).

Mental Health Foundation (1996) *Building Expectations: Opportunities and Services for People with a Learning Disability* (London: Mental Health Foundation).

Mental Health Foundation (2005) *Revolutionising Mental Health Services* (London: Mental Health Foundation).

Millar, J. and Warman, A. (1996) *Family Obligations in Europe* (London: Family Policy Studies Centre).

Miller, C. (2004) *Producing Welfare: A Modern Agenda* (Basingstoke: Palgrave).

Miller, E. and Gwynne, G. (1972) *A Life Apart* (London: Tavistock).

Milner, J. and Madigan, R. (2001) 'The politics of accessible housing in the UK', in S. Peace and C. Holland (eds), *Inclusive Housing in an Ageing Society* (Bristol: Policy Press), pp. 77–100.

Ministry of Health (1957) *Local Authority Services for the Chronic Sick and Infirm*, Circular 14/57 (London: Ministry of Health).

Ministry of Health (1965) *The Care of the Elderly in Hospitals and Residential Homes*, Circular 18/65 (London: Ministry of Health).

Mitchell, S. (2000) 'Modernising social services: the management challenge of the 1998 social services White Paper', in M. Hill (ed.), *Local Authority Social Services* (Oxford: Blackwell), pp. 179–201.

Mooney, G. and Williams, C. (2006) 'Forging new "ways of life"? Social policy and nation building in devolved Scotland and Wales', *Critical Social Policy*, vol. 26, no. 3, pp. 608–29.

Moroney, R. (1976) *The Family and the State* (London: Longman).

Morris, C. (1940) 'Public health during the first three months of war', *Social Work* (London), January, pp. 186–96.

Morris, J. (1990) 'Women and disability', *Social Work Today*, 8 November, p. 22.

Morris, J. (1993) *Community Care or Independent Living* (York: Joseph Rowntree Foundation/London: Community Care).

Morris, J. (2002) *Young Disabled People Moving into Adulthood* (York: Joseph Rowntree Foundation).

Morris, J. (2004) 'Independent living and community care: a disempowering framework', *Disability and Society*, vol. 19, no. 5, pp. 427–42.

Morris, P. (1969) *Put Away: A Sociological Study of Institutions for the Mentally Retarded* (London: Routledge & Kegan Paul).

Munday, B. (1996) 'Social care in the member states of the European Union: contexts and overview', in B. Munday and P. Ely (eds), *Social Care in Europe* (Hemel Hempstead: Prentice-Hall), pp. 21–66.

Munro, E. (2004) 'The impact of audit on social work practice', *British Journal of Social Work*, vol. 34, pp. 1075–95.

Murphy, E. (1991) *After the Asylums: Community Care for People with Mental Illness* (London: Faber & Faber).

Murray, P (2002a) 'Lessons of leisure', *Community Care*, 25–31 July, pp. 42–3.

Murray, P. (2002b) *Hello! Are You Listening? Disabled Teenagers' Experience of Access to Inclusive Leisure* (York: York Publishing Services).

Naegele, G. (1999) 'The politics of old age in Germany', in A. Walker and G. Naegele (eds), *The Politics of Old Age in Europe* (Buckingham: Open University Press), pp. 93–109.

National Council on Disability (2005) *NCD and the Americans with Disabilities Act: 15 Years of Progress* (http://www.acd.gov/newsroom/publications/2005/15yearsprogress.htm, accessed 23 June 2006).

Netten, A., Williams, J. and Darton, R. (2005) 'Care-home closures in England: causes and implications', *Ageing and Society*, vol. 25, no. 3, pp. 319–38.

Nolan, M. and Caldock, K. (1996) 'Assessment: identifying the barriers to good practice', *Health and Social Care in the Community*, vol. 4, no. 2, pp. 77–85.

Nolan, M., Grant, G. and Keady, J. (1996) *Understanding Family Care* (Buckingham: Open University Press).

Northern Ireland Housing Executive (2006) *Welfare Adaptations Survey 2005* (Belfast: Northern Ireland Housing Executive).

Nuffield Provincial Hospitals Trust (1946) *The Hospital Surveys: The Domesday Book of the Hospital Services* (Oxford: Oxford University Press).

Office for National Statistics (1997) *Social Trends 27* (London: HMSO).

Office of the Deputy Prime Minister (2004a) *Review of the Supporting People Programme* (London: Office of the Deputy Prime Minister).

Office of the Deputy Prime Minister (2004b) *Supporting People: Review of the Policy and Costs of Housing Related Support since 1997* (London: Office of the Deputy Prime Minister).

Office of the Deputy Prime Minister (2004c) *Sustainable Communities: Building for the Future* (London: Office of the Deputy Prime Minister).

Office of the Deputy Prime Minister (2004d) *A Decent Home: The Definition and Guidance for Implementation* (London: Office of the Deputy Prime Minister).

Office of the Deputy Prime Minister (2005) *Creating Sustainable Communities: Supporting Independence – Consultation on a Strategy for the Supporting People Programme* (London: Office of the Deputy Prime Minister).

Office of the Deputy Prime Minister (2006) *A Sure Start to Later Life: Ending Inequalities for Older People* (London: Office of the Deputy Prime Minister).

Oldman, C. (2000) *Blurring the Boundaries: A Fresh Look at Housing Provision and Care for Older People* (Brighton: Pavilion).

Oldman, C. and Quilgars, D. (1999) 'The Last Resort? Revisiting ideas about older people's living arrangements', *Ageing and Society*, vol. 19, part 4, pp. 363–84.

Oliver, M. (1990) *The Politics of Disablement* (Basingstoke: Macmillan).

Oliver, M. (1996) *Understanding Disability: From Theory to Practice* (Basingstoke: Macmillan).

Organisation for Economic Co–operation and Development (1996) *Caring for Frail Elderly People: Policies in Evolution* (Paris: OECD).

Orme, J. (2001a) 'Regulation or fragmentation? Directions for social work under New Labour', *British Journal of Social Work*, vol. 31, no. 4, pp. 611–24.

Orme, J. (2001b) *Gender and Community Care: Social Work and Social Care Perspectives* (Basingstoke: Palgrave Macmillan).

Ormerod, M. and Thomas, P. (2006) *Implementing Decent Homes Standards: How Housing Associations are Addressing Accessibility Issues* (York: Joseph Rowntree Foundation).

Pacolet, J., Bouten, R., Lauoye, H. and Verseick, K. (1999) *Social Protection for Dependency in Old Age in the Fifteen Member States and Norway: Synthesis Report Commissioned by the European Commission and the Belgian Minister of Social Affairs* (Luxembourg: Office of Official Publications of the European Communities).

Pannell, J., Morbey, H. and Means, R. (2002) *'Surviving at the Margins': Older Homeless People and the Organisations That Support Them* (London: Help the Aged).

Parker, J. (1965) *Local Health and Welfare Services* (London: Allen & Unwin).

Parker, R. (1988) 'An historical background', in I. Sinclair (ed.), *Residential Care: The Research Reviewed* (London: HMSO), pp. 1–38.

Parton, N. (1991) *Governing the Family* (Basingstoke: Macmillan).

Payne, M. (1995) *Social Work and Community Care* (Basingstoke: Macmillan).

Payne, S. (1999) 'Outside the walls of the asylum? Psychiatric treatment in the 1980s and 1990s', in P. Bartlett and D. Wright (eds), *Outside the Walls of the Asylum: The History of Care in the Community, 1750–2000* (London: The Athlone Press), pp. 245–65.

Peace, S. and Holland, C. (eds) (2001) *Inclusive Housing in an Ageing Society* (Bristol: Policy Press).

Peace, S., Holland, C. and Kellaher, L. (2006) *Environment and Identity in Later Life* (Maidenhead: Open University Press).

Peace, S., Kellaher, L. and Willcocks, D. (1997) *Re-evaluating Residential Care* (Buckingham: Open University Press).

Pearce, D. (2007) 'Family, gender and class in psychiatric patient care during the 1930s: the 1930 Mental Treatment Act and the Devon Mental Hospital', in P. Dale and J. Melling (eds), *Mental Illness and Learning Disability since 1850: Finding a Place for Mental Disorder in the United Kingdom* (London: Routledge), pp. 112–30.

Pearce, J. (2001) 'Small print', *Community Care*, 2–8 August, pp. 10–11.

Pease, B. (2002) 'Rethinking empowerment: a postmodern reappraisal for emancipatory practice', *British Journal of Social Work*, vol. 32, no. 2, pp. 135–47.

Peck, E., Gulliver, P. and Towell, D. (2002) *Modernising Partnerships: An Evaluation of Somerset's Innovations in the Commissioning and Organisation of Mental Health Services* (London: King's College).

Pedersen, L. (1998) 'Health and social care for older people in Denmark: a public solution under threat?', in C. Glendinning (ed.), *Rights and Realities: Comparing New Developments in Long Term Care for Older People* (Bristol: Policy Press), pp. 83–103.

Percival, J. and Hanson, J. (2006) 'Big brother or brave new world? Telecare and its implications for older people's independence and social inclusion', *Critical Social Policy*, vol. 24, no. 4, pp. 888–909.

Phillipson, C. (1982) *Capitalism and the Construction of Old Age* (Basingstoke: Macmillan).

Phillipson, C. (1998) *Reconstructing Old Age: New Agendas in Social Theory and Social Policy* (London: Sage).

Phillipson, C., Bernard, M., Phillips, J. and Ogg, J. (2001) *The Family and Community Life of Older People: Social Networks and Social Support in Three Urban Areas* (London: Routledge).

Phillipson, C. and Walker, A. (eds) (1986) *Ageing and Social Policy: A Critical Assessment* (Aldershot: Gower).

Philp, I. (ed.) (2001) *Family Care of Older People in Europe* (Amsterdam: IOF Press).

Philp, I. (2007) *A Recipe for Care – Not a Single Ingredient* (London: Department of Health).

Pickard, L. (1999) 'Policy options for informal carers of elderly people', in Part Two of *Community Care and Informal Care,* Research

Volume 3, The Royal Commission on Long Term Care (London: The Stationery Office), pp. 1–99.

Pilgrim, D. (2007) 'New "mental health" legislation for England and Wales: some aspects of consensus and conflict', *Journal of Social Policy*, vol. 36, part 1, pp. 79–95.

Plank, D. (2000) 'Performance for the people or virtual reality? Social services and modernising local government', *Managing Community Care*, vol. 8, no. 1, pp. 13–21.

Platt, D. (2002) 'Why stars are underrated', *Community Care*, 27 June–3 July, pp. 36–8.

Player, S. and Pollock, A. (2001) 'Long term care: from public responsibility to private good', *Critical Social Policy*, vol. 21, no. 2, pp. 231–55.

Pollock, A. (2004) *NHS Plc: The Privatisation of our Health Care* (London: Verso).

Postle, K. (2001a) 'The social work side is disappearing. It started with us being called care managers', *Practice*, vol. 13, no. 1, pp. 13–26.

Postle, K. (2001b) 'Things fall apart; the centre cannot hold: deconstructing and reconstructing social work with older people for the 21st century', *Issues in Social Work Education*, vol. 19, no. 2, pp. 23–43.

Postle, K. (2002) 'Working "Between the idea and the reality": ambiguities and tensions in care managers' work', *British Journal of Social Work*, vol. 32, no. 3, pp. 335–51.

Power, M. (1997) *The Audit Society: Rituals of Verification* (Oxford: Oxford University Press).

Poxton, R. (ed.) (1999) *Working across the Boundaries: Experiences of Primary Health and Social Care Partnerships in Practice* (London: King's Fund).

Pressman, J. and Wildavsky, A. (1973) *Implementation* (Berkeley: University of California Press).

Preston-Shoot, M. (2004) 'Responding by degrees: surveying the education and practice landscape', *Social Work Education*, vol. 23, no. 6, pp. 667–92.

Priestley, M. and Rabiee, P. (2001) *Building Bridges: Disability and Old Age* (University of Leeds: Centre for Disability Studies).

Prime Minister's Strategy Unit (2005) *Improving the Life Chances of Disabled People* (London: Cabinet Office).

Propper, C., Wilson, D. and Burgess, S. (2006) 'Extending choice in English health care: The implications of the economic evidence', *Journal of Social Policy*, vol. 35, part 4, pp. 537–58.

Race, D. (2005) 'Learning disability, housing and community care', in M. Foord and P. Simic (eds), *Housing, Community Care and Supported Housing – Resolving Contradictions* (Coventry: Chartered Institute of Housing), pp. 100–12.

Rapaport, A. (1995) 'An initial look at the concept of "home"', in D. Benjamin and D. Stea (eds), *The Home Words: Interpretation, Meanings and Environments* (Aldershot: Avebury), pp. 25–52.

Raynes, N., Temple, B., Glenister, C. and Coulthard, L. (2001) *Quality at Home for Older People: Involving Service Users in Defining Home Care Specifications* (Bristol: Policy Press).

Revans, L. (2001a) 'Hutton unveils new care standards', *Community Care*, 8–14 March, pp. 2–3.

Revans, L. (2001b) 'People with learning difficulties in from the cold', *Community Care*, 29 March–4 April, pp. 10–11.

Revans, L. (2002) 'Human Rights Act fails to protect residents in private care home', *Community Care*, 28 March–3 April, p. 8.

Richards, S. (1994) 'Making sense of needs assessment', *Research Policy and Planning*, vol. 12, no. 1, pp. 5–9.

Richards, S. (2000) 'Bridging the divide: elders and the assessment process', *British Journal of Social Work*, vol. 30, no. 1, pp. 37–49.

Richards, S., Donovan, S., Victor, C. and Ross, F. (2007) 'Standing secure amidst a falling world? Practitioner understandings of old age in responses to a case vignette', *Journal of Interprofessional Care*, vol. 21, no. 3, pp. 1–13.

Richards, S., Ruch, G. and Trevithick, P. (2005) 'Communication skills training for practice: the ethical dilemma for social work education', *Social Work Education*, vol. 24, no. 4, pp. 409–22.

Ritchie, J., Dick, D. and Lingham, R. (1994) *Report of the Inquiry into the Care and Treatment of Christopher Clunis* (London: HMSO).

Robb, B. (1967) *Sans Everything: A Case to Answer* (London: Allen & Unwin).

Roberts, G. (1992) 'Legal aspects of community care', paper delivered to the Law Society Conference, 'Community Care: A Challenge to the Legal Profession', 20 November.

Roberts, N. (1970) *Our Future Selves* (London: Allen & Unwin).

Rowlings, C. (1981) *Social Work with Elderly People* (London: Allen & Unwin).

Rowlingson, K. (2006) ' "Living poor to die rich?" or "spending the kids inheritance? Attitudes to assets and inheritance in later life', *Journal of Social Policy*, vol. 35, no. 2, pp. 175–92.

Rowlingson, K. and McKay, S. (2005) *Attitudes to Inheritance in Britain* (Bristol: Policy Press).

Rowntree Report (1980) *Old People: Report of a Survey Committee on the Problems of Ageing and the Care of Old People* (New York: Arno Press).

Rudd, T. (1958) 'Basic problems in the social welfare of the elderly', *The Almoner*, vol. 10, no. 10, pp. 348–9.

Rummery, K. (2002) *Disability, Citizenship and Community Care: A Case for Welfare Rights?* (Aldershot: Ashgate).

Rummery, K. and Glendinning, C. (1999) 'Negotiating needs, access and gatekeeping: developments in health and community care policies in the UK and the rights of disabled and older citizens', *Critical Social Policy*, vol. 19, no. 3, pp. 335–51.

Rummery, K. and Glendinning, C. (2000) *Primary Care and Social Services: Developing New Partnerships for Older People* (Abingdon: Radcliffe Medical Press).

Ryan, J. and Thomas, E. (1980) *The Politics of Mental Handicap* (Harmondsworth: Penguin).

Sainsbury Centre for Mental Health (2002) *Breaking the Circles of Fear: A Review of the Relationship between Mental Health Services and African and Caribbean Communities* (London: Sainsbury Centre for Mental Health).

Salvage, A. (1995) *Who Will Care? Future Prospects for Family Care of Older People in the European Union* (Dublin: European Foundation for the Improvement of Living and Working Conditions).

Samson, E. (1944) *Old Age in the New World* (London: Pilot Press).

Samuel, M. (2005a) 'Will social care play second fiddle when inspections regime merges?', *Community Care*, 24–30 March, pp. 16–17.

Samuel, M. (2005b) 'Ladyman scraps transfer of schemes as relations with SCIE break down', *Community Care*, 10–16 February, p. 6.

Samuel, M. (2005c) 'Hackles raised after inspectors accuse councils of "coasting"', *Community Care*, 8–14 December, pp. 16–18.

Samuel, M. (2005d) 'Profession becoming less focussed on clients and more on paperwork', *Community Care*, 15 December–4 January, p. 6.

Samuel, M. (2005e) 'Local authority figures labelled as "fantasy" in row over budgets', *Community Care*, 10–16 November, pp. 18–19.

Samuel, M. (2006) 'High Court joins chorus of criticism of "unclear" continuing care system', *Community Care*, 2–8 February, p. 13.

Saunders, P. (1990) *A Nation of Home Owners* (London: Unwin Hyman).

Sayce, L. and O'Brien, N. (2004) 'The future of equality and human rights in Britain – opportunities and risks for disabled people', *Disability and Society*, vol. 19, no. 6, pp. 663–8.

Schneider, U. (1999) 'Germany's long-term care insurance: design, implementation and evaluation', *International Social Security Review*, vol. 52, no. 2, pp. 31–74.

Schunk, M. (1998) 'The social insurance model of care for older people in Germany', in C. Glendinning (ed.), *Rights and Realities: Comparing New Developments in Long Term Care for Older People* (Bristol: Policy Press), pp. 29–46.

SCIE (2007) *The Participation of Adult Service Users, Including Older People, in Developing Social Care, Practice Guide 11* (London: Social Care Institute for Excellence).

Scott, V. (1994) *Lessons from America* (London: Royal Association for Disability and Rehabilitation).

Scottish Executive (2006) *Changing Lives: Report of the 21st Century Social Work Review* (Edinburgh: Scottish Executive).

Scourfield, P. (2005) 'Implementing the Community Care (Direct Payments) Act: Will the supply of personal assistants meet the demand and at what price?', *Journal of Social Policy*, vol. 34, no. 3, pp. 469–88.

Scourfield, P. (2006) ' "What matters is what works?" How discourses of modernisation have both silenced and limited debate on domiciliary care for older people', *Critical Social Policy*, vol. 26, no. 1, pp. 5–30.

Scull, A. (1993) *The Most Solitary of Afflictions: Madness and Society in Britain, 1700–1900* (New Haven, CT: Yale University Press).

Seabrooke, V. and Milne, A. (2004) *Culture and Care in Dementia: A Study of the Asian Community in North West Kent* (London: Mental Health Foundation).

Seebohm Report (1968) *Report of the Committee on Local Authority and Allied Personal Services* (London: HMSO).

Sennett, R. (1998) *The Concession of Character: The Personal Consequences of Work in the New Capitalism* (New York: Norton & Co.).

Sennett, R. (2006) *The Culture of the New Capitalism* (Yale University Press: New Haven and London).

Servian, R. (1996) *Theorising Empowerment: Individual Power and Community Care* (Bristol: Policy Press).

Shakespeare, T. (2006) *Disability Rights and Wrongs* (Abingdon: Routledge).

Shanas, E., Townsend, P., Wedderburn, D., Friis, H., Milhof, P. and Stehouwer, J. (1968) *Old People in Three Industrialised Societies* (London: Routledge & Kegan Paul).

Shaver, S. and Fine, M. (1995) *Social Policy and Personal Life: Changes in State, Family and Community in the Support of Informal Care*, Discussion Paper No 65 (Sydney: Social Policy Research Centre, University of New South Wales).

Shaw, I. (2000) 'Mental health', in M. Hill (ed.), *Local Authority Social Services: An Introduction* (Oxford: Blackwell), pp. 105–18.

Sheldon, J. (1948) *The Social Medicine of Old Age* (Oxford: Oxford University Press).

Sheppard, M. (1995) *Care Management and the New Social Work: A Critical Analysis* (London: Whiting & Birch).

Simic, P. (2005) 'He went berserk and stabbed his mother 43 times … thinking in headlines: mental health and housing', in M. Foord and P. Simic (eds), *Housing, Community Care and Supported Housing in*

Resolving Contradictions (Coventry: Chartered Institute of Housing), pp. 126–41.

Singh, B. (2005) *Improving Support for Black Disabled People: Lessons from Community Organisations on Making Change Happen* (York: Joseph Rowntree Foundation).

Skills for Care (www.topssengland.net/index.asp, accessed 27 March 2007).

Smith, R. (2005) *Human Rights, Anti-Discrimination and Disability in Britain*, SPS Working Paper 9 (Bristol: School for Policy Studies, University of Bristol).

Social Policy Ageing Information Network (2001) *The Underfunding of Social Care and its Consequences for Older People* (London: Social Policy Ageing Information Network).

Spandler, H. (2004) 'Friend or foe? Towards a critical assessment of direct payments', *Critical Social Policy*, vol. 24, no. 2, pp. 187–209.

Spandler, H. and Vick, N. (2006) 'Opportunities for independent living using direct payments in mental health', *Health and Social Care in the Community*, vol. 14, no. 2, pp. 107–15.

Stainton, T. and Boyce, S. (2004) ' "I have got my life back": users' experience of direct payments', *Disability and Society*, vol. 19, no. 5, pp. 443–54.

Starfish Consulting (2002) *The Elusive Costs of Home Care* (London: Starfish Consulting).

Starkey, F. (2003) 'The "empowerment debate": consumerist, professional and liberational perspectives in health and social care', *Social Policy and Society*, vol. 2, no. 4, pp. 273–84.

Steinfield, E. (1981) 'The place of old age: the meaning of housing for old people', in J. Duncan (ed.), *Housing and Identity: Cross Cultural Perspectives* (London: Croom Helm), pp. 198–246.

Stephenson, P. (2005) 'Sector wants Ladyman to revamp long-term funding criteria', *Community Care*, 10–16 March, pp. 16–17.

Sullivan, H. and Skelcher, C. (2002) *Working Across Boundaries: Collaboration in Public Services* (Basingstoke: Palgrave).

Sumner, G. and Smith, R. (1969) *Planning Local Authority Services for the Elderly* (London: Allen & Unwin).

Sutherland Report (1999a) *With Respect to Old Age: A Report by the Royal Commission on Long Term Care* (London: The Stationery Office).

Sutherland Report (1999b) *With Respect to Old Age*, Research Volume 1, The Royal Commission on Long Term Care (London: The Stationery Office).

Sykes, R., Palier, B. and Prior, P. (eds) (2001) *Globalization and European Welfare States: Challenges and Change* (Basingstoke: Palgrave Macmillan).

Symeonidou, H. (1997) 'Welfare state and informal networks in contemporary Greece', in B. Palier (ed.), *Comparing Social Welfare Systems in Southern Europe, Vol. 3, France, Southern Europe* (Paris: MIRE), pp. 337–62.

Taylor, A. (2005) 'Personalised budgets greeted as leap forward in disability rights', *Community Care*, 27 January–2 February, pp. 18–19.

Taylor, A., McCormack, H. and Brody, S. (2006) 'Special Report: Mental Health', *Community Care*, 23–29 November, p. 12.

Taylor, B.J. and Donnelly, M. (2006) 'Professional perspectives on decision making about the long-term care of older people', *British Journal of Social Work*, vol. 36, pp. 807–26.

Taylor, M. (2003) *Public Policy in the Community* (Basingstoke: Palgrave Macmillan).

Taylor, M., Langan, J. and Hoggett, P. (1995) *Encouraging Diversity: Voluntary and Private Organisations in Community Care* (Aldershot: Arena).

Tester, S. (1996) *Community Care for Older People: A Comparative Perspective* (Basingstoke: Macmillan).

Thane, P. (ed.) (2005a) *The Long History of Old Age* (London: Thames and Hudson).

Thane, P. (2005b) 'The 20th Century', in P. Thane (ed.), *The Long History of Old Age* (London: Thames & Hudson), pp. 263–302.

Thomas, F. (1980) 'Everyday life on the ward', in J. Ryan with F. Thomas (eds), *The Politics of Mental Handicap* (Harmondsworth: Penguin), pp. 30–46.

Thompson, A. (1949) 'Problems of ageing and chronic sickness', *British Medical Journal*, 30 July, pp. 250–1.

Thompson, A. (1997) 'Working to a new rule', *Community Care*, 10–16 July, pp. 20–1.

Thomson, M. (1998) *The Problem of Mental Deficiency: Eugenics, Democracy and Social Policy in Britain, c. 1870–1959* (Oxford: Clarendon Press).

Timmins, N. (1996) 'The politicians take over the asylum', *The Independent*, 21 February, p. 17.

Tinker, A., Wright, F. and Zeilig, H. (1995) *Difficult to Let Sheltered Housing* (London: HMSO).

Titmuss, R. (1968) *Commitment to Welfare* (London: Allen & Unwin).

Titmuss, R. (1976) *Problems of Social Policy* (London: HMSO).

Topliss, E. (1979) *Provision for the Disabled* (Oxford: Basil Blackwell).

Townsend, P. (1957) *The Family Life of Old People* (London: Routledge & Kegan Paul).

Townsend, P. (1964) *The Last Refuge* (London: Routledge & Kegan Paul).

Townsend, P. (1968) 'Welfare services and the family', in E. Shanas, P. Townsend, D. Wedderburn, H. Friis, P. Milhof and J. Stehouwer (eds), *Old People in Three Industrialised Societies* (London: Routledge and Kegan Paul), pp. 102–31.

Townsend, P. (1981) 'The structural dependency of the elderly: the creation of social policy in the twentieth century?', *Ageing and Society*, vol. 1, no. 1, pp. 5–28.

Townsend, P. (1986) 'Ageing and social policy', in C. Phillipson and A. Walker (eds), *Ageing and Social Policy: A Critical Assessment* (Aldershot: Gower), pp. 15–44.

Townsend, P. (2006) 'Policies for the aged in the 21st century: more "structured dependency" or the realisation of human rights?', *Ageing and Society*, vol. 26, part 2, pp. 161–79.

Tredgold, A. (1952) A *Textbook on Mental Deficiency* (London: Baillière, Tindall & Cox).

Tregaskis, C. (2002) 'Social model theory: the story so far ...', *Disability and Society*, vol. 17, no. 4, pp. 457–70.

Triantafillou, J. and Mestheneos, E. (2001) 'Greece (September 1998)', in I. Philp (ed.), *Family Care of Older People in Europe* (Amsterdam: IOS Press), pp. 75–95.

Trivedi, P. (2002) 'Racism, social exclusion and mental health: a Black user's perspective', in K. Bhui (ed.), *Racism and Mental Health* (London: Jessica Kingsley), pp. 71–82.

Tronto, J.C. (1993) *Moral Boundaries: A Political Argument for an Ethic of Care* (London: Routledge).

Tulle, E. and Mooney, E. (2002) 'Moving to "age-appropriate" housing: government and self in later life,' *Sociology*, vol. 36, no. 3, pp. 685–702.

Ungerson, C. (1987) *Policy is Personal: Sex, Gender and Informal Care* (London: Tavistock).

Ungerson, C. (2004) 'Whose empowerment and independence? A cross-national perspective on "cash for care" schemes', *Ageing and Society*, vol. 24, no. 2, pp. 189–212.

United Kingdom's Disabled People's Council (UKDPC) (2007), home page (http://www.bcodp.org.uk, accessed 22 August 2007).

US Department of Health and Human Services (DHHS) (1980) *Application Guidelines for Long-Term Care Systems Development Grants under the National Channelling Demonstration Projects* (Washington, DC: Office of the Assistant Secretary for Planning and Education).

Vallelly, S., Evans, S., Fear, T. and Means, R. (2006) *Opening New Doors to Independence: A Longitudinal Study Exploring the Contribution of Extra Care Housing to the Care and Support of Older People with Dementia* (London: Housing 21).

Valios, N. (2005) 'Staying ahead of the game', *Community Care*, 19–25 May, pp. 38–9.

Verdugo, M., Jimenez, A. and Jordán de Urries, F. (2000) 'Social and employment policies for people with disabilities in Spain', *European Journal of Social Security*, vol. 2, no. 4, pp.323–41.

Vernon, A. and Qureshi, H. (2000) 'Community care and independence: self-sufficiency or empowerment?', *Critical Social Policy*, vol. 20, no. 2, pp. 255–76.

Vincent, J. (1999) *Politics, Power and Old Age* (Buckingham: Open University Press).

Vincent, J. (2006) 'Ageing contested: anti-ageing science and the cultural construction of old age', *Sociology*, vol. 40, no. 4, pp. 681–98.

Waddon, A. and Jaenicke, D. (2006) 'Recent incremental health care reforms in the US: a way forward or false promise?', *Policy and Politics*, vol. 34, no. 2, April, pp. 241–63.

Wagner Committee (1988) *Residential Care: A Positive Choice* (London: HMSO).

Walker, A. (1992) 'Integration, social policy and elderly citizens: towards a European agenda on ageing?', *Generations Review*, vol. 2, no. 4, pp. 2–8.

Walker, A. (1999) 'Political participation and representation of older people in Europe', in A. Walker and G. Naegele (eds), *The Politics of Old Age in Europe* (Buckingham: Open University Press), pp. 7–24.

Walker, A. (2005) 'Towards an international political economy of ageing', *Ageing and Society*, vol. 25, part 6, pp. 815–39.

Walker, A. and Maltby, T. (1997) *Ageing Europe* (Buckingham: Open University Press).

Walker, A. and Naegele, G. (eds) (1999) *The Politics of Old Age in Europe* (Buckingham: Open University Press).

Walker, C., Ryan, T. and Walker, A. (1996) *Fair Shares for All?* (Brighton: Pavilion).

Wanless Review (2006) *Securing Good Care for Older People: Taking the Long-Term View* (London: King's Fund).

Warburton, R. and McCracken, J. (1999) 'An evidence-based perspective from the Department of Health on the impact of the 1993 reforms on the care of frail, elderly people', in Part One of *Community Care and Informal Care*, Research Volume 3, The Royal Commission on Long Term Care (London: The Stationery Office), pp. 25–36.

Ware, T., Matosevic, T., Hardy, B., Knapp, M., Kendall, J. and Forder, J. (2003) 'Commissioning care services for older people in England: the view from care managers, users and carers', *Ageing and Society*, vol. 23, no. 4, pp. 411–28.

Watters, C. (1996) 'Representations and realities: black people, community care and mental illness', in W. Ahmad and K. Atkin (eds), *Race and Community Care* (Buckingham: Open University Press), pp. 105–23.

Webb, A. (1991) 'Co-ordination: a problem in public sector management', *Policy and Politics*, vol. 19, no. 4, pp. 229–41.

Welsh Assembly Government (2003a) *The Strategy for Older People in Wales* (Cardiff: Welsh Assembly Government).

Welsh Assembly Government (2003b) *Health, Social Care and Wellbeing Strategies* (Cardiff: Welsh Assembly Government).

Welsh Assembly Government (2005) *Design for Life: Creating World Class Health and Social Care for Wales in the 21st Century* (Cardiff: Welsh Assembly Government).

Welsh Assembly Government (2006a) *A Strategy for Social Services in Wales over the Next Decade* (Cardiff: Welsh Assembly Government).

Welsh Assembly Government (2006b) *National Service Framework for Older People in Wales* (Cardiff: Welsh Assembly Government).

Welsh Assembly Government (2007) *Fulfilled Lives, Supportive Communities: Improving Social Services in Wales from 2008–2018* (Cardiff: Welsh Assembly Government).

Welshman, J. (1999) 'Rhetoric and reality: community care in England and Wales, 1948–74', in P. Bartlett and D. Wright (eds), *Outside the Walls of the Asylum: The History of Care in the Community, 1750–2000* (London: The Athlone Press), pp. 204–25.

Welshman, J. and Walmsley, J. (eds) (2006) *Community Care in Perspective: Care, Control and Citizenship* (Basingstoke: Palgrave).

Wilcox, S. (1997) *Housing Finance Review, 1997–98* (York: Joseph Rowntree Foundation).

Wild, C., Duff, P., Arber, S. and Davidson, K. (2002) 'Stress and strain of moving', *Community Care*, 18–24 April, pp. 36–7.

Wiles, J. (2005) 'Home as a new site of care provision and consumption', in G. Andrews and D. Phillips (eds), *Ageing and Place: Perspectives, Policy and Practice* (Abingdon: Routledge), pp. 79–97.

Willcocks, D., Peace, S. and Kellaher, L. (1987) *Private Lives in Public Places* (London: Tavistock).

Williams, R. (1976) *Keywords* (Glasgow: Fontana).

Williams, V. and Holman, A. (2006) 'Direct payments and autonomy: issues for people with learning difficulties', in J. Leece and J. Bornat (eds), *Developments in Direct Payments* (Bristol: Policy Press), pp. 65–78.

Willmott, P. and Young, M. (1960) *Family and Class in a London Suburb* (London: Routledge & Kegan Paul).

Wilson, G. (1991) 'Models of ageing and their relation to policy formation and service provision', *Policy and Politics*, vol. 19, no. 1, pp. 37–47.

Wilson, G. (1994) 'Co-production and self-care: new approaches to managing community care services for older people', *Social Policy and Administration*, vol. 28, no. 3, September, pp. 236–50.

Winchester, R. (2001) 'Can residents stop the great homes sell-off?', *Community Care*, 1–7 March, pp. 10–11.

Winchester, R. and Leason, K. (2004) 'The Great Divide', *Community Care*, 1–7 July, pp. 26–9.

Wistow, G. (1995) 'Aspirations and realities: community care at the crossroads', *Health and Social Care in the Community*, vol. 3, no. 4, pp. 227–40.

Wistow, G., Knapp, M., Hardy, B., Forder, J., Kendall, J. and Manning, R. (1996) *Social Care Markets: Progress and Prospects* (Buckingham: Open University Press).

Witton, M. (2005) 'Award not enough', *Community Care*, 27 January–2 February, pp. 38–9.

Wolfensberger, W. and Thomas, S. (1983) *Programme Analysis of Service Systems' Implementations of Normalisation Goals (PASS-ING): A Method of Evaluating the Quality of Human Services* (Toronto: National Institute on Mental Retardation).

Woods, B. (2005) 'Dementia', in M. Johnson (ed.), *The Cambridge Handbook of Age and Ageing* (Cambridge: Cambridge University Press), pp. 261–74.

Young, D. and Quibell, R. (2000) 'Why rights are never enough: rights, intellectual disability and understanding', *Disability and Society*, vol. 15, no. 5, pp. 747–64.

Young, M. and Willmott, P. (1957) *Family and Kinship in East London* (London: Routledge & Kegan Paul).

Young, R. and Wistow, G. (1996) 'Development of independent home care in 1995 UKHCA survey', in *The Mixed Economy of Care*, Bulletin No. 4 (Canterbury: Personal Social Services Research Unit, University of Kent and Leeds: Nuffield Institute for Health, University of Leeds), pp. 14–15.

Index